Ruby of Cochin

Ruby Daniel, late 1940s. (*Collection of Ruby Daniel*)

RUBY
OF
COCHIN

An Indian Jewish Woman Remembers

Ruby Daniel
and
Barbara C. Johnson

JPS

THE JEWISH PUBLICATION SOCIETY
Philadelphia
2002 5762

Publication of this book has been made possible through a gift from
ELIZABETH AND SIDNEY COROB
London, England

© 1995 by Ruby Daniel and Barbara C. Johnson
First cloth edition 1995
Paperback edition 2002

The Jewish Publication Society
2100 Arch Street
Philadelphia, PA 19103

Manufactured in the United States of America

Portions of this book has appeared in slightly different form in *Four Centuries of Jewish Women's
Spirituality: A Sourcebook*, edited by Ellen Umansky and Dianne Ashton, pages 298 to 304
(Boston: Beacon Press, 1992; article © Ruby Daniel and Barbara C. Johnson); *K'fari*
(Cabot,VT), December,1989; *Manushi: A journal About Women and Society*, volume 67, pages
30 to 37 (New Delhi, 1991); and *Points East: A Publication of the Sino-Fudaic Institute*, volume
8, number 1, pages 5 to 6, 1993. We reuse them with permission.

The Library of Congress Cataloging-in-Publication has cataloged the hardcover edition of this
title as:
Daniel, Ruby, 1912–
Ruby of Cochin: An Indian Jewish Woman Remembers / Ruby Daniel and Barbara C.
Johnson.—1st ed.
p. cm
Includes bibliographical references and index.
ISBN 0–8276–0539–0 (hard cover)
ISBN 0–8276–0749–0 (paper0back)
1. Daniel, Ruby, 1912–   2. Jews—India—Cochin—Biography
3. Jewish women—India—Cochin—Biography   4. Jews—India—Cochin—Social life and
customs. L. Johnson, Barbara C., 1940–
II Title
DS135.163D363   1995
954'.83004924'0092—dc20   95-14425
[B]   CIP
06 05 04 03 02   10 9 8 7 6 5 4 3 2 1
Designed by NACHMAN ELSNER
Typeset in Galliard by University Graphics

DEDICATED TO THE MEMORY OF
MY BELOVED GRANDMOTHER

RACHEL (DOCHO) JAPHETH, *z'l*
1864–1944

Without her I would not have known all these stories.

Contents

Acknowledgments

Our gratitude goes first of all to Shirley Isenberg, who encouraged Ruby to write down her stories and who faithfully cheered us on as we turned them into a book. Our thanks also go to Abe David for his enthusiasm and help with the family tree; to Raḥel Kala for her cheerfulness and for cooking the *sambhar* while we worked; and to Artur Isenberg, Lillian David, and Steve Kala for reading the manuscript. Further thanks go to Steve for permission to use so many of his photographs.

To our editor, Ellen Frankel, goes our appreciation for her confidence in us and for the vision and imagination that led her to publish these stories.

Barbara acknowledges the American Council of Learned Societies and the Ithaca College Provost's Fund for financial assistance in my travel to Israel to work with Ruby. Fred Estabrook was gracious with his time in preparing the map and the genealogy chart, and Erich Haesche took unusual care with the photographic reproductions.

I want to thank my friends in the Cochin Paradesi community of Israel and India for their more than twenty-five years of hospitality and patience with my questions; there is not room here to list them all individually, but I hope they know what a difference they have made in my life. Among the *haverim* who made us feel welcome at Kibbutz Neot Mordecai, Nicky and I particularly thank Aliza and Willi Gadni, Hannah Avriel, and the *vatikim* at the apple-packing factory: Balu, Haim, Yosef, Chanan, and Manci. Over the years this book project has been blessed with inspiration and support from a number of my friends and colleagues in the U.S., including Martha Ackelsberg, Penina Adelman, Judy Chalmer, Michele Clark, Dianne Esses, Lyn Fine, Elaine Leeder, Denni Liebowitz, Judith Plaskow, Joel Savishinsky, Rachel Siegel, Ellen Umansky, Lucille Warner, and all my sisters in B'not Esh. Diane Zuckerman at JPS has been a creative and understanding editor.

Finally, both of us express our gratitude to Nicky Morris for her countless rereadings of the manuscript, along with her questions, advice, driving skills, companionship, and humor. As Shirley gave her blessings to the beginning of the project, Nicky made possible its completion.

Transliteration and Notes

Hebrew transliteration follows a standard popular form, with "ḥ" representing *ḥet* and "kh" representing *khaf*, with the following exceptions. In Cochin, the *ḥet* was pronounced like a *heh*; this usage is retained in the spelling of given names (e.g., Haim, Eliyahu Hai). Cochin pronunciation will be apparent also in the use of "b" instead of "v" in certain Hebrew words (e.g., *nabi, tebilah*).

For Malayalam words, I have relied on Ruby Daniel's transliteration, which does not distinguish between long and short vowels, nor between certain retroflex and dental consonants.

The footnotes in my introduction are my own. In the rest of the book, the footnotes are in the words of Ruby Daniel unless they begin with my initials, BJ.

Ruby Daniel's Introduction

It all started in 1978. I suddenly got a letter for my Aunt Dolly Japheth in my care, here in the kibbutz where I live. Shirley Isenberg and then later Barbara Johnson, two anthropologists who are interested in the Cochin Jews, wanted to meet Dolly for the tunes of some Malayalam folk songs which the Jewish women in Kerala used to sing during weddings and parties. They contain a few historical facts and were written hundreds of years ago.

First Shirley and then Barbara came here to see my aunt. But by that time Dolly was old and lost her voice and forgot many of the songs she knew, but she sang a few songs with my help.

Then Shirley wanted to have translations of the songs, but she could not find anyone who knows the language well. I am the only person among the Jews of Cochin who took up the Malayalam language as an optional subject in college. So in a weak moment I said I can help in translating some of the songs. Shirley gave me photocopies of some of the songs from books collected in Cochin and Israel. Only when I opened those old books, I found the seriousness of my mistake. It was a Pandora's box.

The oldest book I found was one that my aunt Dolly had kept, written by my grandmother's great aunt. The letters and words are difficult to understand. There are a few words not in use now. The book is written on both sides of the paper with a strong kind of ink they used to make with a kind of nut called gall. The ink will remain for years, but it is so strong, it eats up the paper. You look on one page and you see the blurred writing from the back page. The people who had copied from that book had, I am sure, the same trouble reading it, and being not well educated in the language, they copied it as they thought it should be and perhaps missed a letter or a word. Then those who copied from that book made the same mistakes. And so, after three or four generations, only the skeleton remains, and people sing without understanding a word of what the song is all about. They say when you translate anything from one language to another, the translation is not what the original is intended to be. But this is worse, with letters and words missing, words that are no longer used, words loaned from other languages like

Tamil, Portuguese, Hebrew, and who knows what.

Then the following year my mother died, and then Aunt Dolly died a violent death from being burned, and their only brother, my uncle Daniel, died in England after a stroke, all in the same year. They were the people who loved me and whom I loved. My only relation who was left here on the kibbutz, my sister Rahel, nearly had a nervous breakdown and her daughter Shula called her to the States for a visit.

I am sitting in my house alone with not a single soul to say a word of consolation. Then I took up this work as a challenge. If I don't do something with my head I would go mad.

Moreover, according to Shirley there is no one who could do anything about these songs, and so all this will disappear. Then I thought, I shall do something for posterity. I sat down for hours with all my heart and soul in this work and translated about thirty or so songs in about two and a half years.

Then Shirley and Barbara coaxed me to write anything I can remember, what I heard from the oldsters in Cochin. At this I got interested. I have heard things from my elders which no one has heard and which will never be heard again, about how the Jews lived in Cochin and what happened to them there. Now almost all of us have come to live in Israel, and we are scattered in many places.

I thought, sometime some day someone will be curious to know where these people came from—some white, some dark, always quarreling about the color but otherwise standing up for one another, following the same customs, praying from the same book to the same God. How we lived in a communal life, peacefully, thanks to the regime of the Hindu Rajas.

When I began to write all these stories, my first intention was to show how good the people of Kerala were, how they welcomed the Jews and treated them well. I did not think I would write very much about my own life. But then I thought, I want to write about the situation of women in my generation, about their sufferings and all. Many of us were poor. The girls were not given a high education. They learned Torah enough for reading the prayers and kept in the house and got married, and they lived in poverty with children. I can't bring it out unless I write about my life too, a little rebel in the closely knit society.

It is important for people today to know about what happened before they were born, to know about the lives of ordinary women, people who were not known in the world. Wildflowers who bloom in the forest. Nobody sees them and they fade.

Barbara Johnson's Introduction

ITHACA, September 1993:

I sit here with the manuscript, contemplating the old old stories and gaz-ing at photos of Ruby Daniel in India more than forty years ago. A graceful, sari-clad young woman, her dark hair pulled back from her face, looks solemnly out from the formal group portraits and from the signed and stamped pass-port photo. My mind is full of images of Ruby today. At age eighty, she rides her three-wheeled cycle vigorously around the kibbutz, her slight figure dressed in comfortable slacks and shirts, her fluffy white hair cut short. Her quick movements, her quick wit, her quick smile—how do they relate to the calm gaze in the photographs? Yes, the deep brown eyes are the same today, intent and very direct.

I see her in the Neot Mordecai dining hall, chatting quietly with one or two friends—easy to spot in the crowd because she is one of only two Indian members on this kibbutz, but not drawing attention to herself in any way. She is quiet too in any large gathering of Cochin Jews, at a party or a holi-day celebration, sitting on the sidelines with the other older women.

But in a smaller group of her relatives or close Cochin friends, Ruby is at the center—waving her hand emphatically as if directing the hearty after-dinner singing on Shabbat, keeping us all spellbound with a ghost story or an item of fifty-year-old gossip, stopping us in our tracks with a teasing in-sult, feeding us royally with her famous filled onions or ultra-rich Cochin cake.

I see her at her kitchen counter under the front window, mixing up the batter for three Cochin cakes and pouring it into three pans of different sizes and shapes. Two cakes are for me to take to America—one to be mailed to her niece Shula in Minnesota and one for my own family and friends. Out-side the window, neighbor children call to each other in Hebrew. Inside, the air conditioner hums valiantly, struggling to combat the heat from the oven and the blazing sun of a July day in northern Israel.

Ruby is asking me to chop the raisins as finely as possible, to grate the nut-meg, and then when I am finished, to clean the red lentils for supper. The sweat runs down my back and my front. The air is rich with the mingled smells of cinnamon, cardamon, cloves, nutmeg. We talk as we work. Ruby's stories never cease.

> I am not a writer, but I write in the same way as I cook, but I am not a cook.

> (September 1986, letter from Ruby to Barbara)

> *Barbara*: What did you mean a few weeks ago when you said, "You can't just write plain, you have to put spices in it"?
> *Ruby*: Ah, spices, that means. . . . Did I say that? If you write only the *point*, you have only one or two sentences to tell about it. You have to expand it!

> (April 1990, taped conversation)

This book is a Cochin cake, full of secret goodies and unexpected surprises and mysterious tastes, exotic and familiar.

Two months ago I was listening to some of Ruby's stories for the third or fourth time. Each story remains the same in its essential ingredients, like a Cochin cake, but the shape of the pan may vary, or one time it may be a bit crisper around the edges, and one time the mixture of spices may be just perfect. And each story gets better with age: the spices bring each other out, the ghee preserves it. Sometimes it's meant to be eaten right away, tasted warm from the oven and then savored over days and days of teatime snacks. Or it can be carried anywhere, even to America, to share with friends and family on a camping trip in the Vermont woods.

Ruby will show me how she makes the cake, but she won't write down the recipe.

Most often I imagine that I'm sitting in Ruby's living room, leaning on the low table pulled up to the foam sofa. The table overflows with papers and books, the telephone and a pair of glasses misplaced somewhere in the confusion, but we're not sure which glasses are whose, as ours look so much alike. Ruby is in her chair at the end of the table. Maybe it's January and the two-element electric heater is close by to ward off the morning chill—in which case I must remember not to plug in the teakettle, or I'll blow the fuse again. This is where most of our conversations have taken place, and this is where most of the book was written.

For me it all started in 1968, when I first visited Cochin. Though I already had been living in South India for three years, this was my first encounter with the ancient Cochin Jewish community on the western coast of Kerala. I was entranced by the narrow street called Jew Town, by the friendliness and hospitality of its people, by their ease and pride in being thoroughly Indian and thoroughly Jewish. I began studying everything that had been written about their history and culture, from old government records and travelers' accounts to more recent reports by Western scholars. I began to learn Hebrew, at least in part so that I could read their own chronicles and community records. In 1974 I went back to Kerala, collecting material for my master's thesis on the origin stories of the Cochin Jews.

Returning to Cochin again in 1977, I tape-recorded Jewish women singing their own traditional folk songs in Malayalam, the language of Kerala, and I photocopied the old, handwritten notebooks from which they sang. "But you must go to Israel and meet Dolly Japheth," they told me. "She taught us the songs, and she knows more than we do." I had already begun corresponding with anthropologist Shirley Isenberg, who was undertaking a similar project of recording women's songs from the Cochin Jews in Israel, so I sent her the name of Dolly Japheth. We didn't yet know about Dolly's niece Ruby Daniel, who had left for Israel long before Dolly.

In 1981 I arrived in Israel to work on my doctoral dissertation. One of the first things I did was to visit Dolly Japheth, who was staying with her niece Ruby at Kibbutz Neot Mordecai. I soon discovered that Ruby, rather than her aunt Dolly, was the expert I had been looking for. Not only did she know how to sing the Malayalam women's songs; she could also translate them into fluent English and she could do much more. During the year that followed, I would return to the kibbutz several times, listening with fascination as Ruby told me about her childhood and youth in Cochin and recounted legends and historical memories she had heard, especially from her grandmother. Her version of Cochin Jewish history and of social relations within her community provided an extremely useful balance to stories I was hearing and reading elsewhere.

In 1985 I finally finished my Ph.D. dissertation, on the transition of Cochin Jewish community life from India to Israel. I sent Ruby Daniel a copy of the completed work and then returned to Israel to ask her (and other community members) for their reactions. Ruby responded, "I told you more than that!" With the encouragement of Shirley Isenberg, she had already begun writing down many of her stories that had not appeared in my dissertation, in addition to translating almost thirty of the Malayalam Jewish women's songs into English.* She showed me the stories she had written and I took them back home with me to type them up for her.

*I have cooperated with Shirley Isenberg and with P. M. Jussay (of Ernakulam, Kerala) in photocopying and tape-recording Cochin Jewish women's songs. Our copies of tapes and of handwritten song notebooks have been placed in the Phonoteque Archives of the Israel National and Hebrew University Library in Jerusalem. In 1984, Ruby Daniel's translations and transliterations into Hebrew of nine of these songs were compiled in photocopied pamphlets (Shirley Isenberg, Rivkah [Ruby] Daniel and Miriam Dekel-Squires, "*Tishah Shirei-Am Yehudiim beMalayalam*" [Jerusalem: 1984]).

(*Top*) Ruby Daniel and her aunt Dolly (Hannah) Japheth, examining copies of Malayalam-language Jewish songs, Kibbutz Neot Mordecai, 1981; (*bottom*) The notebook of Malayalam-language Jewish songs copied in the nineteenth century by Grandmother Docho's great aunt, the eldest daughter of Hannah and Shelomi Mudaliar. (*Photos, Barbara Johnson*)

Almost a year later Ruby wrote to me, not so gently, that *SHE* was going to write about a certain controversy in Cochin Jewish history that had been seriously misrepresented in some of the sources I had cited. "For your information," she wrote, "a few months ago some of us sat down together and talked and decided that all that you wrote was bull shit. I am sorry for telling you the truth. But don't be discouraged. Get on" (March 3, 1986).

I was of course intrigued by Ruby's forthright letter. No one else in the community had been so direct with me about their reactions to my work. It was clear that Ruby's stories were historically important as well as fascinating. I urged her to write more about her own life, in addition to the historical stories and song translations. It would make a wonderful book, I said.

She replied, "What interest have people got about my life? . . . . As for publishing all the things I have written, I myself don't know what to do with it. If you and Shirley don't do anything about it, it will all go a waste. I cannot write a book" (November 11, 1986). We began a back-and-forth process, in which she wrote, I typed and asked questions, and she wrote more. But it was not very efficient working by mail. In 1987 she wrote to me, "I am sorry you have done nothing about the book. Try your best and do something about it. I would like to see it too. I will be 75 in December. . . . Now I am writing about my life, all the rubbish. . . . I shall send it to you one of these days" (November 21, 1987).

By this time Ruby had written and I had typed almost one hundred pages, including historical legends, ghost tales, descriptions of Jewish celebrations in Cochin, song translations and a short personal memoir. The growing manuscript was a collection of stories and fragments, much in need of what Ruby called "arranging." It was clear there were more stories she could tell, especially about her own life, and it was clear that we needed to sit together for an extended time to work on editing them into a book.

Finally, in 1990, I received a small grant which enabled me to spend two months in Israel. A friend and I stayed most of that time on Ruby's kibbutz, packing apples in the apple factory to help earn our keep and eating most of our meals in the communal dining hall. The daily life of the kibbutz became much more familiar to me, balancing my memories of daily life in South India.

Almost every afternoon, Ruby and I sat and talked together in her apartment, at the table pulled up to the sofa. We tape-recorded our conversations and I transcribed them while she wrote more. Each night I typed and "arranged" her words, weaving together the written and oral stories. We read through the growing text together, adding and eliminating words, sentences, and sections. My friend Nicky asked questions too, contributing a third perspective.

Ruby complained and teased about my insatiable desire to know more and more about her life. "Too much engraving makes holes in the pot," she grumbled, quoting one of her many Malayalam proverbs. But she acknowledged, "I wrote such a lot more after you came. When I say one story, then suddenly I think of another story. . . ." When I insisted that she read over the final version of each section and chapter, she sometimes rolled her eyes about that too, but this step remained part of our work together.

Sometimes Ruby worried aloud about how others in the Cochin Jewish community might react to the book, especially to some of her criticisms of the white Jews. After one such conversation, she invited her younger cousin Abe from Tiberias to visit for the week-end. Abe and his wife read much of the manuscript and cheered her on: "You must tell the story Ruby-Aunty. Don't worry what others might say!" Their visit reassured both of us.

On the last day of our stay on the kibbutz, Nicky interviewed Ruby and me about how we had worked together, and that taped conversation provided still more material for both the book and this introduction. One of the issues we discussed was Ruby's view of herself as a writer.

Nicky: Ruby, where did you learn to write so well? In school?
Ruby: No, no. That they can't teach you. It is natural.
Nicky: So you were born with it?
Ruby: Maybe. Maybe. I am telling you, all the examinations I passed, it's only by the way I write. I forget what I have learned in the books. I just have an idea, and I just go on writing three pages at least. . . . But the English I write, it is a very easy language, very low. I haven't got a high language, only a high school English.
Barbara: But I think one reason this book is so interesting is because it's written the way people talk. It's like a conversation, so someone who reads it can just relax and enjoy it, because—
Ruby (laughing): Because it's like a story. But I am trying to compare this with all these books of classical English. Samuel Johnson writes, just for going for a walk, he is "perambulating," and so I think my language is poor.

This question of language usage has come up at several stages in the process of my editing the manuscript. I have edited Ruby's writing only for clarity, leaving in her interjections and repetitions along with idiomatic features of South Indian English, which may be unfamiliar to American readers, including the colloquial habit of frequently switching between past and present tenses. To me this is part of the charm of the book, that it preserves the rhythm and flavor of everyday South Indian speech along with the frequent poetic turns of phrase that characterize the style of a particularly gifted story-teller.

English is Ruby's second language. Her first was Malayalam, the language of Kerala's 29 million people, and she now speaks and reads Hebrew fluently. But like other educated Indians of her generation, she studied in English-medium schools and college. The way Ruby speaks and writes English is very much affected by her rich knowledge of Malayalam. Her everyday speech is peppered with Malayalam sayings and proverbs: "As my grandmother used to say. . . ." Also Ruby was unique among educated Cochin Jews in choosing

Malayalam language and literature as an optional subject in college (equivalent in some ways to an undergraduate minor in the U.S.). This advanced study gave her an acquaintance with classical literary Malayalam, making it possible for her to translate some obscure words and phrases in the old Malayalam Jewish songs that are incomprehensible to others who sing them.

"Malayalam has comparisons, very beautiful, and always some parables," she explained to Nicky and me. "The literature is difficult. The poetry is written eight hundred or a thousand years ago, and of course it is all wisdom. We had to memorize the poetry in school. But to translate the songs I must use my dictionary. In Cochin I had a dictionary and many books in the house, but I left everything behind. Then when I stayed in Bombay, on my way to Israel, I lived a while in my cousin's house. He said, 'Ruby, I've got a dictionary I brought from Cochin. You take it with you. Nobody wants it here, because in Bombay we don't need Malayalam.' I said, 'I am going to Israel! Why the hell should I take this Malayalam dictionary?' Then all of a sudden I thought, I don't like to throw away books, so I brought it. It's lying down here for thirty years. Every day I thought, What's the use of keeping this old book? But I didn't throw it away, and after thirty years it came to use. I was in a great predicament translating those songs and it helped me. (She pats the book lovingly.) Thank you!"

(April 1990, taped conversation)

As I contemplate the wider significance of this book that Ruby Daniel and I have produced together, I realize that a key issue is methodology.* From the beginning our process has been different from that of traditional oral history, for it is grounded in Ruby's *written* memoirs, with supplementary material from interviews. It also differs from the methods of many of my fellow anthropologists, who have chosen their "informants" and "collected" their oral narratives from them during ethnographic fieldwork, then gone back to their academic worlds where they edited (and often translated) the narratives themselves, sometimes shaping them to fit one anthropological theme or another.† Critical scholars of life story methodology have begun to note the perils of transforming an oral narrative into a written text in this way, point-

---

*For an expanded discussion of our methodology, in the context of the rapidly expanding field of life story scholarship, see my article "Bold Enough to Put Pen on Paper: Collaborative Method in an Ethnographic Life Story," in *Gender, Race and Political Activism: The Legacy of Sylvia Forman,* Dena Shenk, editor (Washington, DC: American Anthropology Association, forthcoming).

†There is a new anthropological questioning of traditional methods, with some scholars working toward more collaborative and reflexive life story methodology—for example Lila Abu-Lughod (*Writing Women's Worlds: Bedouin Stories,* Berkeley: University of California Press, 1993), Ruth Behar (*Translated Woman: Crossing the Border with Esperanza's Story,* Boston: Beacon Press, 1993), Karen Brown (*Mama Lola: A Vodou Priestess in Brooklyn,* Berkeley: University of California Press, 1991), and Greg Sarris (*Mabel McKay: Weaving the Dream,* Berkeley: University of California, 1994).

ing out the imbalance of power between the narrator and the interviewer/ editor, and the alienation of ownership that is likely to result.*

Ruby Daniel and I have tried to avoid these pitfalls. Basically Ruby initiated the project herself, and it began and has remained grounded in her writing. Our extended time together in 1990 was invaluable for eliciting a large quantity of new material and for editing most of the manuscript together. Since then, the challenge of completing the manuscript, weaving together the final version of her oral and her written stories, has been left mostly to me. But Ruby has continued to be involved in the process by mail and during my several brief visits to the kibbutz this year. Following our original understanding, she has maintained final say over the written text, at least up to the point that it reached the JPS editor. It's clear that Ruby Daniel sees herself as a writer and as the author of her own book.

In my extensive reading of other life stories, I was pleased and inspired to find one with a methodology similar to ours. *Lemon Swamp and Other Places: A Carolina Memoir* (New York: The Free Press, 1983), by Mamie Garvin Fields and her granddaughter, sociologist Karen Fields, began with a set of childhood memoirs written by Mamie Fields to give as a Christmas present— "an armful of looseleaf pages . . . wrapped in a big, red folder marked with the words 'Letters to My Three Granddaughters.' " The two women eventually worked out a lengthy process of talking, tape-recording, writing and editing together which sounds familiar to me, as I look back on my own work with Ruby Daniel.

Unlike Karen and Mamie Fields, Ruby and I are not members of the same family. If we were, our working relationship and our book would surely be quite different. But I have sometimes felt myself sliding into the role of a younger relation of some sort, first as an eager audience for her stories and then gradually as the person responsible for helping her preserve them. There's a sense that I myself didn't choose this project, with its intertwined privileges and obligations, as much as Ruby chose me for it. It's not a bad model for collaborative life story work.

Another significant aspect of this book is the light it sheds on Cochin Jewish history. A skeptic might question the accuracy of stories passed on orally from generation to generation, compared with those written down closer to the time of past events. In fact many of Ruby's orally transmitted stories match

---

*See for example the challenging work of Greg Sarris (*Keeping Slug Woman Alive: A Holistic Approach to American Indian Texts*, Berkeley: University of California Press, 1993) and various interdisciplinary anthologies, including Sherna Berger Gluck and Daphne Patai, eds., *Women's Words: The Feminist Practice of Oral History* (New York: Routledge, 1991); The Personal Narratives Group, eds., *Interpreting Women's Lives* (Bloomington: Indiana University Press, 1989); and Sidonie Smith and Julia Watson, eds., *De/Colonizing the Subject* (Minneapolis: University of Minnesota, 1992).

up quite precisely with historical documents of which she was unaware. I have noted a few examples in footnotes.

Furthermore, as Ruby notes, one cannot always trust the accounts of those who are too much involved: "Those who want to write about the history of the Cochin Jews, beware! Because they would not find an honest commentator, and the result will be a distortion of facts."

The controversy Ruby mentioned in her 1986 "bull shit" letter to me was that concerning the status of the so-called "freed slaves" or "*meshuḥrarim*" in Cochin. On this topic, Ruby is an expert, and her book provides a particularly important corrective to the historical record.

Ruby's family was part of one small congregation of Kerala Jews, those of the Paradesi Synagogue, dominated by the so-called white Jews of Cochin. The Daniels and Japheths belonged to the group of people within that community who were denied equal rights in the synagogue. The whites labeled them "*meshuḥrarim*" because their ancestors were said to have been converts or the children of white Jewish men and slave or servant women. "*Meshuḥrar*" was a label Ruby's family firmly rejected. Part of Ruby's motivation in writing this book is the desire to set the record straight about her family's origins and about all the controversies over their status.

Those controversies have been documented again and again for more than a hundred and fifty years. Waves of conflict within the Paradesi community have been set off or intensified by the questions and interference of curious Westerners, Jews and non-Jews alike. Outsiders have been fascinated, if not obsessed, by evidence of social inequality and prejudice among the Cochin Jews—as if such distinctions are not found in Jewish communities elsewhere!*

Earlier writings on the community have included varied points of view found among the white Jews—some who supported the discrimination against the

---

*I count myself among those scholars who have focused in the past on how the Hindu caste system influenced Jewish social structure in Kerala. This approach is seen in my earlier writings, but I am working now on a critique and revision of that perspective. It seems clear that the Jews did think of themselves (that is, all Kerala Jews together) as a *jati*, or caste, distinct from the Hindu, Muslim, and Christian castes surrounding them. But they did not regard their internal divisions as constituting separate castes or subcastes—not the distinction between the Paradesi congregation and the more ancient communities of Malabari or so-called "black" Jews, and certainly not the differences between the "white" Jews and other members of the Paradesi congregation.

Likewise I am reassessing my earlier views on "slavery" in Cochin Jewish history. Various forms of servitude (both land-based and personal) were known in ancient Kerala; beginning in medieval times, Arab and eventually Portuguese merchants brought to the area Middle Eastern and European versions of slavery. The picture was further complicated by the Cochin Jewish application of biblical and rabbinic laws of slavery and manumission to a cultural situation very different from that in which these laws were compiled—also by the limitations of Hebrew vocabulary (in which *eved* can be translated as slave, bondsman, servant or serf)—and not least by the peculiar Cochin Jewish practice of accepting converts to Judaism only through the ritual for the manumission of slaves. Furthermore, British interpretations of internal Jewish divisions in Cochin must be viewed in the light of their 19th century "anti-slavery" ideology and colonial policy.

other faction and some who advocated ending all distinctions. But until now, the viewpoint of the so-called "*meshuḥrarim*" has been portrayed monolithically from the perspective of two of their male leaders: Avraham (called Avo), who led a 19th century exodus of his followers from Jew Town to Fort Cochin, and Avo's grandson A. B. Salem.* In the following pages Ruby gives credit to both of these men for the roles they played in Cochin Jewish history, but she adds a critical perspective passed down through the women in her own family, who descend from two of Avo's sisters. Her family's viewpoint might be summed up in one statement: "We were never slaves, so we should not be called freed slaves."

To tell the story of the Cochin Jews from an essentially male perspective, as most writers have done, is of course to tell only part of the story. In addition, this approach distorts the realities of the larger Kerala culture, in which women hold a relatively high status and have often been well educated and influential. The ruling Hindu dynasty of Cochin Maharajas, along with a powerful group of high-caste Hindus called the Nayars, traditionally practiced a form of matrilineal inheritance and family structure that still influences the women of the entire culture.

Kerala women have been literate to a much higher degree than women elsewhere in India. Among the Cochin Jews, members of Ruby Daniel's family were pioneers in literacy for women, beginning with Avo's sisters in Fort Cochin, who "were educated at a time when the rich girls back in Jew Town did not know how to read or write their names." Ruby inherits her expertise in the Malayalam Jewish songs from her grandmother Docho, and that expertise can be traced back to Docho's great-aunt in Fort Cochin, who wrote by hand one of the oldest collected notebooks of women's songs. Thanks to the insistence of her mother (Docho's daughter Leah), Ruby was the first girl in her own generation to continue her studies outside Jew Town, and the first Jewish woman in Kerala to enter college. I believe that this intellectual inheritance partially explains why Ruby Daniel is also the first Cochin Jewish woman to write and publish a book.

One day on the kibbutz Ruby asked me, "Why do *you* take so much trouble with this work?" My first response was to remind her of the complaints

---

*The earliest written sources to tell the story of "Avo" (from a white Jewish perspective) were written in Hebrew by European Jewish travelers. See Jacob Saphir, *Eben Saphir*, vol. 2 (Lyck: Silberman, 1874), pp. 69–72, and Solomon Reinman, *Masaot Shelomo* (Vienna: W. Schur, 1884), pp. 161–162. The earliest source to link A. B. Salem's story with that of his grandfather Avo was David Mandelbaum, "The Jewish Way of Life in Cochin," *Jewish Social Studies* 1, no. 4 (1939), pp. 449–450; later expanded as "Social Stratification among the Jews of Cochin in India and in Israel," *Jewish Journal of Sociology* 17, no. 2 (1975), pp. 165–210. Saphir, Reinman, and Mandelbaum (1975) were recently reprinted and widely read among the Cochin community in Israel; see Shalva Weil, ed., *MeCochin leEretz Israel* (Jerusalem, 1984).

by her and by others about my dissertation—about what I had written and about what I had left out. "I realize that an outsider like me can't tell the story the way a member of the community can. So now you are telling the story in your own words," I said, "and I am glad to help you with that process. . . ."

She snapped back, "So you want *me* to be the *korban* [sacrificial offering]?"

Startled, I laughed: "Yes, I suppose that's right."

This was my first response, but I've been trying to answer her question on many levels ever since. This work certainly represents more than a scholarly project for me. I think Ruby was asking quite specifically, Why Cochin? Why her story?

Part of the answer is that I am a Jew—and as a convert, in some sense a marginal one. When I first went to Cochin for extended visits in the 1970s, I was not yet a Jew, so according to Paradesi custom I couldn't sit with the other women in the synagogue, upstairs in the women's section. When I prayed in the Paradesi Synagogue, I sat down in the entrance room, where members of Ruby's family used to sit. In some sense my intense personal engagement began then.

It also began further back in my life, during the four years I lived in South India during the 1960s—first teaching at a women's college and then living closely with a large Indian extended family. The stories Ruby tells of herself as a child, as a student, and as a young woman feel familiar to me. I connect them with the lives of my students and close personal friends, and sometimes with my own life. The South Indian style of conversation and friendship is comfortable too. I feel at ease in Ruby's home.

The particular Jew Town landscape of Ruby's childhood has also become familiar to me. The narrow street with houses all connected so everyone knows everyone's business, the hanging glass lamps in the synagogue, the swishing sound of coconut palms bending in the wind, the sticky heat and the welcome first drops of monsoon rain—all these have worked their way into my being.

Familiar also is Ruby's sense of displacement, the loneliness of living among people who have never been in India and who construct it as a fantasy world or do not acknowledge that such a world exists. In helping her to tell her story, I am somehow reclaiming a piece of my own, a part that was very formative but that is usually invisible.

And then there are the ghosts.

I identify with Ruby and her grandfather in what she calls their "scientific" attitude toward matters of life and death, but I have never asked her how she reconciles these beliefs with her ghost stories. One night the two of us were talking late in her apartment, without the tape recorder, as we sometimes did. I was feeling very troubled about what to do with the spirits who seemed to appear so frequently in the streets and courtyards and houses of Cochin—and with people's mysterious dreams that brought messages from the dead. Ruby had written a whole chapter of stories about these Cochin Jewish ghosts and dreams, writing them down in no particular order, just as they occurred to her. At this point they seemed to defy being "arranged," and they were invading both my waking and my sleeping hours.

"Have you any experiences like these?" Ruby asked. Hesitantly I described sensing my father's presence, a few years after his death, on a dark icy road in Vermont as my car spun out of control and righted itself just in time to avoid a serious crash. She listened attentively.

Then much more hesitantly I recounted a waking dream, which had come to me some years earlier while I was still struggling to write my dissertation: I stood before a whitewashed wall. My eyes were fixed on the outline of an old door. A door that had been plastered over long ago, but I knew it led to the next-door house in Jew Town. A door like the one between her family's two houses, where the ghost of her grandmother's aunt had tried to cross through as Ruby's mother watched from the veranda. In my dream there was just the outline of a door. I knew I could pass through it, but I stood there, unable to move.

"That's all?" Ruby seemed to ask, though she didn't speak.
"I'm not sure what that dream meant, Ruby."
More silence.
"It could be about this book," she said.

Part One

THE LIFE STORY OF RUBY DANIEL

Chapter 1

STORIES FROM THE PAST, TOLD TO ME BY MY ELDERS

I t has been suggested that I should write down everything I have heard from my grandparents and from other old people who have heard stories from their own grandparents. So I make myself bold enough to put pen on paper to say what I can remember from what I heard, mostly from my grandmother Rachel (Docho), the daughter of Daniel Haim and the wife of Eliyahu Japheth, both of whom were *rabbanim*, learned in the Law. They were very Orthodox people, but she was a foot above them. The following stories may contain some grains of truth. Everything cannot be fiction. There is no smoke without fire, they say. But there are no records which I can show you.

In the city of Cochin in Malabar, on the southwest coast of India, there is a street located in between the towns of Mattanchery and Kochangadi. It is called Jew Town or Jews Street because for many centuries only Jews lived there. The houses are built on both sides of a narrow road as a block. There are only two or three openings to get in and get out of this Town. When I was growing up in Cochin there were three synagogues in that street, one at each end and one in the middle, for three separate Jewish communities. At the northern end is the Palace of the Maharaja with the Hindu temple. Next to the temple wall is the Paradesi Synagogue, where my ancestors worshiped for hundreds of years, and Jew Town reaches from there to the Kadavumbagam Synagogue at the southern end of the street, near the small house where I lived with my family. The middle synagogue, called Tekkumbagam, was located closer to the northern end of the Town.

The city of Cochin is on an island surrounded by water, and it has one of

Jew Town, Cochin, in the 1930s. The bell tower of the Paradesi Synagogue stands at the northern end of the street. The bamboo screen (*vesha*) hanging in front of each door was doused with water to cool the interior of the house. (*Wonderful India*. New Delhi: *The Statesman* and *Times of India* Book Depot, 1938)

the safest harbors. The backwaters touch the courtyards of the buildings on the eastern side of Jew Town. The Arabian Sea is about three miles to the west, with the backwater river joining the sea in the north near Fort Cochin. On the mainland across the harbor is the city of Ernakulam.

Before the 1950s, when almost all of us immigrated to Israel, there were about two thousand Jews living in this part of Kerala. In addition to the three synagogues in Cochin, there were two synagogues in Ernakulam and one each in the villages of Parur, Chendamangalam, and Mala. All of these Jews were referred to as Cochin Jews, because they lived in Cochin State, the part of Kerala ruled by the Cochin maharaja (except for Parur, which was in Travancore State). The people of Malabar, especially those of Cochin, are friendly

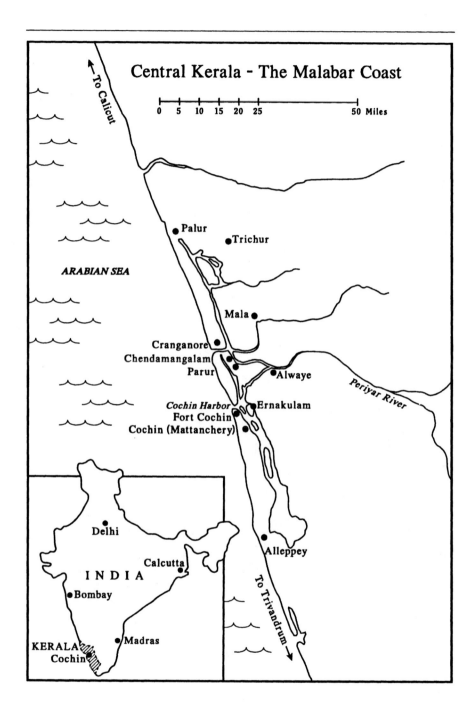

Central Kerala - The Malabar Coast

0 5 10 15 20 25   50 Miles

To Calicut

ARABIAN SEA

Palur

Trichur

Mala

Cranganore

Chendamangalam

Parur

Alwaye

Periyar River

Cochin Harbor

Fort Cochin

Cochin (Mattanchery)

Ernakulam

Delhi

INDIA

Calcutta

Bombay

KERALA
Cochin

Madras

Alleppey

To Trivandrum

Coconut palm trees in the Kerala countryside, from an 1860 drawing. (Charles A. Lawson, *British and Native Cochin*. Cochin: Courier Press, 1860)

and tolerant, so we lived in peace with our Hindu, Muslim, and Christian neighbors.

THE COAST OF MALABAR OR KERALA

In Hindu mythology there was a mighty king called Parasurama. He once threw his hatchet from a place called Gokarnam and it fell in Cape Comorin (now the southern tip of India). Then a land rose up from the sea, and this piece of land from Gokarnam till Cape Comorin is called Malabar or Kerala. Its climate is mild, with plenty of rainfall. Fresh fish is abundant, vegetables in numerous varieties, fresh fruit in plenty, and everything inexpensive. When I was young, labor was cheap too, but those who could not afford meat ate fish or vegetables, which cost very little. Rice is cultivated there and is the main food, and coconut is a principal ingredient in many kinds of preparations of food and sweetmeats.

Kerala takes its name from the *kera* or coconut tree, which grows there in plenty. Another name for that tree in the Malayalam language is "the tree that gives everything," because every part of the tree is useful. The white kernel of the coconut is used in making curry or chutney or sweet dishes, or oil is extracted from it for cooking or for the hair. When the fruit is not ready to be plucked, when it is still tender, there is more water inside and the kernel is very soft and sweet like ice cream. If a traveler is thirsty on the way and asks at any house for a drink of water, the householder doesn't give water. Instead he calls one of the servants and asks him to pluck a couple of tender nuts, cut off the top, and give him to drink and to eat the tender kernel inside. Also a kind of liquor is tapped out of the coconut tree, called "toddy" by the English. It is collected in pots attached to the tree. A certain caste of people used to have the job of climbing high into the trees and emptying the pots three times a day.

The trunk of this tall palm tree is cut into planks and used in building houses, and the leaves are plaited and tied around instead of walls. Still there are huts like this in remote villages. Those who have brick or stone houses also used to thatch the roofs with coconut leaves, to protect the roof from falling coconuts, because there are usually a few coconut trees in every compound or yard where a house stands. The leaves are also used to make baskets. The fruit is covered by a hard shell, which is burned as firewood. Now they make all kinds of articles from the shell, such as cups and saucers, vases and spoons. This shell is covered with fiber, from which is made rope, carpets and rugs, brushes, and a filling for the bedding.

No wonder the land of Kerala is named for this tree, which satisfies your appetite, quenches your thirst, gives you a shelter, fire to cook your food, a drink if you need it and a cup to drink from, sugar jaggery to sweeten your coffee or make sweetmeats, an umbrella to keep off the rain, a carpet and a broom for the floor, and even a toothpick or a brush for your teeth.

ORIGINS OF THE COCHIN JEWS

It has been a question why and how the Cochin Jews are unique, living far away from the bulk of the Jewish people in Europe and America, or even in the Middle East. There in the southernmost part of India we kept up the Jewish tradition, always longing for the Land of Israel in spite of the quiet and peaceful life we led in Malabar.

Tradition says that the Jews were in Malabar even during the time of King Solomon and had arrived there as traders in gold, ivory, and peacock feathers, for which the area of Travancore is still famous. That may be one of the reasons Jewish refugees found this place many years later after the Destruction of the Temple. Ten thousand Jewish families are said to have come to Kerala. Where are they, I wonder? What happened to them? By the year 1940 there remained only about two thousand souls. I think they must have assimilated or left the country, but no one knows.

From early times, about 1000 C.E., the Jews were granted certain privileges by the then ruler of Malabar, called Cheraman Perumal. These rights are engraved on copper plates said to have been presented to one Joseph Rabban, the then leader of the Jews. These privileges are the same as those allowed to the Hindu ruling class in Malabar. To quote a few: a cloth spread before the bridegroom in a wedding procession or before the child taken in a procession to the synagogue for his circumcision; a brass lamp with lights around carried on a chain; a silk umbrella or a piece of silk spread on an umbrella made from the fronds of the palm trees; to ride on an elephant; to be carried in a palanquin. Also to use wooden slippers which have a piece of wood attached on the top which is held between the first two toes, this stump to be made of gold; and so on. These are the signs of nobility. These privileges were granted to the class of people whom the rulers favored. There are a class among the Christians and Muslims who have these privileges also.

CRANGANORE

A few traditions about the origin of these Kerala Jews are centered around Cranganore, an ancient port city north of Cochin. The ruler of Cranganore was very good to the Jews. They were given many privileges and they lived in their own colony. It is said that a rich widow from somewhere in Palestine came with her daughter and eight hundred people and settled in Cranganore.

At that time widows stayed put in the house and never showed their faces outside their homes. So this lady, known as Kadambath-Achi (*Achi* means lady), got a six-year-old boy to marry her so that she would no longer be a widow, and she would no longer be stuck inside her house. She must have been a courageous and enterprising woman.

It happened one morning as the ruler's son was taking his daily horse ride, he saw the daughter of Kadambath-Achi and fell in love with her at first sight. He confessed this to his father and he wanted to marry her. So the raja went to the mother and requested her daughter's hand in marriage to his son. But she utterly refused to give her daughter to a gentile. King or emperor did not make any difference to her. The raja's son pined for the daughter and fell ill. So the raja got angry and ordered the Jews out of his country overnight, under pain of death. So all the people ran away. This lady and her daughter ground all their jewelry and precious stones into powder and threw it into a pool. They themselves swallowed diamonds and died. The name of that pool is still called the Jewish Pool (*Jutha Kulam*) and the hill nearby is called the Jewish Hill (*Jutha Kunna*). No Jews remain there, only the names of these places. People living there still say they sometimes find tiny pieces of gold in the sand of that pool.

Other traditions about Cranganore are found in songs and history books. I have heard just a few lines of one Malayalam song which recounts how the Cranganore Jews were having a big party to celebrate the building of a new synagogue. As they were celebrating, an old man came—some say he was Eliyahu Hanabi—and he told them, "You will live here only three times thirty years, and after that the synagogue will be destroyed."

Then there is the historical fact that in the sixteenth century Jews were driven away from Cranganore by the Portuguese and the Moors. Then the Jews settled in several places south of Cranganore, such as Mala, Chendamangalam, and Parur, and went from place to place. They also settled and built synagogues in Palur, Muttath, and Southi, as is mentioned in Malayalam songs and folklore. These latter places they left eventually. Some found a haven in the city of Cochin, where they found favor in the eyes of the rulers.

Whether from Cranganore or other places, the Jewish refugees did not arrive as paupers. They brought with them fabulous amounts of gold coins, diamonds, rubies, gold dust, and other such things. When they went to see the rulers they presented them with a small packet of diamonds, which was placed before the ruler and cut open with a golden knife. At once the ruler wrote out the ownership of an island, or a hill to the newcomer, who had to pay only a nominal tax to the government. Thus many islands and hills came into the possession of the Jews, and like other landowners they had to spend money and develop the land and cultivate it.

The first synagogue in the island of Cochin was in Kochangadi, a few furlongs to the south of where Jew Town ends today. It was abandoned long ago. After that the Jews came and built the Kadavumbagam Synagogue, which stands at the southern end of Jew Town. Then the synagogue which stands at the northern end of Jew Town in Cochin, next to the palace of the maharaja, was built by *Paradesi* (a Malayalam word for foreigners).

These Paradesi Jews escaped the pogroms of Spain and Portugal and found asylum in that remote corner of India, among the Jews who had settled in Malabar nearly two thousand years before them. They joined a few of the rich Jews there and others from Syria and Turkistan and other places, and they stayed in Cochin as a separate community. They were known as the white Jews because they were fair-skinned. The Jews who came earlier to Malabar had lost their color after hundreds of years of settlement and hard work in a very hot country, and of course by some mix with the natives, just like the Jews in Europe got their blond hair and blue eyes. Nowhere is it written that the color of the original Jews was white. Was Sippora the wife of Moses white? The color of Queen Esther also was not white.

Anyway, these Paradesis didn't marry among the Jews of the other seven synagogues. Sometimes they called the others "black Jews," though in fact most of them are not very black in color. And sometimes they spoke of them as their converts and slaves, even though those Jews had been in Kerala hundreds of years before them.

Some of the Paradesis became very wealthy. Chellanam, Neendakara, Irimbanam, Maruvakadu, Ponnankadu, Mulavukadu, Venduruthi, Vettaka, Pathuruthi, Manakodum were a few of the islands in the possession of the Paradesi Jews till lately. It is said that Ponnankadu was such a fertile land that the rice that is cultivated there yields such a lot that there won't be enough place to store it in the whole of Jew Town.

The rich Paradesi masters did not spare the young women who came to do domestic work for them in their poverty, and the children thus begotten they called in Hebrew *yelide bayit* (children born in the house). They also called them their "slaves" which was not correct, and then after some years they called their descendants *meshuḥrarim* or "freed slaves," but that was also not correct. I have never seen any evidence that the Jews bought slaves with money, or that there was slave trade in Cochin, as for instance there was in Africa.

It is true that there were castes in Kerala called Parayas and Pulayas, who were brought from some other places and given hard work in agriculture. There is also a class of Hindus called Cherumies who are blond with blue eyes, and another class called Thiyan who are fair skinned, and a caste called

Kanakas. The Kanakas are the people employed to climb up the coconut tree to pluck the nuts.* Anyway, all these castes were kept in their places and branded as "untouchables" or "slaves" by the Hindus. Just because they were weak people, they were put in this position. Why do people look down on them? The people who treat them like animals, they are called "masters" and looked on as big people. I think they should be given a name worse than slaves.

But there were no slaves like these people among the Jews.

SOME DISTORTIONS CORRECTED: THE ORIGINS OF MY FAMILY

Those who want to write about the history of the Cochin Jews and their customs, beware! Because they would not find an honest commentator, and the result will be a distortion of facts. Most of the stories written by modern writers are the stories told by the so-called white Jews, the ones who brought this "slavery" craze and felt themselves to be superior to other Jews in Cochin. I am glad to write what I heard from my grandparents and others, to correct some of these distortions. Following is the true story.

At one time it so happened that a beautiful woman with a small daughter came to Cochin Jew Town looking for work. There was war in her country and she escaped from the hands of the enemies. This woman by the name of Kadoori was the great-great-great grandmother of my grandmother Docho. She was hired as a domestic help by one of the Paradesis, and she and her daughter stayed with that family.

The daughter (whose name is forgotten) grew up to be a beautiful girl, and the master or his son took her as his mistress. This man's name was "Daikachan," maybe David. He did not marry another woman but remained with her. Kadoori's daughter had one daughter and four sons from him. He took great care of his children, and his idea was to send them away from Cochin to find good wives for the sons and a husband for his beloved daughter, whose name was Hannah. But Daikachan died and the sons took care of their sister, hoping to save her from this gang of "slave" producers in Jew Town.

There was a cousin of Daikachan named Shelomi Mudaliar. He was Solomon Hallegua, the ancestor of the present Hallegua family in Cochin.† Shelomi

---

*Now I find that there is an island called New Caledonia in the Pacific and natives there are called Kanakas, so perhaps they came from there.

†*Mudaliar* (headman) was a title given by the maharaja to the leader of the Paradesi Jews, and it was held for several generations in the Hallegua family. In fact the name Hallegua was originally Alleva. When they found out that somewhere in Europe there was a family called Hallegua, they changed the Alleva to Hallegua. In our house we had a few chairs handed down from Shelomi Mudaliar, on which were written the initials S.A., for Solomon Alleva.

fell in love with this girl Hannah and wanted her, but her father and the brothers after him will not agree to it. Shelomi was lovesick and was bedridden with no food and drink, so his friends and relatives made a scheme. All the young girls joined together and made a party. They invited Hannah to join them. As they were all her friends, the brothers let her join them. At the end of the party all the girls suddenly disappeared and she was left alone in the room. Before this young girl could realize what was happening, Shelomi went into the room. At that time, being alone with a man was the greatest disgrace for a woman and her family. In fact her four brothers all left Cochin afterward.

But Shelomi Hallegua did not want to spoil her. He took her to Vettaka, an island he possessed, and there he invited a few of his friends and read the Hebrew words "*Are at mekudeshet li*" ("Behold you are holy to me"), which is equal to a marriage. Hannah lived with him for forty years as the mistress of the house and got five children—a son and four daughters. The son's name was Abraham and the sisters Rachel, Sarah, Leah, and Rivka. In her old age Hannah was called Annochimuthi for respect. Abraham was called Avo or Avomutha; this was the Avo so many writers are incorrectly calling a "slave." The Paradesis referred to this family and their descendants as *meshuhrarim*, without any basis for that name.

After some forty years, Shelomi Mudaliar got married to another woman. Annochimuthi persuaded him to do it, perhaps because the other white Jews didn't accept her as his wife, or perhaps she became crazy. This girl from the community used to come to visit, and Annochimuthi liked her very much. Suddenly she had the craziness to tell Shelomi to marry the girl. He said, "Why should I? I've got a wife and five children." But Annochimuthi forced him to marry her. The other white Jews were just waiting, and when the second wife got pregnant, they all joined together to take Annochimuthi out. Shelomi didn't want her to go. He said, "Stay, you are the mistress of the house." She could have stayed with the other wife, but no, she wanted to get out. For nothing at all. One by one the daughters came to stay with her too. They moved to the house where I grew up, and the house next to it.

Shelomi Mudaliar's new wife gave birth to a son named Isaac Hallegua. When Shelomi was on his deathbed, he asked his son Abraham to take care of this young boy, his stepbrother. Avo got married to the daughter of a very rich man named Doika, who was from one of the Jewish families who had come away from Cranganore. Abraham and his wife had six children, including one son named Itzhak, who became a scholar and wrote Sefer Torahs (Torah scrolls). Some of their daughters married *hakhamim* (Jewish scholars) who came from Yemen and other places.

Anyway, Abraham must have thought he needed no money from his father, Shelomi Mudaliar, because he gave everything to his stepbrother when the boy came of age. Perhaps he did not realize that his own sisters, who became widows early, with one or two children, would need help. One sister, Leah, lost her husband when she was only sixteen; he was trading in Hongkong or Shanghai when he was lost from the ship. A second sister, Rivka, also had a husband who died at sea. She had only one daughter, who died in childbirth, and Rivka raised her daughter's son, Koko. After some time he went to Bombay or Calcutta.

Another sister, Sarah, was married to a Yemenite named Binyamin Benaya, who came to Cochin from Aden. They got a son named Benaya Benjamin and a daughter named Rivka. Their daughter, Rivka, was the mother of both my grandmother Docho and my father, Eliyahu Hai Daniel, and I am named Rivka after her. The other sister, Rachel, married a man named Haim, and their son was my grandfather Daniel.*

FROM JEW TOWN TO FORT COCHIN

These people, whom the white Jews called "slaves," were not given equal rights in the Paradesi Synagogue. After some time they refused to go to the synagogue and started praying in a private house. But the white Jews would not accept this, because then they won't have anybody to be called their slaves. So they filed a suit to stop them from praying where they wanted. Their complaint was that the sound of the blowing of their shofar disturbed the prayers in the Paradesi Synagogue. But the Thekkumbagam Synagogue was next door to the Paradesis and that did not disturb them, and the place where the so-called "slaves" prayed was double the distance from their synagogue.

The case went up to the British resident governor. He could not understand why a group of people cannot pray where they want. One of the white Jews' complaints was that there should not be a fourth synagogue in the Town. So the resident governor himself came to find out. The white Jews told him that anyway these people don't need another synagogue, because they are welcome at our synagogue. A few of the Paradesi noblemen took him to see the place where the other group were praying. When the governor went back, he told the white Jews that he measured the distance by foot and found how far it was and it was a lie to say that their prayers disturbed the Paradesi Synagogue and that they should keep quiet to save their honor. So these noblemen removed their caps and put them at his feet and requested him not to disgrace them, as they are white people like him. But he could

---

*BJ: It is sure that the names of these four sisters were Leah, Rivka, Sarah, and Rachel, but there is no one remaining alive who is absolutely sure which one was which. The names assigned here and in the family tree are Ruby's best guess.

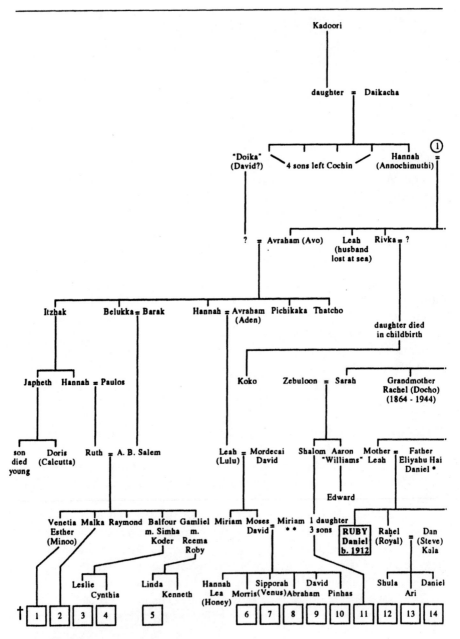

† See "Supplement to Family Tree," page 193.

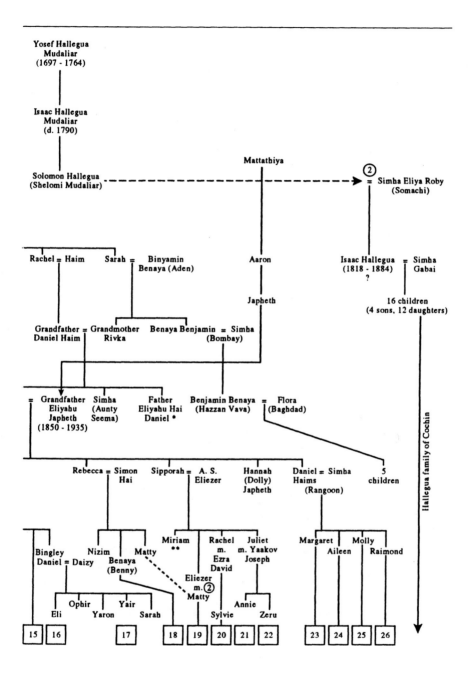

not do anything for them, because it was the time when religious freedom was proclaimed by Queen Victoria's government.

The governor told the other party that if they wanted to build a synagogue, he will get for them permission from the British parliament. But they did not do so at that time, maybe because they didn't have enough people to conduct a synagogue. I have heard that at one time the white Jews were willing to make a synagogue and write on it "Synagogue of the *Meshuḥrarim*," just to establish that they had slaves, but people were not willing to accept this. Maybe that was what happened at this time.

Anyway, when all these things were happening, the white Jews became very angry. They hired some thugs from the Kadavumbagam community and asked them to capture Itzhak, who was the son of Abraham and the grandson of Shelomi Hallegua. "Bring Itzhak and the Sefer Torah!" they told them. They just wanted to get rid of Itzhak because he was a scholar and the one who wrote the Sefer Torah. So on a Purim day when these people were at their prayers in a large house opposite to our house, these thugs went in suddenly, pulled out all the jewelry from the ladies, and hit them. But an old lady saved Itzhak. They were using this hall as a school also, so there was a stand from the blackboard. She took this stand to a room where there was an opening in the wooden ceiling to a storage space under the roof. She helped him up there and pushed up the Sefer Torah too, and then she closed the board. When she finished her work, she found herself surrounded by these drunkards, with no way to escape. So she jumped out of the window of the top floor rather than fall into their hands. She broke her legs. But anyway they did not find Itzhak or the Sefer Torah.*

Then these people whom the white Jews called "slaves" ran away to Fort Cochin, which was under the direct jurisdiction of the British, so they were safe there. There is no record of exactly when this happened, but I have heard that my grandfather Eliyahu Japheth was a young boy of about twelve or thirteen at the time he went to Fort Cochin, and he was born in 1850 or 1851.

The Arabian Sea was very close to the buildings in Fort Cochin, which were built in the time of the Portuguese. There is a graveyard there in which there is a tomb supposed to be that of Vasco da Gama.† There is a wall around that graveyard, and the waves now come up to its walls. It so happened that when this group of Jews went to live in Fort Cochin, the sea started receding and stayed half a kilometer away, revealing the remains of the old Dutch fortress there. It made a beautiful beach of cream-colored soft sand. One could travel on this beach, on foot or by bicycle, as far as Cape Comorin at

---

*BJ: This Purim disturbance probably was the one referred to in Ezekiel N. Musleah, *On the Banks of the Ganga: The Sojourn of Jews in Calcutta* (North Quincy, MA: Christopher Publishing House, 1975), p. 374.
†Or maybe it is just a monument or memorial stone.

the southern tip of India. So the people of the place were very happy. They believed it is by the luck which the Jews brought that this miracle happened.

At that time there was a bishop in Fort Cochin called Lazron Padre, who became very fond of these Jews.* He took them under his wings and helped them a lot, together with the Anglo-Indians who had more or less the same problem like those people. They also were born to the mistresses of the European masters of the houses where they worked. Their fathers were not only British; Frankies (French) and the Dutch were also partners, only there was nobody to call them slaves. The Indians insulted the Anglo-Indians. The epithet concerning them was "disowned by the East and disinherited by the West: the permanent monument of British adultery." Many of the Anglo-Indian women were left without husbands, and no one to marry them, so they were starving and living in huts. These people were helped by the Christian missionaries, who taught them to support themselves. There was a school in Fort Cochin called Santa Cruz High School, taught by European monks. Many of the Jewish girls were taught sewing and embroidery work by the European nuns in their convent called St. Mary's High School.

These missionaries were glad to get a group of Jewish refugees. The missionaries did not know that their belief was rooted in the religion of Abraham, and that they were not interested in becoming Christians. Anyway they taught these Jews to read and write in English, before most of the Paradesis learned, and the women became self-supporting because they knew needlework. My grandmother Docho's great-aunt, the oldest daughter of Annochimuthi and Shelomi Mudaliar, was one of the women who learned to write in Fort Cochin. She copied down many of the Malayalam songs which the Cochin Jewish women sing, in a notebook which I have today. She also learned to make pillow lace.

There were many Jews living in Fort Cochin at that time. Avomutha and the others made a synagogue there. When I was growing up, our family had three shofars from that synagogue. Then there was a terrible epidemic, and I have heard that about seventy-five of the Jews in Fort Cochin died. Many of the others went away to Bombay and Calcutta. Some of those families are still known, but we don't know what became of the others. So there were not enough people left to conduct the synagogue separately in Fort Cochin, and most of the few Jews who remained there returned to live again in Jew Town. The daughters of Shelomi Mudaliar and Annochimuthi were among those who returned to Cochin. They had no husbands. What else could they do?

---

*BJ: This must have been a Church of Scotland missionary named Rev. Edward Laseron, who supervised a school in Jew Town during the 1840s. The school did not last long, as he became embroiled in quarrels with the white Jews, insisting that the so-called meshuḥrarim should be allowed to attend his school. See excerpts from the Diwan's Diary for 1845–1849 in the S. S. Koder manuscript collection, Cochin, vol. III, mss. nos. 6–17.

Avo and Itzhak and many of the others are buried in the Jewish cemetery in Fort Cochin near the beach. Itzhak had a son named Japheth. He went to Calcutta to do business as a young man, and then he went to England and opened a hotel there. But he lost all his money and came back to Cochin. At his wish he was buried next to his father, Itzhak, through the influence of Mr. A. B. Salem, as the Jewish cemetery in Fort Cochin was closed by the time he died.

TROUBLES IN BOMBAY AND COCHIN

One of the men who left Cochin was Benaya Benjamin, my grandmother Docho's uncle, who went to Bombay and engaged in trade. He had an only son, Benjamin Benaya, who was well versed in Torah.* In order that his son should learn, the father kept a hostel for the ḥakhamim who came from Palestine and other places to collect money. Many men of learning gathered there. They had free board and lodge as long as they stayed. In a midrash (Hebrew school) in Jerusalem there was kept a board saying that the one who is receiving and taking care of Jewish guests in Bombay is Benaya Benjamin.

Benaya's son Benjamin became a ḥazzan (prayer leader) for the Bene Israel, who called him "Ḥazzan Vava." Benjamin married a lady named Flora from Baghdad. It was the time of the famous Sassoons and Ezras in Bombay, and Benjamin's family was on friendly terms with them. There were also white Jews from Cochin living in Bombay at that time, and they became so jealous of Benjamin's social success that they did everything in their power to ruin him. They ordered globes and lamps from him for the Paradesi Synagogue and many other things to sell. He gave them what they ordered but they did not pay him.

The Paradesi Jews insulted Benjamin in every way possible and wrote to the Bombay synagogue that he was their slave and that they didn't give any privileges to him in Cochin, so the Jews of Bombay should do the same. But these Bombay Jews who came from Iraq had no such prejudices. So they wanted to find out what it was all about. They wrote to the Chief Rabbi of Palestine or Egypt. He sent his assistant Asher Levy to Bombay with powers to do what was necessary to purify this set of people if necessary.

When he reached Bombay, Asher Levy brought all these people together. He investigated and found them like any other Jews, versed in Torah and observant of the Law. Some people said that many were the children of white

*This Benaya Benjamin was the brother of my grandmother Rivka. Their father, Binyamin Benaya, came from Yemen and married one of the daughters of Annochimuthi and Shelomi Mudaliar. Benaya's son was named Benjamin for the grandfather. He had an only son named Benaya, but when this child died, Benaya said that he was the seventh generation of Benaya Benjamins, and he was grieved why he had died, and the line of the Binyamin Benayas came to an end on his side. Perhaps he still has some relations in Yemen from another line.

Jews and non-Jewish women, and some said they were converted in Cochin, and some said they were not. Asher Levy said if you are once converted there is no dispute. A Jew is a Jew, not a slave or a *meshuhrar*. To clear any doubt, he asked them to do *tebilah* (ritual bath), which made them equal to any *ger*, or convert, and everyone of this group in Bombay and Cochin did so. As for the so-called "black Jews" from Cochin, he said that there was no need for them to do *tebilah* because they were pure Jews in every way.

While he was still in Bombay he went to a synagogue on Saturday and gave a lecture. He said if a gentile converts into Judaism he is equal to the other Jews, and we can give them our daughters to marry and marry their daughters, and so on. Then one of the white Jews from Cochin insulted him by saying, "You can give them your mother and your sisters and daughters." Asher Levy was so disgraced that he cursed this fellow, saying that he was speaking the Laws of the Torah and since this fellow lost his temper, may his own blood go up his head. And it seems this man died the same week by hemorrhage. The blood oozed even from the pores of his skin.

This Asher Levy was called by the nickname "Sheddar" (maybe from the term *shaliah* for messenger). After he finished what he had to do in Bombay, he was sent to Cochin with a man who was born in Cochin but was living in Bombay. He was a *hazzan* in a Bene Israel synagogue, a member of the Kadavumbagam Synagogue, named Isaac Nehemia. Because he came with Sheddar, the white Jews nicknamed him as "Baddar" and this name stuck till he died at a ripe old age in Cochin.

When Asher Levy came to Cochin, he arranged for this set of people in Cochin to do *tebilah*, and he talked to the white Jews in the Paradesi Synagogue on Saturday, explaining that they should accept them as their equals. The white Jews in Cochin also abused and insulted him, as had their relatives in Bombay. Some of the youngsters even tried to hit him. He said that he was speaking the one Torah and they did not have to insult him. He got out of the synagogue and went to the Tekkumbagam Synagogue and from that time he did not set foot in the Paradesi Synagogue again.

When this gentleman Asher Levy went back home, he or the Chief Rabbi wrote a book *Pesaq Din* [Judgment] on these people of Cochin. All this happened not more than a hundred ten to a hundred twenty years ago. My father was a baby when Asher Levy came to Cochin, so it must have been in 1880 or 1881.*

*BJ: For an account of *Hakham* Asher Abraham Halevy's visits to Cochin, Bombay and Calcutta in 1881, see Naphtali Bar Giora, "Sources-Material for the History of the Relations between the White Jews and the Black Jews of Cochin," *Sefunot* 1(1957):260–265 (Hebrew). This material is summarized in English in Musleah, ibid., pp. 373–374. Asher Halevy's nickname "Sheddar" must have come from the acronym for *shaliah de-rabanan* (emissary from an institution of Jewish learning).

It so happened a few years after the Sheddar affair that Asher Levy's grandson went to Bombay. So all the rich people went to receive him at the station in their double-horse carts, he being a grand person. Among them was Benaya Benjamin with his single-horse cart. The rich people had arranged a grand bungalow for the visitor to stay, and they wanted to take him there. Then he asked, "You all have come to receive me because I am an important person. Please tell me where the poor ḥakhamim, who come to collect money for the poor Jews in Palestine, usually stay." They told him that the poor ḥakhamim usually stay in Benaya Benjamin's place. Then he said, "Then I am also going there first. After that I shall come to you." So Benaya took him in his single-horse cart, and all the rest of the people escorted him to Benaya's place. After taking refreshments there, the visitor went with the others.

Then those people in Bombay asked Sheddar's grandson to go to Cochin. But he refused. He said, "If you show me any record that the white Jews of Cochin have accepted my grandfather's ruling, only then I shall go to Cochin, because the white Jewish community there was excommunicated by the Chief Rabbi when they refused to accept his ruling."

When what I have written above comes to the notice of the white Jews, there is going to be great controversy. But this is what I have heard from reliable sources.

I should also mention that it was not only in the Paradesi community that converts had to suffer disgrace. There was a case that happened not many years ago in Ernakulam. There was among them a boy who very much wanted to learn Torah. But some people in that community said that there were converts in his family, so they should not be allowed to study Torah. They said if someone converts, for seven generations they should not be given any rights. So he was not allowed into the class where the other Jewish boys were learning. The teacher was a scholar called Harsulla, who came from Aden or somewhere from the Middle East. This boy came every day to the school and sat at the bottom of the staircase listening to the teaching. He was not even allowed to sit at the top of the staircase. The teacher, seeing this, called him up. The community protested violently, but the teacher said, "Anyone who wants to learn Torah must not be turned away," and he started teaching him against the protest of the community. This boy grew up to become one of the greatest Hebrew scholars of the time there, and many of the learned men of today used to be his pupils. I heard this story from one of them, an old man in Kefar Yuval.

DIFFERENT REACTIONS

In my time not everyone agreed on what to do about this problem in our community, as could be seen in the differences between my grandfather Eliyahu Japheth and Mr. A. B. Salem.

At about the time when Asher Levy came to Cochin (1882), A. B. Salem was born in Fort Cochin to Belukka the daughter of Avomutha. He grew up to be the first advocate [lawyer] among the Jews of India. His mother was very poor, and she worked hard to educate her only son. They suffered a lot in the house. When he wanted to study at night he had to go out on the street and read by the light of the municipal oil lamp, because they had no light in the house. The great-grandson of Shelomi Mudaliar! The so-called rich relatives of his great-grandfather refused to help him because they did not want him to be bigger than their sons.

Mr. Salem finished his university studies in Madras, so he became friendly with all the boys who later became great politicians and leaders of India. One of these was Rajagopalacharia, who became the governor of Madras at the time when Lord Mountbatten (the last Viceroy) left, when India was granted independence. Mr. Salem came back to live in Jew Town after he finished his studies. He was acquainted with all the members of the Congress Party and worked for them during the satyagraha movement of Gandhiji. He was the leader of the Workers Association in Cochin, and when he stood for election all those people worked for him without compensation. He was famous and popular. Even those who opposed his ideas were fond of him.

But contrary to what has been written in a number of books, Mr. Salem was not the "leader of the *meshuḥrarim*." There were no slaves or freed slaves in his time! He fought for himself and for his family. In 1950, when his son wanted to marry one of their girls, the white Jews did not allow them to marry in the Paradesi Synagogue, so they got married in Bombay. When a son was born to them, the white Jews did not allow him to be circumcised in the synagogue, so it was done in one of the synagogues in Ernakulam. But when this boy grew up, not long ago, he got married to the granddaughter of Mr. Salem's arch enemy Dr. Simon. At that time I was wondering what was happening between the two grandfathers in their graves!

Before all this, when I was living in Cochin, both the Salem family and our family had to sit separately from the others in the Paradesi Synagogue, the men in the *azarah* (entrance room) and the women in the separate building just in front of the synagogue. We could see everything from there, but it was a shame for us. So my grandfather Eliyahu Japheth, who was the teacher of many of the white Jews, usually didn't go to the synagogue, only on Yom Kippur and other special times. We would pray at home instead.

Mr. Salem was not like us. He began fighting for his rights in the synagogue, and he was willing to do whatever he could to get them. His character was like Gandhi's: you hit him on one cheek and he turns the other. He has skin like an elephant. My grandfather was not like that. When A. B. Salem was asking for rights, the white Jews told him to ask Eliyahu Japheth to sign a petition to the synagogue in which it was written, "I am *meshuḥrar*." Salem was willing to say anything, even to say "I am *meshuḥrar*," but my Grandfather would not. He said, "They want us to bring it in the record that we accept this status, to make this record ourselves." Mr. Salem came to our house a few times and they argued, but Grandfather and Father won't sign.

Anyway, when the white Jews finally decided to give the synagogue rights to our families, the first *aliyah* to the Torah was given to their teacher, my grandfather Eliyahu Japheth.

Chapter 2

A CHILDHOOD IN JEW TOWN

Sometimes I wish I was born fifty years earlier or fifty years later. But it happened in December 1912. Once I read somewhere that those who are born at that period of the year will feel lonely even when among a thousand people. How true it is of me!

I was the first daughter born to my mother, and the only child born that year in the whole of Jew Town, so I was a pet of the whole Town, not only of my grandparents. In our Town it was the custom when a baby is born that another woman who had a suckling baby went and gave suck to the newborn till the mother was able to feed the child. Two neighbor women, I was told, did this for me when I was born. Recently my brother told me that Father used to send him with a glass of arrack to one of these ladies on my birthday each year. That lady did not drink, but her husband drank it. Once it seems he asked my brother, "Don't you ever forget us."

Nobody will forget my birthday, because I was born during Hanukkah, on the first day of the month of Tebet. Every year when they light the seventh candle, everybody in the Town knows that it is my birthday. It is supposed to be an auspicious day because it is after Rosh Hodesh (the new moon), but that did not bring me any luck. During that time each year my father bought a bottle of arrack and kept it in the house. His friends who passed the house called to my Father, "Eliyahu Hai! Today is your daughter's birthday." Then Father brought a glass of arrack and gave them. They drank it on the roadside where they stood and went away.

In Jew Town there were parties for all the eight nights of Hanukkah. In our house the seventh night celebration was an established fact. We did not have to invite anybody, they would just come. Grandmother was a good cook. If Father asked her to prepare for ten people, Grandma did for thirty. People invited themselves. They will just tell my father, "Eliyahu Hai, tonight is your daughter's birthday. I am coming." Our house is cosmopolitan, for white, black, and gentile. One year I don't know what happened but Father did not make the party. So one of the family's friends asked, "Why did he not make the party? Perhaps he has no money?" So she made the party in her house and invited all of us.

A surprising thing happened on the day of my birth. My mother always gave birth in the house. When she was screaming and crying, my grandfather couldn't stand it so he went into the backyard of the house, where we had coconut trees on the other side. Suddenly he heard the new baby crying, and at the same moment there fell a nest from the top of the tree and in it a small bird crying "craw-craw." So he took the baby crow and started petting it and then growing it up. It grew up with me and lived about six years.

I remember that crow very well. When Grandfather would feed me, then he used to give the crow something to eat too. At one time when I was small I didn't like to drink milk. In the front of our door there was a screen, called a *vesha*, made of bamboo. The crow used to come and sit on the top and cock his head and look at us. So my aunty Sarah used to shout at my grandfather, "Your crow is casting the evil eye on the child. That's why she doesn't drink the milk." So they would quarrel. At last she brought some alum, a salty substance that looks like rock sugar candy. They used to pass it around the body or the head of a person and then throw it in the fire, where suddenly it pops up and takes one shape or another when it is melted. My aunty did it to me, passing it around my head, and when she took it out of the fire, it was in the shape of the bamboo stick with something like a crow standing on it. She said, "See, it is the crow that is casting the evil eye."

But Grandfather still kept it. Anyway, the crow would not go away. Whenever he is outside he will call out, "Cacaji!" and the crow answers, "craw-craw" and comes and stands on his shoulder. It won't come to anyone else. One day I remember Grandfather was lying down on his easy chair by the window and reading the newspaper. He used to put the paper on the window seat next to the chair. The crow came to the veranda and called out. It wanted Grandfather to go and play with it. Grandfather didn't pay attention, so it came and snatched the paper and flew away with it. Then Grandfather had to get up and play. He would take it in his hand and feed it. The crow comes and goes, flies away and then comes back.

As One Family

When I was a small baby, there were many people around me. We were all living together in the house which had belonged to my father's father, Daniel, and in the house next to that one. We cooked and ate together as one family. In addition to my parents there were Grandfather Eliyahu Japheth and Grandmother Docho, my mother's parents. They had raised my father from the time he was a small boy, because he was the baby brother of Docho; his parents, Daniel and Rivka—after whom I was named—died when he was young, so I never knew them.

Also living with us was my father's unmarried sister, Aunty Seema. Aunty lived with us all the rest of her life. She looked after all the children and grandchildren of her sister and brother. We could not do without her. We went to her when hungry, to give us a wash, to mend our dress, and so on. When we were small we used to sit around her and she hand-fed all of us. There were also other aunts—my mother's younger sisters Sipporah, Rebecca, and Dolly. Her brother, Daniel Haim, went away to Rangoon to work when he was a young man. My father's other sister, Sarah, who was married, lived in a house near us. Later she went to Bombay, as did Sipporah when she was married, and when Rebecca married she went to Rangoon with her husband. But when I was a baby they were still young, and they loved me, you know. All of them wanted to wash my napkins [diapers]. "I will wash, I will wash," they said, because there were no other children in the house.

After my birth my mother had three babies: Daniel, who was born after me, lived till the age of two and a half years, when he died of whooping cough and pneumonia. My brother Bingley was born when I was ten years old and he lived, but then two more brothers died before my sister Rachel was born, twenty years after me.

Grandmother was a very good-looking woman, with long hair which fell in curls like rollers when she let it down. One time after a bath she was sitting at the table copying songs when a friend came to visit. That woman took a ruler and put it inside one roll of Grandmother's hair, and the hair was so heavy she didn't feel it until she moved her head and the ruler fell out. Of course women who have such hair are pretty. But when she was seventeen years old, during her first pregnancy, she had very bad smallpox all over her face, so she lost her color.

Grandmother could read and write in Malayalam, and she was an expert in the songs which the Jewish women sing for weddings and other celebrations. She was a perfect wife, keeping up all the traditions for Shabbat and the holidays and keeping kashrut (the laws regarding food) in the house. I learned all this from her. That's called domestic culture; you talk about things, just as when I am telling about something and I suddenly think of a story, so I say the story. Religious observance for us was a daily affair like cooking. We all learned from the grandparents to keep the Shabbat, to keep kashrut. Even now if I do a mistake, I know I am doing a mistake, and if I have to do it, still I feel guilty.

Ruby's beloved Grandmother "Docho," Rachel Japheth (1864–1944). (*Collection of Ruby Daniel*)

Also Grandmother was crazy about the children. I remember how she used to carry me on her shoulder. I had asthma when I was a baby, and for twenty or twenty-two days she would not let me down.

I was always very attached to Grandfather. Though he was over sixty years old when I was born, he was still very strong. He used to exercise with dumbbells and all, and he did karate too. He and some of his Muslim and Christian friends would stand out on the veranda and have competitions, holding a chair by one leg or holding a glass of water steady for a very long time. Once I remember Grandfather put a whole coconut in the bend of his arm, inside his elbow. When he suddenly closed his arm, he crushed the coconut completely, so that the milk ran out. He was a good marksman too. He had a double-barreled gun and he would go shooting rabbits and crocodiles with his friends.

Grandfather was also very musical. He played the violin and he could sing so nicely, in Hebrew and Malayalam and English. He wrote a few songs, translating prayers from Hebrew into Malayalam. One of my earliest memories was when I was small, very small, lying on Grandfather's arms. I couldn't have been more than three or four, because after that age men don't go very near a child. Not even my father; I never remember kissing my father. Anyway, we were staying in Alwaye at the time. My grandfather was lying on the bed and I was lying on his arms when he taught me my first song, "Twinkle, twinkle, little star, how I wonder what you are."

I remember too when Grandfather came from the work, he used to play with me—because the meal was not yet ready—to be sure I won't fall asleep before eating. He would lift me up and carry me, putting a stick over our shoulders like a gun, and all the children from the neighborhood would come in. We would go round and round the table singing "John Brown's body lies a-moldering in the grave." And my aunts, they were not very old at the time, he would take them too and go marching around the table.

Grandfather was a very learned man. Elders from all the Jewish communities used to come and learn halakhah and Gemara from him. The big boys and the married men too would come to the house of Joseph Hallegua, who was a rich man with a big house, and they would study in the evenings on the top floor there. My grandfather taught them, though he had learned everything by himself. Someone must have taught him to read and write, but the rest he learned from his own study. Even the Christian bishop would come and study with him. They walked together on the beach in Fort Cochin and discussed religious matters. Grandfather also studied the Koran as well as the New Testament.

But all his learning I didn't inherit, only his stubbornness. Ooh, he was stubborn. The whole town was afraid of him, just to be on the safe side, just to please him. They respected him a lot. If you ask him about the Koran or the New Testament or anything, he will tell you on which page it is written, but if he puts something down, he will say, "It is not here, I put it somewhere else." Once I remember he said he put an envelope between the glasses of the Shabbat lamp, a pink envelope it was, a promissory note. "And when was that?" we asked. It was six months ago, he said, and now he can't find it. Every week Aunty was cleaning that lamp. So somebody must have taken and put it somewhere. Now who can remember? I am telling you, the whole house was upside-down, looking through all his books and papers. At last when we found it, it was not a pink envelope, it was a blue one. And that was his memory!

Most of the time, Grandfather was not in the house. He was working as an agent for a rich woman who dealt in planks for making boxes. They had a big house in Jew Town, in the middle part of the Town, but she lived three miles away, in Fort Cochin, and this house in Jew Town was empty, so he used to stay most of the time there. How can he sleep in our house with so many women and girls? He likes to sleep alone. I am the same; I also like to sleep alone.

Grandfather was the *shohet*, who slaughtered chicken and animals for all of Jew Town, according to the Jewish law. He even had the right to give *shehitah* (authority to be a *shohet*) to others, which he got from one of the *hakhamim* who came from Egypt or Palestine. There was one fellow in Cochin who wanted *shehitah*. Grandfather asked him some questions and found that he knows nothing. "How can I give him *shehitah*?" he said. "There are thirty-four names for the places on the neck, and you must know where to cut so the animal won't feel it." So many things they had to learn.

After some time Grandfather went to work in Fort Cochin for the Koders, a rich family of white Jews living there. He stayed in their house and taught Hebrew to their sons. He was the *shohet* there too. There was a great *rab* who came to visit in Cochin, and he would not eat any meat or chicken because he was not sure it was kosher. He stayed at the Koders' house too. One day he and Grandfather went for a walk on the beach. Only Grandfather could talk with him in Hebrew. They started talking, and the *rab* put all sorts of questions to him about *shehitah* and other matters. The *rab* said for everything he was satisfied. Back at the Koders' house they asked the rab what he wanted to eat and he answered, "Kabob." From that time he ate meat in their house. One time another man invited him to his house for Shabbat. The *rab* came to his house but said he won't eat meat. "But I saw you eating meat in Koder's house," the man said. "Why can't you eat it here?" The *rab* replied, "Ah, that is a *shohet* there." His host told him, "The same *shohet* cut this meat," so then he ate.

Once it was discovered that there was something wrong with one of the Torah scrolls in the Paradesi Synagogue. If there is one mistake in the writing of a Sefer Torah, the belief is that something bad might happen to the community. The mistake had to be corrected, but everybody was afraid to touch it, for fear something might happen to them. So my grandfather had to do it, taking a bath first and saying certain prayers. He was learned and pure enough to correct the Sefer Torah, but still they would not call him to the Torah during prayers.

When it was finally decided after many years that our section of the community should be called to the Torah, Grandfather was the first to be called. One of the rich men in the Hallegua family sent word that Grandfather should come to the synagogue for the Feast of *Shemini Atzeret*. He never used to go because of the discrimination, so he didn't have a *kapa*, the long white robe which the men wore for Festivals. Suddenly we had to make him a *kapa*. There was a tailor shop in front of our house, and they did it overnight. When Grandfather went into the synagogue the next day, this Hallegua went and kissed his hand. After all, Grandfather was his teacher! Then all the men came and kissed his hand. They had to give the honor first to Eliyahu Japheth.

A House Full of Light

All the houses in Jew Town are so close and the road is so narrow, you can see everything that is happening in the houses. Our house didn't have a top floor, but it is a little above the ground. Our lights will be burning from six o'clock to twelve o'clock at night. We had a number fourteen chimney for our lamp, which uses half a bottle of kerosene, so the whole house is full of light. Others use a number ten or number eight chimney, just to light their house, but we are many people in the house and we want to study. We talk and we sing. We have nothing to hide. We are living just like rich people, so people didn't think that we are poor people.

The house where we lived was a small one, but it has been standing for about three hundred years. It is made of stone blocks from the mountains, stronger than granite. If you want to break one of the walls and you hit it with an iron, sparks of fire will come out. The walls are so thick, if you want to sit down, there is a place under the window that is wide enough for a seat. We had one big room and a hall. The hall was divided in two at the back, with one room for sleeping. People would sit on the veranda when they wanted to talk. The kitchen and bathroom were outside in a courtyard in the back, and there was a well on the side and a wall around. After some time the wall fell down, but who had the money to repair it?

The next-door house, which we rented from someone else, was arranged in the same pattern. There was a door connecting the two houses, which we usually covered with a large cupboard, but for feasts and parties we would open the door and have one large room. Later on when my aunts would come from Bombay and Rangoon to give birth, they stayed for several months. All these people had to be fed. When I was a bit older I used to worry always, "Will there be enough for the others?" so I wouldn't take more food for myself. Sometimes I was called the "daughter-in-law" of the family because I acted more like a daughter-in-law than a daughter. (In India the daughter-in-law is the one who always comes last.)

I have always hated to take things from people, especially outside my house. I remember when I was small, about five years old, my mother took me to the home of a rich lady in Jew Town. Her daughter had studied with my mother and they were good friends. So one day she called my mother to her house and I went along. The mother brought me a piece of fried banana and offered it to me, but I refused to take it. She gave it to me in her hand, not on a plate as we always did in my house. I said I don't want it and then Mother forced me to take it. Finally I took it in my hand but I didn't eat it, just held it while we were there, and then I put it down when we left.

My mother wouldn't let me go out to play with other children. She always kept me in the house. But I had a lot of toys which my aunts from Bombay and Rangoon used to send me, Japanese toys which at that time you can't see anywhere, all made of porcelain. I had a few dogs, each with a big head on a spring, which was all the time nodding. So I put them there on our veranda, and people who were passing by would stand and watch the heads nodding. I also had a ship, which my uncle took apart because he wanted to know what was inside. He always takes everything to pieces, and then it's gone. There was also a beautiful sofa made of glass with long beads at the back, and on it was a lady made of porcelain, lying down and feeding her baby. They also sent me a lot of dolls. I remember there was one beautiful doll, and one day I was just standing outside rocking that doll in my hands. Suddenly it flew off into the middle of the road, and both its eyes rolled back into its head. I was so sad! I can't forget the feeling, to see the doll which looked like a human being, and the eyes went down like that. How can you look at its face without eyes?

The other children would come and play, but I didn't know how to play with them. What can I play with them? All the things I put there on the veranda and the children would come and play with them and some of the toys disappeared.

Next door to our house on one side my aunts were living, and on the other side lived a Muslim family. They were a big family with many daughters, who did not show their faces outside. When they went out they covered their faces with a cloth which they called *burkha*. So when we wanted to sit with the women it could be done only at night, sitting at the veranda. During the day my grandfather and their father sat at the veranda and talked. He was a religious man and they talked about the Koran and the Bible. During the time of their Ramadan celebration, this Muslim family got up at twelve o'clock at night and the men started praying while the women went to the kitchen to cook. It lasted till three or four o'clock in the morning. There was only a wall dividing the houses, but neither they nor we imagined that as a disturbance, whether it was their prayers for Ramadan or our singing late on Shabbat and Festival nights, or our early morning *Selihot* prayers before Rosh Hashanah.

In our family we were friendly with many people from Kadavumbagam Synagogue, which was close to us at the southern end of the street. My father used to go and write letters for them. Many of the women had husbands working in Bombay and other places and they didn't know how to write, so he had to write for them. They knew nothing will get out. Whatever my father hears, the secrets of the whole Town, they will not come out of his mouth. They all liked my grandmother too. Sometimes they came for advice, if a child was ill or many other things, or to gossip and talk about ghosts and spirits. Myself, as a little girl I loved to hear their stories, specially about ghosts.

On Friday night all the children and grandchildren in our family sat together. We made a lot of nice food. On Shabbat (and also for Feasts) we didn't feel that we were poor, because we had everything on the table. Then we would sing Sabbath songs. Our gentile servants also learned these songs by heart. Next morning sometimes the parents got up early and sang the *bakashot* [petitionary hymns], then the morning prayers. Then there was the midday meal, when we also sang the Sabbath songs. Then the women were free to go visiting. The men and a few women (those who had time, without small children) had such a lot of prayers to read afterwards before *Minḥah*, each of them reading alone. This was during the time when my family did not go to the Paradesi Synagogue, because they were not given equal privileges. There were not enough of them for a minyan in the house, but we would sing all the tunes and everything. Sometimes children from the neighborhood would join us. One of our neighbors used to say, "I learned all these things from your house."

STORIES AFTER DARK

Most of the time I was with my grandmother and Aunty Seema. They, specially Grandma, taught me tunes of prayers and told stories she heard from her grandmother. When the ladies came to visit, I always sat in a corner and listened to the ghost stories, which I loved to hear then as now. The other children went out to play with their friends.

On Saturday we lit the lamps very late in the evenings, waiting for the light to be brought from the synagogue. The servants lit the lamp from the synagogue after the prayers and brought home the lighted candles to every house. After the visitors left but before the lamps were lit, when the houses started getting dark, I became nervous thinking about ghosts and spirits, as if they were in every corner of the house. I caught hold of my mother's or Aunty's hand and was afraid to move about alone. But it was below my dignity to tell them I was afraid.

There was an open place a few houses south of our house. No one seems to remember what was in that place. There was only a piece of wall standing when I saw it. Some said that it was once a Hebrew school and some thought it was a prayer house. It was called Misro Palli. *Palli* means synagogue but nobody knows the meaning of the other word, though some said it was really midrash (school). Anyway that place remained empty for ages. A few people have seen a man standing by the side of the road in white clothes like those used to dress up the dead body.

The curry we usually ate on Saturday night was eggs cooked in sauce and dried salt fish fried, as we must have a hot meal and there is no time to cook meat. We had to cook quickly after dark on Saturday, as we couldn't light a fire during the Sabbath. There was a woman selling the salt fish, who lived on the other side of the Misro Palli, and it fell to my lot to go and buy the fish from her. I was so afraid to cross that place! There was no electricity and the streets were not well lighted at the time I am speaking of. Whatever one sees at night in darkness is distorted and sometimes double in size, and the stable things seem to be moving, or one sees one's own shadow from all sides. Even sounds play their own game.

Anyway, when I was sent there at night, I stood a house further back from the Misro Palli and waited for someone to come. Traffic was rare at that time of night. As soon as somebody came, I ran with them to the other side, and I did the same on my return trip. I was too shy to say I was afraid, so it was always my lot to pass that place every Saturday night.

Our family's houses were thought to be haunted. Some said this was because they had been coveted by many people, ever since they were first given by Shelomi Mudaliar, the rich white Jew who married my great-great-grandmother Annochimuthi. When he took a second wife after forty years of marriage, Annochimuthi left his house and came to live in this small house at the other end of Jew Town. I do not know what happened to the house when many of the family went to live in Fort Cochin for some time. But eventually the house came to Annochimuthi's eldest daughter, the one whose husband was lost at sea when she was only fifteen or sixteen years old. She never had children, but one of her sisters had a son, my grandfather Daniel, and another sister had a son and a daughter, Benaya and Rivka. The oldest sister said, "If these children marry from outside, when I am old they will not take care of me," so she made the one sister's son, Daniel, marry the other sister's daughter, Rivka, who was my grandmother. I have heard that Grandmother Rivka suffered a lot because of these three aunts. When they became old they were laid up with rheumatism and all, and she had to do everything for them. When the oldest aunt became very old, her sisters thought they should all share the house, but she said, "How can I throw out all these little pups?" and she gave the house to my grandfather Daniel.

From that time on, if someone in the family died young, it was said that he could not get his share in the house. Sometimes his ghost would appear in the house, though I have not seen any ghosts myself.

When each of my three baby brothers died, my mother would see a shadow near the child's bed. Sometimes somebody would have a dream before the child died. Once when I was very young I had a dream in which I saw a small tomb nicely built. My mother was standing near and crying, "My son, my son!" Within six months of that dream, my baby brother died, and when I visited the grave after some time I saw the same pattern of the built-up grave I had seen in my dream.

My mother had a younger brother named Japheth, who died when they were living in this same house, at the age of about thirteen. While he was still alive there was a party in the house. The women had fried some pastry puffs which we call *pastels* and kept them inside the back room, which had a window with wooden bars on the back side. There was one door on the side and another opening from the hall at the front. In the evening Japheth wanted to take some of the *pastels*, so he entered the room, which was dark inside. He suddenly screamed. He saw his uncle, who had died in Bombay a long time before, standing in the other room and looking in through the bars of the window. Just a few months later Japheth died.

My father was afraid to sleep alone in that back room. He said that his mother was in that room, though he never said why he thought so.

In the front veranda of our house there were three benches. My mother always sat in the corner where the benches from two sides meet. That was her favorite place. From there one can see the back door of the house through the window. One late afternoon she was sitting in that corner and looked inside the house. Then she saw an old lady in a white dress and close-cut graying hair coming into the hall from the back door and going to the side wall, where there was a cupboard covering the door to the next-door house. Well! Later my mother told her mother about what she had seen, and she described how the lady looked. At once my grandmother said that she was her grand-mother's sister, the one of Annochimuthi's daughters who lived in the next door house many years before (when she was alive of course). I wonder why she took a roundabout way to go there that afternoon?

This next-door house was haunted too. At one time, when our family did not live there, it was rented to a lady and her husband. They had no children. She was very fond of my mother's brother Japheth, who was then a boy of eight or so. One day when she was taking a bath at the well, she saw a boy making faces at her and laughing at her. She got angry at him for making fun of her, and she shouted at him and he went away. After she finished her bath she wanted to tell my grandmother about it. They were living in the adjoining house. She called to her and asked, "Where is Japheth?" The mother said he was sleeping. She said, "No, he came and made fun of me." She must have felt something was wrong, or there was no reason to ask his mother if he went to her home.

Years later my grandfather rented this same house to two Muslim brothers. They were selling spare parts for carts and nails and pieces of tin, etc. At night there was a big chimney lamp burning in the middle of their salon. One of the brothers went out to eat, so the other one stayed to watch. He was sitting in the veranda. When he looked in, he saw a young boy dancing under the lamp, going round and round for a little while, and then he disappeared. This he told my grandfather. Then they remembered about what the other lady had told them years before.

Some years later both my aunties Rebecca and Sippora were living there with their children. One evening as they were sitting out in the veranda they saw a small boy entering the house. They were frightened when he went near one of their children, who was sleeping on the bed. Suddenly the ghost disappeared. Fortunately nothing bad happened after that.

MISCHIEVOUS SPIRITS

Sometimes ghosts or spirits could be mischievous too. There are stories of mysterious beings in all places, like the pixies in Cornwall, leprechauns in Ireland, fairies in the woods, dwarfs in some other places, and in Cochin we have *kapiris*. They are depicted as short, black, with curly hair and a set of white small teeth, quite harmless unless they are harmed. They play tricks on human beings. Sometimes they are not seen but felt. Sometimes they are said to be living in some corners of the houses or outside in the far end corner of a courtyard or inside a cupboard. They also live in families of men, women, and children. Their places of abode are often abandoned houses and guava or jumbo trees. If those places are polluted, then you have had it. They even throw excrement at you.

There are stories about the master of the house when he is in the lavatory and needs some water. He calls out, "Isn't there anybody to bring me some water?" Then he hears the jingle of the bells which are under the brass jugs. The water is brought and put near the doorstep but one does not see anyone. Sometimes people feel as if someone is just passing from behind. Sometimes they see a shadow. But I have never heard of any harm being done to anyone, so the people were not so afraid of the *kapiris*. Still they could cause problems.

One time while my grandfather was working for the woman who sold planks for making boxes, a strange thing happened in that house. The planks were sawed and cut into size and arranged in a storeroom behind the house. It was full from top to bottom, arranged in such a way that it was impossible to push even a hand into it. At the time I am talking about, the owners were vacationing in Alwaye, and they left their housekeeper in charge. She was a woman named Katzina. One day she just disappeared. People looked everywhere for her but could not find her. On the third day the mistress in Alwaye dreamt that a *neshamah*, a spirit or soul, was struggling in the well of her Cochin house, and then she was sure Katzina was there somewhere. They decided to clear the planks of wood from the storeroom, and they found her pushed into a corner behind the planks, standing flat against the wall, barely breathing and without being able to move. She did not know how she got in there.

This was the house where my grandfather used to sleep alone when it was empty. He did not believe in devils and spirits. In the backyard of that house there was a tree bearing a sort of sour fruit, and it was supposed to be the abode of the *kapiri* of that house. This tree had not borne fruit for a long time, so Grandfather had told Katzina that it will help if she clears the night pot at its base. She did it a few times, and then this thing happened to her. Katzina became a little touched after this. Grandfather said she was crazy even before, and that is why she managed to squeeze herself into the storeroom. But others think that the *kapiri* did it.

In Ruby Hallegua's mother's house there was a tree producing a sour kind of fruit. There was a *kapiri* living in that tree. They had a servant woman who used to clean and sweep the yard around this tree. Every time she did so, she found a small silver two-anna piece near the tree. There are many stories of *kapiris* leaving small amounts of money for people who keep the places around some trees or rooms clean, but once they tell anyone about it no more money is left.

Once my aunt Rebecca, who was staying in the house next door to ours, threw her wet cloth over the back fence by mistake, and it fell into the well of the next house, two houses away from ours. That well was built with a breast-high wall, and the ground all around it was paved with cement tiles. One had to put in a ladder in order to get in for cleaning or anything. She could not find someone to take the cloth out for her, and she wouldn't stop talking about it because it was a new cloth. After a week or two, she, her sister, her children, and the servant were working in the kitchen. Suddenly something came flying out of the well and fell in front of them. It was the wet cloth twisted on a rotten piece of bamboo. From the well to that place there were drops of water. If Aunt Rebecca was alone there I would not have believed her, but the others saw it too.

In this same house next door to ours, many years before, there was another family living. Like every house in Jew Town it had a well in the backyard of the house. The astrologers told them that there was a treasure hidden in that well, so they tried to pull it out. First they gathered a few people to draw the water out, and when they nearly finished they saw a big pot at the bottom. Suddenly a kind of thorny fish were thrown up from the bottom so the people could not work anymore. Still they did not give up.

They saw two handles for the pot, which they supposed must contain the treasure, but however much they tried, they could not pull it out. So they brought an elephant, put a loop into the handle, and made the elephant pull. The handle broke and came up with the rope. Just then they heard the treasure pot being dragged underground far away. They say that from this handle, which was pure gold, they made a crown for the Sefer Torah in the Thekkumbagam Synagogue, which was in Jew Town Cochin. This was talked about, and all heard, but nobody contradicted.

In India, superstition is paramount. I think it is from the Hindus, who believe in reincarnation and ghosts and spirits. So it is stamped upon the Jews also, who were living among them for thousands of years. There are so many stories of ghosts and spirits seen by people in Jew Town, one would think that when the body of the dead is taken out through the front door, their spirits enter by the back door. Jew Town has a definite attraction. The Jews who lived there for seven or eight hundred years did not want to get out, even though most of us have now come to Israel. The ghosts and spirits of the dead also were not willing to leave entirely. Their presence is still felt by those living—in their houses, or in the streets or in the synagogue.

Chapter 3

EAGER FOR EDUCATION

My family has always been eager for education. Over a hundred years ago my grandmother's great-aunt took a few Jewish girls into her home in Fort Cochin and taught them Malayalam songs and needlework. She would spread a sheet to cover the table and teach them embroidery on that cloth. Thus they learned all the fine arts of needlework, and she would also sing Malayalam songs to them, which they learned by heart. Afterward they would earn money in their house, for instance by making drawn-thread work (like lace) for Christian wedding garments, or special embroidery for Muslim caps. A few of these girls also learned to read and write in Malayalam. They would bring a Hindu or some person from another caste, who taught them to write letters in the sand with the finger. So it happened that these women were educated at a time when the rich girls back in Jew Town did not know how to read or write their names.

In later years the young girls and boys in Jew Town were sent to learn Torah in the *ḥeder*, the Jewish school. But by the time the girls reached the age of puberty they were stopped and stayed at home. When my mother was a girl, at the end of the nineteenth century, there were only three or four boys in the white Jews community who had gone for higher studies. During that time a British missionary established a lower secondary school in Jew Town only for the Jews. It was in that school that my mother and others of her generation went to learn. One of the rich white Jews fought for my mother to be admitted, along with one girl from the Kadavumbagam community.

When my mother was learning in the school, some of the white Jewish girls wanted to give her trouble. In those days the children all learned with slates. They sat on the benches and put their slates and books on the floor in front of them. Sometimes the other girls would pass by and step on my mother's slate and break it as if by accident, but really it was because they were jealous. My mother was first in her class all the time. Once she even got double promotion, but they gave all the prizes to another Jewish girl. The teachers were always influenced by the white Jews. The only prize they couldn't deny to my mother was her double promotion.

My father also was a good student. When he passed first in his class, he was given a prize of three books, beautifully bound with green binding and golden colors. Inside was written "Presented to E. H. Daniel." As soon as he got the book, a man named Naphtali Roby came and took it from him, saying, "This is not meant for you to keep." Naphtali Roby kept it in his own library. I know this is true because many years later when I was in school I was friendly with Naphtali Roby's son, Samuchi. One day I asked him to lend me a book to read from his father's books, and he lent me the one in which my father's name was written. It said something about black and white in it, so probably that was why Naphtali Roby didn't want us to read it. When I asked Samuchi to lend me some more books like that, he said, "No, you must give back that book. Father is getting angry."

When my parents were children there were thirty-two boys and girls, all Jewish, studying in Jew Town. When the first group finished the sixth grade, the missionary in charge suggested raising the lower secondary school to matriculation level, and they asked the rich Jewish people and the three synagogues to contribute half the expenses. But for one reason or the other the rich people refused. So the missionary closed down the school, after my mother had completed the sixth grade. Some of the rich families hired private tutors to teach their daughters at home, but only one of those girls passed the matriculation exam.

Then the government took over the girls' school and made it a preparatory school where the younger ones attended. It was no longer a Jewish school. When the Jewish girls finished the four classes in that school, they stayed at home because no one could imagine sending them outside the Town to study. Many got married and forgot about learning. By the time the Jews came to their senses, they had become a backward class, along with the Muslims, who did the same with their daughters.

Mother regretted that she could not continue her education past the sixth grade, and she was determined that I should have the opportunity. She was always reading the newspapers, and she also used to read English novels and translate them to her friends. She was expecting at the time she was reading the novel *Pride and Prejudice* by Jane Austen. She liked the qualities of Mr. Bingley, the hero of the novel. So when her son was born she called him Bingley though his given name was Mathathiyahu. This son, my brother, got all the good qualities of Mr. Bingley except a very important thing—money.

My father also had to interrupt his studies when he was young, because his parents died and he had to look after the family. But he was first in his class when he passed out of the school in Jew Town, and then he studied for a few years in the school in Ernakulam, across the harbor. He always made use of his learning to help others by writing letters for them. And of course my grandfather was a very learned man, having educated himself in so many subjects. But the men in my family did not think it was so important to educate a daughter. It was my mother who insisted.

MY EARLY EDUCATION

I started speaking from the age of ten months. I remember when I was two or three years old we used to say the prayers and for the prayer "*Vatitpalel . . . gevua gevua*" I would say "Gevuduvah, gevuduvah." Everyone was so amused they would come and ask me to repeat it. My cousin Daniel Hai used to ask me to pray, and when I said, "Gevuduvah, gevuduvah," he would buy me a banana. Then I would say it to get the banana!

From the age of two my mother started teaching me English, with pinching and hitting if it did not go her way. She also taught me to read the Hebrew letters, the *alef-bet*. When I was six years old I began to study in the government school for girls in Jew Town. I was very shy and quiet. I couldn't speak to people easily. Once a Hindu friend of my father's said, "Why do you want to educate this one? If someone carries her off, she won't even cry out."

The rich Jewish girls were jealous of me in the school. They thought I shouldn't learn, as if it was their privilege or something. It was a government school with children from all the different communities. The others weren't jealous, only those Jewish girls.

Anyway, I learned nicely. Even now I remember about the examinations. Once in the first standard we had a dictation, and I was careless, so I misspelled the word "window." I took my slate to the teacher, and she checked off that first word, which I wrote as "windo." The other children got twelve correct and I got only eleven. Then the teacher took one look at my face and she wrote "12" on the slate.

At the end of each year they used to give a prize for the first and second high marks. In the first class they gave one rupee, for the second class two rupees, then so forth for the third and fourth class. Every year another Jewish girl—Rebecca Elias—and myself got the prizes. Either she is first and I second or I am first and she second. But when we finished the fourth class I was neither first nor second but third. Then I don't know how the headmistress managed. She made three prizes so that I should get one, because she knew I was a bright student in class and something must have happened in the exam. Or maybe they decided to give three prizes that year.

When I was in that school there was also a *ḥeder* for teaching Torah, on the opposite side of the school. There the Jewish boys and girls all sat together on benches, under the supervision of the teacher, who was a man from the Tekkumbagam community. We learned to read Hebrew and to read the *parashah* (the Torah portion of the week) with the correct tune. We memorized some of the portions in Hebrew, and then we also learned the translation in Malayalam. The whole week we learned the *parashah* for the following Shabbat. Then when Shabbat comes, you remember.

Also we learned to understand a few things in the prayers. The women could sing nicely, even better than the men, so all these prayer tunes the youngsters had to learn from the women.

I remember when we learned the translation of the *parashah* where it is told about Abraham sacrificing Isaac, I used to cry. Everybody made fun of me. So every time we had to study that portion, I made an excuse and did not go to the *ḥeder*. Some sixty or more years later I went to a synagogue here in Israel for Rosh Hashanah, and my old Hebrew teacher was there. The *parashah* of that day was of Abraham sacrificing Isaac. Though so many years had passed, when my teacher Eliyahu Meyer saw me, he started showing me signs with his hand, making motions for cutting the throat and shedding the tears.

We started *ḥeder* at 8 o'clock and when the school bells rang at ten o'clock I went to the girls' school. We finished at four o'clock with a break for lunch. Then we went back to the *ḥeder* which finished at five o'clock. All day long I was busy, then home in the evening to take a bath, eat, do my homework, and sleep. Who had time for friends or playmates? By this time there were movies and theaters, which were an abomination at the time of our grandparents. The parents who were a little lenient were afraid of their own parents. When I wanted to go somewhere for a picnic or an excursion with the other school children I asked my mother's permission. If she does not approve of it she will say, "Ask your Father." If Father does not like it, he will say, "Ask your Grandfather." Then it is a foregone conclusion. So I never asked and never went.

FAMILY VACATIONS IN ALWAYE

However there was one time in the year for a family excursion. That was after Passover, midsummer in Cochin, when the children have school vacation and even the offices have one month. The weather is very hot at that time, and many of the families from Jew Town spend a few weeks in Alwaye. Those who have got money, they go every year, and the others once in a blue moon. Everybody will be dying to go. We didn't go every year, but it happened that we were there the year of the great flood.

Alwaye is a health resort some miles from Cochin, where the Periyar River comes down from the mountains. The river is a little bit wide there, and on both sides it is just like a beach—all beautiful, cream-colored sand. The water is fresh and sweet, good for drinking, and it is said to have sulphurine curing properties. Three or four times a day you bathe in the river or it won't be effective. You are always in the water. Even in the evening it is not cold. Some of the rich people have a house there. If people can't get a house, they make a hut and stay there or they stay on a *vallam*, a big country boat with a covering over the top. Our family used to stay in the Koders' house, or sometimes in the Halleguas' house nearby, if they weren't there. On both sides of the river are hills—one very high and one not so high. From the Koders' house going down to the water you have to climb thirty-two steps. Only the Koders have steps down to the river. Their house was a big one with a veranda, with mango trees and jackfruit trees all around.

There were many beautiful pebbles in the river, some of them valuable stones. One of the richest men in Cochin was a Muslim named Abdul Satar. He had a hundred and one wives. Everywhere he goes he gets another one, and the eldest wife will look after all the others. They all used to come to Alwaye. The women won't show their faces out, so they make a fence from coconut leaves—on both sides from the house to the middle of the river—and there they sit down and put on oil. It takes hours, and we don't like to go after them because the river will be full of oil. Once one of the wives found a beautiful bright stone in the river. She took it to a goldsmith or someone who knows about these things, and he made something out of it and got a hundred rupees.

The Jews go to Alwaye only after *Pesaḥ*, and some stay until the feast of Shavuot 50 days later. That's the best season. We always make so much food for *Pesaḥ*, and a lot will be remaining to take with us. Alwaye is a remote place, like a village, so you can't buy many things there. So we load all our things on a *vallam* to carry them there, and we stay for a few weeks, until the money runs out or until the rains begin. A few days before, you can see the water in the river is getting darker. The color changes, it becomes muddy, and there is a kind of foam on the water. Then you know the rain has started in the mountains and in a few days there will be a flood. You can't stay any longer. In the rainy season all the beauty is gone.

THE GREAT FLOOD

In the year of the flood I was ten or twelve years old. Some of our relatives had come down from Bombay—the daughter-in-law of Benaya Benjamin and two or three of her children. Her son had been hurt on the leg. A horse

Covered boats in the Kerala backwaters in the 1930s. In such a *vallam* Ruby's family (but not Ruby!) traveled to Alwaye for vacations. (*Wonderful India*. New Delhi: *The Statesman* and *Times of India* Book Depot, 1938)

hit him or something and he had pus all the time. Whatever they did, it didn't help, so somebody said, "Better go bathe in that river at Alwaye; perhaps it will cure it." That's why they came down, and really it helped him. We went along with them to stay for a few weeks, and suddenly it started: the flood is coming up, the water is rising. It was the great flood of the early 1920s, which caused devastation in Cochin State, but we didn't know it then. What a story it is!

Before the flood started, I had already left Alwaye. I am damned afraid of this *vallam*; I don't ever want to go in one. If you go by railway, you have to walk a lot and you can't bring such a lot of things, but in a *vallam* you can take so many things. So I knew they would go back by *vallam*, because they are bringing the luggage and all. So I thought I must get away from Alwaye before they leave. I didn't know what to do. Who can save me? Then my aunt Rebecca had to go to Cochin to celebrate the Feast of Shimon Bar Yohai. She must have made a *neder* or vow to celebrate that Feast, so she was going to do it in the house in Cochin. She asked if we want to come. My aunt Dolly and my cousin Mary's father also were there in Alwaye, and they were going to return to Cochin by rail, but my grandmother and mother and uncle and the relatives from Bombay, all of them don't want to leave yet. So this is my opportunity! Mother said, "You go with them." Then after the celebration the rest of them returned back to Alwaye, but I said, "I won't go back, I'll stay here in Cochin with my aunt." I didn't tell them why.

And then let me tell you what happened in Alwaye, which I heard afterwards from my family who stayed there. It was on a Friday, and the water was getting a little bit black so they didn't bathe that day. That night the water was rising, and then there was a breeze. When the wind started, they closed the door. They didn't think what is happening down at the river, where there was a Christian family staying in a hut on the beach and a *vallam* tied next to it.

Suddenly they hear screaming and crying. They open the door and find the veranda and all around it full of people. "What happened?" they asked. That Christian lady said she knew that there was going to be something bad, so she thought, "I'll feed the children soon; then we'll go up." So she put out the plates, and before the children could finish eating, the plates started floating, the water started coming, and they all came running up. And this *vallam* was swept away, with one boy left inside it. He was the younger brother of their boatman, who had wanted to come with him to Alwaye, but their mother didn't want to send him. So that Christian lady took the responsibility for the child, saying, "I will look after him, because he is crying." That boy was left inside the boat, and everybody ran. The *vallam* was tied there and suddenly it came loose, and the hut they had on the shore fell onto the *vallam*, and the boat and the child and the hut went down the river, and he was screaming and crying, and they can't do anything. At last he was saved by somebody who heard his voice, a long distance away from there. A *vallam* will not sink so soon; it just rides with the current. But such a current you have no idea: if you just put your finger in the water, it will cut your finger.

The next night my family decided to leave, so they brought their *vallam* and filled all the things inside. It was a moonlight night and there is nothing wrong, but what happened on the way! Suddenly the boatman said, "I see a little cloud somewhere in the sky. That side it is a little bit dangerous. So there is a place nearby where we can tie the boat. Then if the cloud goes away we can leave. If we don't tie it there it is a long distance to go before we find a place." My relatives from Bombay said, "Oh there's nothing wrong. See how bright it is." But my mother said, "No, we are in his hands. They know all these things. What he says we have to do." Another boat also came along, and both of them were tying up together. Before they could finish tying, the storm started. As my mother said, "Storm means storm!" Thunder and lightning—from one side the lightning goes in, and out the other side. And these two boats were just rolling and rolling. So many boats were sunk that night. Back in Alwaye a mango tree fell down where my uncle used to sleep on the veranda, and the flood came up on both sides of the hill until the top. Early in the morning they saw the government waterboat passing by, and then they knew it was safe to go.

And I, in Cochin, could see the storm blowing. Suddenly the little lamp we used to keep at night went off. And I started crying. I know they are on the way. The whole night I was crying, in the morning I was crying. Father said, "Why are you crying? Tell me." I will not tell them why I am crying. Even if I tell them, what can they do? I am standing outside, crying crying crying, till nine o'clock, when the boat finally arrived. I will never forget that!

That's the first time we have seen such a flood. We found out later that it did not happen just because of the weather. There was a dam built in the mountains across the Periyar River, turning the water toward Pondicherry. The dam was so full that it was feared that it might break, in which case the whole country would be under water. So two inches of water was let out. If that could cause such destruction, imagine what would have happened if it was broken!

In some places the water rose up to the top of the coconut palms. I heard a story of two brothers who got hold of the top of a coconut tree. How did they manage to live? They caught hold of a chicken cage which was floating by. They ate the chicken raw, and stayed alive for three days until help arrived.

My relatives who came down from Bombay were staying in Fort Cochin, in Gladys David's father's house, along with my mother and my small brother Bingley. The flood did not come there, because there is an opening to the sea. Everything that goes from the river to the sea, you can see from there. They could see people and all kinds of huts and animals, all floating from the river toward the sea. There was no harbor built then, so the ships stayed in the open sea about three miles from the shore. All that far the sea had a color of blood mixed with water. The captain of one ship phoned to the Port Officer by wireless, "What is happening in Malabar? Is it a war? We are seeing so many dead bodies, we have sunk today thirty bodies. What's happening in Malabar?" That village is washed out, this village is washed out, that's what they say. And then people stopped eating fish, because they find when they open it, inside there will be some piece of a human body, in some cases a finger with a ring on it. For six months we didn't eat any fish. All the stories you hear, all round! But I was too young to be told of all the havoc caused at the time.

I was staying in Jew Town, and there the flood came only up to our houses. At high tide the water started coming from the market in front of Kadavumbagam Synagogue. For three days it was coming more and more. I used to go and buy things from that side, like coconut shells for firewood, and I had to wade with the water up above my knees, carrying a big basket on my head. If my mother was there, she wouldn't have sent me, but she was in Fort Cochin. So I can see what's happening there. Not far away they were using a boat to cross. From both sides of the Town the water is coming, coming, coming. But then it stopped in the middle of Jew Town, right by the road going to the old cemetery. Some people say it was because the Jews were there, the water didn't come in and flood the Town.

Some time after this the British built a good harbor in Cochin, between Ernakulam and the island where Jew Town is located. Previously the river between had contained a quagmire, and it was said that if anyone drowned there he would never come up. When the harbor was built they reclaimed this part of the river and made an island called Willingdon Island, so there could be a wharf where the ships could come near. I remember the time they started this. They brought trunks of teakwood for the foundation and built a wall of granite stone all round. Then they brought dredgers. From one side they dug the sea to make it deep for the ships to come in, and they filled this place with the sand and mud. One side of the island is joined to another island called Venduruthy. They made a long bridge from Cochin to Venduruthy and from there to Ernakulam. Then cars could go over the bridge, whereas before the only way to go was by ferryboat. But after the harbor was built we still went by ferryboat, though it became more dangerous because the water was very, very deep. It was the mouth of the sea. If there was a little wind the waves could rise very high. It was this place I had to cross twice a day for about twenty years, because all the big schools and hospitals and the university were in Ernakulam, as well as the government offices.

ACROSS THE HARBOR TO ST. THERESA'S

When I finished school in Jew Town, my mother wanted to send me to school in Ernakulam or to the mixed school in Cochin. But Grandfather put his foot down. No sending far away and certainly not in the mixed school. Grandfather was a very stubborn man. But my mother was more stubborn than her father. So she put both her feet down. She said that she will do whatever she wants with her daughter and not spoil her life as her father did it to her. My father was ill in bed with typhoid fever at the time. Mother had no money. So she mortgaged her gold chain and with that money took me on the steamboat to Ernakulam and registered me in the St. Theresa's Convent School there.

The ferry to Ernakulam, which I now had to ride every day, was a large boat holding four hundred people, with separate rooms, upstairs second-class and downstairs two rooms inside—one for ladies and one for gents. At nine o'clock in the morning all the children on their way to school would fill the boat, and at 4:30 there would be the same pandemonium when we all returned to Cochin. The first year, I was the only Jewish girl going on the boat, but I would meet other girls who were also going to the school. The next year my aunt Dolly and a girl named Essie joined me at St. Theresa's, so they would cross on the boat too. I remember one day in the winter it was raining and there was a lot of mud on the jetty where the boat was tied. There was no paved road, just mud, brown mud, and so slippery. We had to go down two steps to get into the boat. I got in first, and then after me Essie comes. She slips and falls down. Then after that comes Raymond, laughing "Ha ha ha, Essie fell down," because it's a disgrace to fall, and then he also fell down. And the next one comes, and he also fell down! I just sat there laughing like anything.

All the teachers at St. Theresa's were nuns, who were just as strict as my grandfather, so that did it for me. From the frying pan to the fire. It was a completely English school. Up to this time I had studied in Malayalam, with English as a separate subject. Now *all* the lessons were in English, with Malayalam as a second language. We were not allowed to talk anything but English in the school, but I didn't talk very much anyway. Only many years later when I went into the army I was bound to talk in English, because the officers could not talk our language, being foreigners.

St. Theresa's was a convent as well as a school, with the nuns' quarters in the same compound. Most of the children were Christian and Hindu. I was the first Jewish girl to go there, but they didn't have any prejudice against anyone. They were just teaching, and they liked the children who were learning well. Mother Mary was the mother superior, and she was my teacher in the sixth grade. The other girls used to say "You are Mother Mary's pet."

At the end of lower secondary school I got the first prize for my class. The day the awards were announced I wasn't at the school, because I had gone to sit for a scholarship exam for the higher secondary school. Hundreds of children sat for that exam, and I didn't get a scholarship. But when I returned to school the next day, Mother Mary gave me my prize. She was so happy I won the prize, she pinned it on her breast and told everyone "I am keeping it for Ruby." I still have that prize today. It is a medal with a portrait of Edward VIII, with the words "Our Empire Prince" and the date of the award, 24 May 1927.

After that I went on to complete higher secondary school. When I finished, my grandfather, who had been opposed from the start, was so happy that he gave me a gold chain with a pendant. The entire six years of high school I had peace because I was the only Jew in my class. The white Jewish girls who followed me, with their color and their money, were one class below me.

The medal awarded to Ruby in 1927 for standing first in her class at the conclusion of lower secondary school, St. Theresa's Convent, in Ernakulam. (*Photo, Barbara Johnson*)

Some of the rich white Jewish girls went to St. Mary's Convent in Fort Cochin, but I was glad to be going to Ernakulam instead. Only when they joined me at St. Theresa's College, then I felt discrimination again. It was just when I completed high school in 1931 that St. Theresa's College was opened, and I was a member of the first university class to study there.

A College Excursion

One happy event from college I will never forget. The nuns who were our professors arranged to take us for an excursion to see the mountains and the forests of Chalakudi. It was the fourth station by train. There they cut the trees from the forests, and elephants drag them to the shore of the river, where they pile it up with a precision as if it is done by machine. When the suitable time comes the trunks are dropped into the river, and the current floats them down to where the sawing machines are. You could see all this from the train when you pass by. We were to leave for our excursion in the early morning and come back by night. We had to sleep in the school the night before. We were sixty-four grown up college girls and a few nuns, our teachers, and one or two male helpers. But as usual, Grandfather put a stop. I was so aggrieved and angry that tears burst out of my eyes when I had to tell my friends I was not going. When can I get a better opportunity to get out of that damned town just to see what was around? Who has seen a mountain or a forest?

The two other Jewish girls in my class were Gladys David and Lily Koder, the daughters of the two richest men in the community. Gladys told my predicament to her father. My grandfather was the agent for his business, staying in Fort Cochin at that time. Both Grandfather's and Mr. David's handwriting looked alike. He was not afraid. He wrote a letter to my parents in Grandfather's name asking them to send me because the other two girls were going. I was so happy I took the money from Mother and ran. I took the steamboat, which takes half an hour to cross the harbor, and when I arrived at the college it was nearly dark. No bed was prepared for me. I don't remember if I had supper. So the other two girls put their beds together and let me sleep in the middle, with the edges of the bed poking up.

We started early in the morning and went by train to go up the mountains, looking out the window all of the time. I remember we saw elephants and one man sitting on top of the elephant. We kept asking when we would reach the place. The conductor would say, "One more incline"; "Another incline"; and every time we asked him, he would say, "Another incline." There was no end of inclines. My friend Lily said "When is the last incline?" Finally we reached a flat place and got down from the train. We had to climb up a little bit, then we sat down and ate something.

We returned to town in the afternoon. Three times my father had gone to the boat jetty to see if I had come back. I came by the last ferryboat. Then he brought me home in a rickshaw. It was a few days later that Grandfather came to know that I went. He shouted at my mother. She said that it was because *he* wrote the letter that she had sent me. Then it was revealed that it was his boss who wrote the letter. So he could not say anything. But I did not know whether he went and shouted at Mr. David also. He was capable of that.

Sad Endings

That excursion was memorable, but much of my college life was not so happy. By that time we were having a lot of troubles at home. My father became ill, and Grandfather was quite old and not in very good health. Two more of my younger brothers had died while I was in secondary school—both under two years of age—and Bingley was still a young boy studying in the school. We were in need of money, but we had no help from anyone.

I suddenly became weaker in class. What I studied at night I forgot the next morning. I began to get mixed up with things I read. I was studying history at the time, and there was so much to read: modern history, ancient history, European history, Indian history. With all these troubles in the house it was a terrible time, but nobody at the college knew why my loss of memory, so it was branded as laziness and idleness. The Anglo-Indian lady professors always made much of the white Jewish girls, and I felt the discrimination against me again. How I hated one Anglo-Indian lady who is the color of charcoal! So proud she was. They did not take any interest in me, and I had no help in the house. At the end of the year I completed two subjects successfully—English and Malayalam (my second language)—but I didn't pass the paper in history. Having passed two of the three papers, it was possible to try again for the third. Many students did that. At first I thought I would try, but the troubles at home continued and it was very difficult to study. Whatever plans you make, I am telling you, somebody else is making it happen. Man proposes and God disposes.

Then my father became so ill that he could not go to his work at the Ferry and Transport. The director of that company was Mr. Samuel Koder, one of the wealthiest men in the Jewish community. He said, "The daughter is staying at home, let her do the work." He told the others, "I consider her as my own daughter. Nothing will happen to her." Otherwise, people were afraid for me, seeing a young girl selling and collecting tickets at the boat jetty.

Father was put into the hospital in Ernakulam, at first with dysentery, but I think it must have turned into cancer. Mother was taking care of him there when she began to get pains for the birth of their last child. She took the ferry back to Cochin, then had pains for the next eight days. One rainy night she sent me out to call the doctor, Dr. Ruth Salem, and I went in the dark sharing an umbrella with an old woman who was one of our relations. Finally at three o'clock in the morning my sister Rachel was born, and from the beginning she was like a doll for me. We called her Royal.

Ruby Daniel holding her sister Raḥel (Royal), behind their family's home in Jew Town, 1935. (*Collection of Ruby Daniel*)

One day I remember I came home from work, when my father was still living. It was terribly hot, about two o'clock in the afternoon. You won't feel like eating when you come home from work, but my mother had already put the food on the table. "Eat, eat," she said. "I can't eat now, I'll eat afterward," I said. Then she scolded me, saying I am not eating, and this and that. "I'll eat afterward," but she won't listen. She started shouting, "Eat, eat," until finally I said, "I don't want it." That was my only way to punish her, by not eating. My father came out of the room and said, "Daughter, eat. One day you will cry for this food. A mother and two children are on your shoulders." He knew he was going to die. Good thing he didn't curse me something worse! Even now when I am sitting down to eat in the afternoon, I think of that. If anybody is around I tell them the story. It was nice food— rice and fish curry. Grandmother cooks so nicely. But I couldn't eat at that time, so what could I do? And my mother couldn't understand.

Then after Father said that, I thought, What shall I do? There is my father, who gave me everything—education and food and everything—until he became ill. Now whatever he gave me, I'll give to his children. That was my idea. I don't want anything from anybody. I'm telling you, I don't owe anything to anybody. Even these kibbutz people in Israel, I don't owe them anything.

My father and my grandfather died within two months of each other. They were always very close. My father will never say anything against him. Grandfather is like a judge and Father is like an advocate. When Grandfather was more than eighty years old my father knew he was going to die, and he too was very ill. Father thought, He has done such a lot for me, and even when he dies I am not able to do the rites for his death. Grandfather would say, "Oh, don't show me the death of this boy, I don't want to see it." Those were their prayers all the time.

Then suddenly one day Grandfather had a heart attack and died. He was ill in the morning and everyone came round to see how he was. While Dr. Ruth Salem was feeling his pulse, at that moment his heart stopped beating. Father was so ill he didn't have the strength to say the *Shema Israel* for him, so he made Bingley, who had completed his Bar Minyan, do all these rites, even the prayers at the end of the thirty days of mourning. Father sat near him and told him what to do. Then in another month Father died, and this thirteen-year-old boy had to say the last rites for his own father, and some years later for our grandmother and then for Aunty Seema. Father and Grandfather were buried one beside the other. I loved my grandfather even more than my father, and he loved me. With the loss of the two of them together, it was a terrible time.

Chapter 4

MYSTERIES OF LIFE AND DEATH: A WORLD OF DREAMS

My grandfather Eliyahu Japheth was a very learned man in the Torah, but he also had a scientific attitude. He was not a kabbalist like some of the other learned men in the Town, including my other grandfather, Daniel. It is said that the two of them used to argue about their different beliefs. Both of them were *rabbanim*. These people were not fools like the present generation. This generation knows nothing. They don't care. At that time everybody was interested in learning Torah and all the things connected with it.

Kabbalah is not for everybody. You should not learn alone. Grandfather Daniel and the men of his generation learned from a man called Yaakocha.

There was one man from the Jewish community in Mala who used to sit in the synagogue alone and study. One day he saw something that made him afraid and from that time his mind was not right. When all the other Jews left Mala for Israel, this man stayed behind and lived in Jew Town until he died. My grandfather knew him when he was younger. Grandfather said that he knew many things, but he should not read alone. That often happened with these kabbalists. They don't know that to go deep, you must have a teacher. Also *Kabbalah* is not for young men. Until you are forty-five you should not read *Kabbalah*.

CONTACT WITH THE UNDERWORLD

There were also some men in the Town who were said to have connections with the underworld, perhaps like Shelomo Hamelekh, who called up Ashmodai, king of the *shedim*, or devils. I heard about one learned man who was a teacher for the big boys, and this man had contact with the underworld. He had many books on the subject, which he had stacked away in a far corner with explicit instructions to the pupils never to touch them. But he did not lock them away. In those days children usually would do what they were told.

It so happened the master had to go away for a few days. At the time, two of the boys became inquisitive. They wanted to find out the reason why the master forbade them to touch those books, as is usual with youngsters. So when there was nobody in that place they took a book and read a passage without understanding what they were reading. At night they went to sleep. When they opened their eyes they saw a phantom, a form of a man, standing at the door of their room. They were frightened and did not know what to do. They huddled up together, but when they opened their eyes, the form was there the whole night through. Three nights passed and the form was still there. They were afraid to tell anyone—more afraid of the punishment for disobedience than of the phantom, I believe.

On the fourth night, the form came to their bedside and stood silently with folded hands. So they ran away to Alwaye. These boys could not drink or eat, neither could they sleep. They became pale and thin, and the parents were worried. Still the boys wouldn't tell them. On the fifth night, the phantom started making a humming sound, as if asking why he was called. The boys couldn't stand it anymore, so they confided to their parents what was happening. The parents quickly contacted their teacher. When he asked the boys for the truth, they told him what they had done and which page they had read in the book. Then the master showed them another passage in the book to read, and from that day the phantom did not appear.

In Cochin there was a belief that Ashmodai rode in his chariot with his retinue, once a week or once a month at a certain time of the night, across the Street of Jew Town. A lame fellow ran before his chariot. It seems once a woman and her daughter lived in the Town. Suddenly this daughter became mad, and after much treatment she still did not get well. Then it was told that one night she had cleared the night pot into the street, being lazy to go to the right place to empty it. It was just at that moment when Ashmodai rode across the Town, and a drop of the dirty liquid chanced to fall on this lame fellow. He got angry and put his spell on the girl.

The learned people told the mother that there was only one remedy. Though this lame fellow is supposed to be wicked, Ashmodai was said to be good-hearted. So they told the mother to wait for the occasion when Ashmodai came again in procession and to run and fall at his feet and beg his pardon for the ignorant crime of her daughter. For the sake of her love for the daughter, the mother waited for the procession and did as she was advised, falling down and begging for her daughter to be made well. Ashmodai at once stopped the chariot and inquired as to who was responsible for this act of cruelty. When he found out that it was the lame fellow, he ordered him to cure the girl at once. It was done and she became her normal self again. So the story was told.

GRANDFATHER THE SKEPTIC

But my grandfather Eliyahu Japheth did not believe in ghosts and devils. He said nowhere is it said in the Torah that God created the devil. Once he was talking with some non-Jewish men who tried to convince him of the existence of devils, which are sometimes seen with a pot of burning coals on the head, jumping and dancing in some remote part of some glen where there are no people. They are seen only from far away, usually in the middle of the night. One fellow among them told Grandfather that if he wants to see one of these devils, he should go to such-and-such a place one night and look in a particular direction. So Grandfather went alone, as he was instructed, and he saw the devil from afar, just as it had been described. It was pitch dark in that place.

Grandfather went slowly around the hill and caught hold of the devil from behind, holding him in such a way that he couldn't move. He found it was that man who had challenged him that there was a devil. He started begging Grandfather's pardon and asking him not to kill him. But if that man and his gang had had the upper hand, they would not have spared my grandfather. They would have said the devil took him.

Grandfather had a scientific attitude about death too. Once he said, "Suppose a candle is burning. You put out the fire. Where does it go? Death is like that." Once when he was not well, we sent for Dr. Ruth Salem, who was our relative. As she was leaving, he blessed her, saying, "May you live to one hundred and twenty years." She said she didn't want to live like that, as she was already fed up with life. Then he replied, "Don't say so. Even if you are in great difficulty, no one wants to die. Why do you want to die? Our body and soul are made out of a combination of different elements, like everything else in the world. When one dies, those elements will be integrated into the other elements from which they came." Then a part of one might become a worm or a frog or such things. Even one's soul, what we call the *neshamah*, is the same. After death the components join their own elements. That is why I think people say there is no heaven or hell. Everything is in this world itself.

Well! I am not qualified to discuss this thing. But I don't think Moshe

Rabenu has said anything about the other world. Everywhere he said if you follow the precepts of the Torah, your life will be prolonged in the land which I give you, and you will have a good life. I don't think he said you will go to heaven when you die, or to hell. You will get the reward of your good deeds towards the end perhaps, if you deserve it.

Nevertheless, after Grandfather died, some people felt his presence. My brother Bingley had his Bar Mitzvah only four months before, and he had to do the last rites for him because my father was so ill. We were all shaken at the time. Our family slept on the floor, one next to the other. My aunt Rebecca and her daughter were staying with us so we sent Bingley to sleep in the next house, where my aunt Sippora and children lived. Putting a mat under the bed which stood in the front of the room, he slept off. Suddenly in the middle of the night he opened his eyes and saw Grandfather standing at the door of the room, looking at him. He closed his eyes and slept again, and didn't tell anyone what he had seen. The next night my aunt Dolly dreamt her father. She cried to him, "Why are you not visiting us?" Then he replied, "Yes! I did come last night, and I saw Bingley and I waved to him." When she told us about the dream, Bingley said yes, that was what happened.

Then Grandmother dreamed that Grandfather came and told her, "If you go with me, then I will take you straight to paradise." She asked him, "How can I go to paradise?" and he said, "I will carry you on my back." She said, "If I go away, people will talk when they don't find me in the morning, and say I eloped with someone." Then he said, "What do you care? I am the one who is taking you away. You are going with me!" She said, "Why should I go just now? When I die, will I not go to paradise?" He said of course she will go to paradise, but if she waits it will be a little painful. She said anyway she would wait and go when she died.

GREAT-GRANDFATHER HAIM'S DREAM

I was told that my great-grandfather Haim once had a wonderful dream about paradise. He was the father of Grandfather Daniel the kabbalist, but he himself was not a learned man. This dream came to him when he was a young man of about eighteen. One Shabbat afternoon he was resting in his house on a bench near the open door, hoping to enjoy a cool breeze, and he slept off.

He dreamed he was chased by a policeman. When he was running in fright, his cap was flying away, so he put the cap in his pocket. He ran and came to a graveyard. There he jumped over a grave, and the policeman jumped after him. Suddenly an old man came and took hold of his hand. "Why are you running, son?" the old man asked. He wailed, "Grandpa, the policeman is chasing me." Then the old man said, "Look, there is no policeman," and he saw that the policeman was gone. Then the old man asked him, "What is your religion?" He said, "I am a Jew." "Then where is your cap?" He pulled it out of his pocket. "Put it on," the old man said, and he put it on.

Then the old man called out to another man, who brought him a bunch of keys. With these keys he opened each and every room and showed him all that was to be seen during the time of the Temple and what is going on in the other world. I was told all that he saw, but unfortunately I forgot—even the name of the man who brought the keys. Only one thing I remember is that he was taken to a place surrounded by high walls, where he could hear the sound of sawing. So he asked the old man what the sound was. He was told that it was the sound of sawing diamond sheets to use in the building of the Third Temple. It is the work of young girls who died before they reached puberty.

Then they came to a river which the old man said was the River Jordan. There he saw a friend of his named Murdai, a fisherman who had died in Cochin a few years before. He was fishing in the Jordan. Great-grandfather turned to his friend and asked him, "You died in Cochin some time ago. How did you come here?" He replied, "Wherever you die, you'll come here." As he was talking to his friend, the old man disappeared. Suddenly a mynah bird flew over Haim's head, a kind of bird which did not exist in South India. He caught hold of it in his dream, then his eyes opened, and he found himself in his house in Jew Town, still holding the mynah bird in his hands. He tended this bird for some time, and the people seeing it believed in his dream. If not for the bird, who would have believed that a young man who was not learned would have such a dream? It is said that good dreams also come to people who are pure and innocent.

A few years later my great-grandfather Haim was living near the Paradesi Synagogue. The *shamash* (caretaker) of that synagogue was his friend. During the *selihot* period of forty days before Rosh Hashanah, this friend had to open the Synagogue at three o'clock at night. When Haim heard his friend shaking his bunch of iron keys, he would get up and go to the synagogue to help his friend by lighting the lamps while the *shamash* went to call people for prayers. That was the practice in Cochin. One night Haim thought that he heard the sound of the keys, so he got up and hurried to the synagogue. As he drew close, he saw the light burning outside the door of the synagogue. He thought he must have slept late, so his poor friend had to do all the work alone. As he came still closer, he saw an old man sitting on the steps of the synagogue with his head bent as if reading from the big book in his hand. Suddenly he recognized him as the same old man he had seen in his dream a few years before. He got frightened and walked backwards till he fell into the doorway of his house. The time was much earlier than three o'clock. He was laid up with fever for a long time after that.

Because great-grandfather Haim was not a learned man in Torah, he was not able to ask the old man to see any special places he wanted to see. In his dream he saw only what the man showed him. So people started talking: "Why did you not go and say shalom to him? Perhaps *Mashiah* would have come." Others said, "Why did you not go and prostrate before him? He would have taught you the whole Torah." I wonder what their reaction would have been if they were in his place?

Well, a few years passed. There was an old man in Jew Town who was very learned. He was on his deathbed. He dreamt the same dream that my great-grandfather dreamt. In his dream he saw the same old man, who called out a name, and someone came with a bunch of keys. So he went with him and was shown many places. He was asked what he wanted to see and was shown whatever he wanted to see. At last the old man opened an inner door. There was such a bright light in that room that the man's eyes became dim. At the time someone called out, "Tishbi, Tishbi" (one of the names for Eliyahu Hanabi). The old man replied, "*El rahum vehanun*" (God compassionate and merciful). Then the old man said he is not permitted to show him any more.

When he woke up in Jew Town, the man's eyes were red and swollen. Then he sent word to the three synagogues requesting all the men to come to him after the morning prayers. When they came, he related to them his dream and asked them to find out who was the man who brought the key to the old man when he called him by such a name. They searched in the books and found out that was the name of the *shamash* of the First Temple.

Then this man, who was on his deathbed, warned them that three days after his death a great cry will come from the north and told them to be careful. It so happened three days after his death thieves got into the Paradesi Synagogue, which was in the north of the Town, and they robbed covers of the Sifre Torah, threw Torah scrolls on the ground, and dirtied them. It was really a terrible cry. The whole Town's people fasted and prayed because the Torah scroll was desecrated.

DREAM MESSAGES

Many people in Cochin had dreams which came true in time. People dream so many hundreds of things that are not important, but there are also important dreams, in which they feel the presence of someone who has died. Usually it is the women who talk about these dreams. Most of the men don't speak about them, even if they see something. Sometimes it's a good dream and sometimes it is not. Sometimes the dream comes when a person is worried, as when someone is ill or has a great problem, but sometimes such a dream comes when one is not thinking about anything in particular. I don't know—who can explain all these things?

Once my father's mother was saved from danger by a dream. She was a young woman at the time and she was lying down at night feeding the baby. The double door was open and the kerosene lamp was burning. Her husband, Daniel, always used to come late, because he was learning and teaching with people in the Town. Anyway, she slept off and dreamt that her mother, who had been dead for a long time, came and called her by name: "Rivka, are you sleeping? The door on the top floor is open." It was a one-story building and there was no door on the top, only a window. Suddenly she woke up and saw that it was midnight and the door in front of her was open. She was so frightened from the dream that she got up and closed the door. Just as she was drawing the iron bolt, there was a very loud noise of someone from the other side hitting on the door with both hands. Grandmother said perhaps somebody was waiting there to rob her, and she woke from the dream just in time.

A young man in the Rahabi family was also saved by a dream, many years ago. I have forgotten his name. When his father died, this man was very young. He was left with a lot of money, but no experience. A man filed a suit against him, claiming that his father had borrowed a lot of money from him many years ago and did not return it. So he claimed the money with interest and compound interest. It was such a big amount, the whole of his property could not fetch the value to clear his debt. This young man was so worried, he could not eat or sleep. One night his father came in his dream, so he cried to him and told him the story. Then the father said, "Don't worry, my son. I have written down all his account in the account book of so-and-so number on such-and-such a page." The next morning the son told his dream and the advocates found the book of which the number was said and found on the same pages his account and how it had all been paid. They presented the book in court and won the case.

This happened quite recently. A woman died in Cochin, a spinster who bequeathed all her jewelry to her niece. The niece was married and lived in Bombay. So the sister of the deceased woman took the jewelry with her when she visited her daughter. One night while she was staying in Bombay, the mother dreamt that her sister came and told her a pair of her earrings was missing from the jewelry and that their servant has robbed it. Next morning she and her daughter looked into the jewelry box and found that the earrings were really missing. They searched everywhere, and at last the police caught that particular servant and found the earrings in her possession.

Sometimes a dream brings a bad message, like the dream I had about my baby brother's tomb. I also dreamed once that someone died on the Kadavumbagam side of the Town, and suddenly the next day or two I heard there was a funeral. Seema Salem's mother told her she should always say "ḥalom tob" (a good dream) when telling about a dream, to prevent any bad message from coming true. Years before, her mother dreamt that her young son died, and in the dream when she saw her friend sitting at the window of her house she cried and told her that her son had died. A short time later her son in fact became ill and died, and when her mother got out and saw that friend of hers sitting at the window, she cried and told her how her dream had come true.

This happened in the family of the Halleguas. A gentleman in that family had only one son, who became very ill and the doctors had given up hope. The father was always praying and asking for his son's life. One night he had a dream. A police inspector and two policemen came to arrest his son. Suddenly the inspector shouted at the policeman. He said, "You are not asked to arrest him. But arrest this man," pointing at the father. "He shall be imprisoned for eleven months." From then on the son became better, but the father was laid up with a stroke. He was taken to Vettaka for treatment. After eleven months he died. His body was brought back to Cochin with great pomp by boat. Both sides of the river were decorated with lights. Most of the property belonged to him. His boat was accompanied by small boats called *odi* fore and aft, just like the funeral of a maharaja.

My friend Koko Roby told me that at one time her sister Reema was very ill. She was in the hospital and was very serious. One night Koko dreamt an old man. He told her, "Don't you worry. Your sister will be all right. Moses died." Koko didn't know which Moses. Her husband's name was Moses, but he was not ill. Next day a telegram arrived in Jew Town from Bombay, saying that a Cochin Jew named Moses Ashkenazi had suddenly died there of a heart attack.

Often a dream brings a message which is hopeful. My cousin Mary was very ill after the birth of her third child, Venus. The doctors were afraid for her life. Everyone was worried. One night she dreamt her grandmother, who died a few years before. She told her, "Don't worry, child, your grandmother is taking away all your illness. You will be all right." From then on she improved.

A number of years ago my cousin Juliet was in Bombay, living with her parents. She had two small children and she was separated from her husband. Her married sister and husband were also in Bombay. They were a help for her. She was also working but did not earn much. Then her sister immigrated to Israel and her father lost his job. She was in much difficulty and was very much worried. One night she dreamt that she was standing on a seashore.

Suddenly the water parted and far away at the other end a man was standing. He bent down and picked up a sheaf of grain and waved to her. She says from then on she got a better-paid job and things became easy for her and she never had to starve.

There is also a remarkable story about Benaya Benjamin, my grandmother Docho's uncle, who was a businessman in Bombay. He got cash from many different sources, and once he found a forged hundred-rupee note among the money he had collected. It was lying there on the table when the man from whom he buys rice for the family came to collect the money. He had no cash at the moment to pay him. So he asked him to come the next day. But the rice merchant saw the hundred-rupee note. He was told that it was a forged note, but he said it does not matter, he will change it anyhow, and he took the note and went away.

Benaya knew he could be prosecuted, and that is what happened. The rice merchant was caught, and he said he got the note from Benaya. So Benaya was arrested. I think there was some foul play. The only way he can escape is to tell a lie. His advocates advised him to do so, but he would never tell a lie. Anyway, he was shut up in prison, even though he had friends among the famous Sassoons and Ezras who were ready to swear of his innocence. His nephew Williams, who was only a boy then, used to bring his meals to the prison three times a day, because Benaya ate only kosher food. Back in Cochin all his relatives were very concerned about him.

The night before the trial, Benaya was so worried, as no one could predict the result. He was sitting on his bed when he heard the sound of someone opening the iron doors, which had been locked by the jailers awhile before for the night. He was wondering who could come in the middle of the night, when he saw his mother, who had died a few years before, coming through the door. She said, "Why are you wearing this prisoner's cap, my son?" She pulled off the cap from his head and threw it on the floor and said, "Your case number nine is dismissed," and then disappeared. He did not even know the number of his case. When Williams came the next morning he asked him to find out the number of his case, and it was indeed number nine. The next day, the case was dismissed.

That same night in Cochin my grandmother dreamt that she went out of the house. She saw a light. When she looked up she saw a door open in the sky from where the light was coming. I don't remember if she saw anyone. She woke Grandfather and told him about her dream. This Eliyahu Japheth, the man who never believed in dreams and ghosts, listened to her. He said, "That is salvation for Benaya."

Chapter 5

THE SITUATION OF
WOMEN IN COCHIN

H ere I want to write something
about the lives of many women in my generation, not just myself. Times were
beginning to change and we were in the middle. If I had been born fifty years
earlier I would not have had these things to think about. The earlier generations took life as it came. Nowadays women seem to have a better situation.
But we were in the middle and that was very, very difficult. People didn't talk
about it then: they just suffered in the house. If I explain what has happened
to me, it may give an idea about other women who were born at that time.

By the time my grandfather and father died, I was at an age when most
young women in India would have been married for at least a few years. But
that did not seem to be an option for me. First of all, to tell you the truth I
was not personally interested in getting married. My young cousins and their
friends used to talk about men and marriage and all these things, but I never
had girls of my own age as friends to talk with. I didn't know much about
sex, but the idea did not appeal to me. Also there were no appropriate men
in Cochin who could make me change my mind.

There were many women among the Paradesi Jews who remained single.
As I have explained, the white Jews would not marry outside their own group.
Also, some of the rich white Jewish families would not even marry from the
poorer families of white Jews. In my mother's generation there were seventy-
two men and women in the Paradesi community who remained single, largely
because of all these restrictions. Think how large the community would have
been if they had married! Many of the single Paradesi men went to Bombay
and other places looking for work. The unmarried women had to stay at home.
They were given a small amount of money from the synagogue, just enough

The Situation of Women in Cochin / 61

to eat. I can remember they used to knit caps for Muslim gentlemen, then do some embroidery kerchiefs, and so on, and that is the way they made clothes and other things. They were good-looking women too.

Many families were ruined by their daughters' marriage celebrations. People thought it a shame if they cannot celebrate a marriage as their neighbors did. Those who had a big house might mortgage half of it and before they could redeem it, there came the second daughter's marriage. Then they sold it and were in debt for the third one. Many women had to wait to get married because of this financial problem.

My mother was the eldest daughter of my grandfather, and her marriage was celebrated for a couple of weeks, I don't know with how much trouble. When it was time for my aunt Rebecca to marry, my grandfather and his rich friends decided to solve this problem by reducing the celebration to one day. But who is to start this? My grandfather said he was willing to do it for his daughter's wedding if all the rich friends whose daughters were to get married soon should do the same. Otherwise, it would be a disgrace for him. So all of them made a vow to follow suit. It was done so for all public celebrations—the norm is one day. But those who can afford, they called friends to their home for Shabbat, and everybody celebrated the night before the wedding as a bachelor's party and did *Sheva Berakhot* (the traditional seven blessings) every night of the wedding week.

Some of my relations married non-Jews, including Mr. Salem's two daughters, both of whom were medical doctors. Several of my aunts and cousins married Jews from Bombay or Rangoon, but when I saw the difficult lives they led in those places, I was not at all interested.

TRADITIONAL INDIAN WOMEN

People in Cochin seemed to think that women are created to suffer and in silence. Not only in Cochin, in the whole of India. In an Indian poem written thousands of years ago, I read about the qualities of an ideal woman. To quote a few: She should have the wisdom of a minister. She should be a slave in her work. In beauty she should be like a fairy. In bed she should be like a prostitute. She should be a perfect mother. In patience she should be like the earth. If women are like this, then why should they be controlled by men?

But the Indians had the idea that a woman should be under the control of the father when she is young, then under the control of the husband when she is married, and then under her sons in case she became a widow. Recently I have read about women in India being burnt because they don't bring enough dowry when they are married, or what was promised to them by their families was not given to the in-laws. And the parents don't care, or they are helpless to do anything. I know the suffering of women is not only in India. I have read and seen pictures about women in other countries, how they suffer. Everywhere these things happen.

It should also be noted that this was not true for all women in India. In Kerala there is a high caste of Hindus called Nayars. They and the royal families and some other castes have the family system called a *tarwad*, in which all the members are supported from the family fund according to their needs, as long as they remain in the family fold. Their marriage system is called *marumakathayam*. Their inheritance was not from the father but from the mother's brother. The Nayar women don't get married to one man. If a man wants to go to a woman (he can be of any caste), he brings betel leaves and a set of clothes, and only if she wants him, he becomes a husband. But he comes in the evening when it is dark and goes in the morning before it is light. He has no rights in the house. That is for the women. Men go and work and make their own living. If children are born, they belong to the mother and her *tarwad*. If a woman decides she doesn't want him, if she wants another man, then she'll keep a pair of his wooden slippers and a brass pot with a handle on the top, full of water, and put them outside on the veranda. When that fellow comes and sees these things, he can't go inside. So these women won't suffer at the hands of men.

Not all of the castes in Kerala follow this custom, and even the Nayars were beginning to change during my generation. When they got educated, they felt that this custom was a sort of shame or disgrace, and they began to take up the practice of marriage. But I think that their old custom was good for the women.

In some of the other castes a woman would be thrown out of the family if she had anything to do with a man before marriage. Some women like this, from very good families, came to Jew Town for refuge, knowing that there were Jewish families there who would take them as servants. I remember a Christian woman who came to the Town looking for work with a week-old baby, soon after she gave birth from the hospital. My aunt Sippora hired her. She was a very good-looking woman. She was so troubled, my grandfather asked her for the cause of her worry, and then she related her story.

She got married to the friend of a notorious thief named Umballi. She was from a good and rich family, but he wanted to marry her, and if she was not given to him he was capable of killing her family and taking her away. He went to jail for some offense, and after some time she got pregnant by somebody else and ran away from the neighborhood. At that time she was expecting her husband to finish his time in jail and come out, and she was so afraid. If he finds her she was sure that he will kill her and the man who betrayed her. She came to Jew Town from the hospital, knowing she can find an asylum among the Jews. Once Grandmother asked, "You are such a beautiful girl; how did such a thing happen to you?" Her reply was, "Madam, if one can peel the beauty and put it in a pot, will there be food?" She went away and we didn't see her again.

SOME PROBLEMS OF JEWISH WOMEN

If you study the Jewish tradition, it seems that women were intended to have more control. When the first woman, Hava, was created, God did not have the idea of her being controlled by the man. Perhaps He had that idea, but it turned out that Hava controlled Adam. When Adam was given the apple, he ate at her hands without a question but then accused her to God, saying, "The woman You gave me as a companion gave it to me and I ate." Sarah the wife of Father Abraham asked him to drive away his mistress Hagar and the son, and without a question he obeyed her. Their daughter-in-law Rebecca told her brother she was going with the stranger Eliezer, who went to fetch her for his master. The two daughters of Lot, who thought after the destruction of Sodom and Gomorrah that all the people of the world were destroyed and they were the only women left, had to save the world, so they begot children from their father. When Barak, one of the judges of Israel, had to go for war, he requested Deborah the prophetess to go with him because he did not have the guts to go alone. There were other women, like Miriam and Hannah, who were prophetesses, and Yael was the one who killed the commander in chief Sisera.

Then what happened? The women reduced themselves to be controlled by men and their in-laws. Well! Now I am writing only of the Jewish women of Cochin. In most cases they were not taught much except the prayers, and then their families got them married away to anyone who was willing to marry them. I knew of girls who used to cry and beat their breasts because they did not want to marry the man the parents chose. But it did not help. The parents arranged the marriage and perhaps there would be a grand wedding. But then the bride had to go to the house of her husband's parents, with other married brothers and unmarried in-laws. There she had to live till the end, through thick and thin. Some men were drunkards, some were very poor, some men enjoyed beating their wives. Still the woman had to give birth and rear the children even under the worst conditions.

The parents wanted to get rid of the daughters soon after they came of age. They are afraid they might do something so their reputation as well as their family's reputation will be at stake. If a family's reputation was damaged, it would affect all the children's chances for marriage. To explain how a whole family could be boycotted by the rest of the Jewish community, let me tell the story of a large family with whom we were friendly in Jew Town. They had come there from another Jewish community because of the great troubles that happened to the mother, Sarah. The following is her story.

Sarah was a beautiful young Jewish woman in Chendamangalam or Parur, who married an elderly fellow, sometime around the beginning of this century. Her husband had a lot of money and much land, including the entire island of Gothuruthi. The following is what one of her daughters told me. Sarah and her husband had two small daughters. One Saturday afternoon the husband told Sarah that men of his family did not have a long life. They usually died when they were in their forties. He told her that in case of his death, she should get one daughter married to his brother's son and one to her brother's son, so that the money will be divided between the two families. That same night he died, and Sarah was left alone.

After that her brothers tried to swindle her. She did not know how to read and write, so whatever documents her brothers brought, she signed. One person who helped her was Eliyahu, who had been an agent for her husband. He found out what her brothers were doing and told her not to sign the documents unless first someone read them and told her what was in them. Her brothers knew it was Eliyahu's doing, and they hated him also. They wanted to take away both of her daughters for their family, but Sarah insisted that the money was her husband's and she will follow his wishes. She was a very determined woman. The brothers were determined to take away the daughters by any means, even if it meant killing Sarah.

Sarah's brothers collected some people from here and there, about six hundred in all, and went to Gothuruthi, where she was living, to take away the children by force. On the island were some rich Christian tenants, who all loved Sarah because she was good to them. They did not want it to happen to her or in their island. So the leader of these people, I think Thoma was his name, hid Sarah in someone's house. When her brother came and took hold of Sarah's daughters, Thoma told him to leave the children for the time being and promised to bring the mother and children himself to his house. But the brother said he will not let the children go. Those people can be very nasty too. So Thoma said if he did not leave the children, he will cut off his hands and take them. When he still refused, he cut his hand off and took away the children.

The people who came from outside to help the brothers did not know the lay of the land in Gothuruthi and the dangerous mud banks, where they used to bury the thick skin of the coconuts to make ropes. So many people have been drowned in that mud. One of Sarah's brothers sank in the mud, and some of the tenants hit him on his head and he died. Anyway, Sarah was saved for the time being, but she had to escape from there, as they brought a murder case against her. She had to run from place to place with the police hot on her heels—from Chendamangalam to Parur to Ernakulam and so on, till at last she came to Cochin.

Then the rich white Jewish men Joseph and Isaac Hallegua and my grandfather and others took her under their wings. Joseph Hallegua gave her a house in British Cochin, which is now the Fort Cochin of today, where the Cochin State police had no jurisdiction. There was a small group of people who had helped her in the village, including the agent Eliyahu and his parents and sister, who also came with her.

The other Jewish communities did not approve of Sarah's relationship with Eliyahu, but she married him and they had a son and three daughters. All this time they never left the Torah. For Festivals and Shabbat they managed to get together a minyan to pray. They used to take a shofar from our house. We had three of the big shofars which came to us from the synagogue in Fort Cochin.

The worst thing Sarah's relatives did was to excommunicate Sarah and all those who helped her, so that if anybody marries her children, that person is also excommunicated by the six communities of Cochin. They stayed on a few years in Fort Cochin, but they could not stay all the time cut away from a community. They had to join with someone, so the Kadavumbagam community agreed to accept them. (That community had also been excommunicated by the six others because of some other quarrel some years before.) That is how Sarah and her family came to stay in Cochin in the south end of Jew Town near where we were living. Anyway, Sarah will not take a woman or a man for her daughters or son from that Kadavumbagam community. She thought after a few years that she and the family would be accepted back by her people, and once they go, they must all go together.

Sarah managed somehow to get the first two daughters married, but the youngest daughter, Seema, was not willing to marry whoever the mother wants. She went to school and college, and in college she met a boy, a relative of hers. But he could not or would not marry her because of what had happened to her mother. He did not want to be thrown out of his community and relations.

Of course not all the women in the Jewish community had problems with their marriages. There were lucky women, who got married to good men, and their lives were happy. With all the poverty and illness in our family, my grandmother and my mother loved their husbands. My father did not open his mouth. Whatever food Mother put before him, he ate. Sometimes when she makes a *cunji*, rice cooked in water, she forgets to put salt in it, and she'll ask, "Is there salt in that?" He'll say, "I don't know, it seems all right." Mother and Father knew each other well before they married, because they grew up in the same family.

Originally, my grandfather did not want to get married. He wanted to leave and go far away from Cochin. His parents died and he had no relations in the Town. But his friends didn't want him to leave, so they said, "Tell us who you want to marry, and we'll arrange it for you." It was the time of my father's *brit milah* (circumcision) and they all went to the party. All the women and girls came dressed up nicely, and my grandmother was the most beautiful and the youngest among them, only twelve or thirteen years old. He was over thirty years old. He pointed to her and said, "If I get this girl, I will marry." Her father said, "What? I give my child to this giant?" But all these rich people—the Halleguas and all—coaxed the father and finally he agreed. She didn't get pregnant right away, and that's a problem. The very year that she gets married, a woman must have a baby. All the others who got married that year were pregnant. Her mother was so worried, she started taking her to the doctor and giving her medicines. My grandmother couldn't tell anybody then what was happening, but when she was old she told us. He never touched her till she was sixteen years old. Until then he brought her up like a daughter.

My grandfather didn't have much money, but he always told his wife, "On Shabbat and Festivals, you must make everything in the house. My children should not feel that we are poor." We didn't feel that. We always had nice things for *Pesah* and all the Festivals. Grandfather was very stubborn, but he loved Grandmother. For Festivals, unless she comes and stands near him, dressed up like she is going to the synagogue, with scarf and all, only then he will start the *berakhah*. She will say, "No, start, I am coming, I am coming," but he will not start. I can still see it. How nice it was! In my family the men had respect for the women.

For some of the other women in my family it was quite different. They married men from different families, with whom we had no relationship at all. One must get married to whom she can get married. They suffered a lot. Aunt Rebecca didn't get beaten or anything like that, only her husband was poor. He had a small shop in the interior in Burma, where she had no contact with any Jews and she was alone there. When she came back to Cochin he couldn't come with her. If he leaves he will have nothing. When she came with the three children, sometimes he sent something, whatever he could send. For some other women in the family, the husbands used to hit them, and drink a lot. I heard about one time, before I was born, when the husband of my aunt Sarah got so angry he hit on the cupboard and broke all the glasses and good things for *Pesah* in my grandfather's house, and he used to hit his wife too.

Even today in Israel there are a few Cochin Jewish women who willingly suffer at the hands of the husbands. A short while ago I was in a nearby town.

I wanted to buy something. Then I saw a Cochin woman from a *moshav* (village) coming toward me. She knows me by sight and I the same. She was crying, so I went to her and asked her why she was crying. Then she started pouring out her troubles. She was married in Ernakulam, and there she did not have children. Her husband did not like her. He used to hit her and curse her. Then after coming to Israel she says she gave him eight children, who are all grown up now. He was drinking and sometimes ill in bed. Then she has to hand-feed him. That day he was ill in bed, still cursing her, when she left the house to go to the market, where she met me. I asked her why she does not leave him or go to her mother and brothers, who always ask her to go to them: "At your age you can do without a man," I said. "The children are grown. Then why are you afraid to leave him? At the rate you are working in the *moshav*, you can work anywhere and be an independent woman." You will be surprised at her reply to me. She said, "Oh Ruby Aunty, *YOU* can say all that to me," emphasizing the *YOU*. I suppose she meant that I couldn't understand her because I never married. But I know that if I were in such a position I wouldn't bear all these things, and anyway it is not necessary in Israel today.

If the situation is not so bad now for women in India, I think it is because more women are being educated. In the past, there were no schools anyway, but once there was an opportunity for education, most of the Jewish families still would not send their daughters to school because of this fear for their reputation. Even some minor thing could ruin a girl's chance for marriage. But without an education, a woman could get trapped in a bad marriage, because she had no way to support herself.

Chapter 6

MY YEARS IN THE GOVERNMENT SERVICE

I remember when my grandfather told us, "We don't want to be supported by our daughters. Stay at home." But Grandfather was seventy years old when these orders were given, and he did not have a penny in his name for us to inherit. He did not think who is going to support us. His only son went to Burma. Before Grandfather died he saw three of his daughters and myself working and supporting themselves and their families. My aunt Rebecca worked as a municipal midwife, Aunt Sippora worked in the Tata Oil mills, Aunt Dolly was a teacher, and I started off working in place of my father in the Ferry and Transport Company.

When my father and grandfather died within two months of each other, I was thrown into an ocean without knowing how to swim or wade. I still don't know how to swim. Then I did not know how to talk to people, request, or even to beg. Thank God I did not have to beg.

At this time, in 1934, the most pressing problem for me was financial. How was I to support the family, including my mother, my young brother in school, my baby sister, Grandmother, and Aunty Seema? My health deteriorated so that I could not go on working at the Ferry and Transport. I would get a catch in my side and have difficulty breathing. No one in the family was employed.

Finally Mother decided that she would go and take my place, so she began working in the job which my father had for so many years, selling and collecting tickets at the boat jetty. She was a very stubborn and strong-hearted woman. At first it was difficult for her, but she got used to it. Every day she came in contact with thousands of people, and they respected her. She started work when she was about forty-five and worked for fifteen years, till the company was taken over by the government.

Ruby's mother, Leah Daniel, early 1940s. (*Collection of Ruby Daniel*)

When I stopped my work at the Ferry and Transport, I went for the Government Service. In Kerala there is an age bar to enter the Government Service. One must enter before age twenty-four in order to get a pension at age fifty. So we had to get in, even only for a month, to replace someone who took leave. We would run from pillar to post wherever there is a vacancy, then get thrown out till finding a permanent place. One cannot pick and choose. There is a percentage of positions for each caste, with only a one percent chance for Jews and Anglo-Indians together in the Government Service. I worked first as a teacher, then in the Judicial Department, the Registration Department, Police Department, Medical Department, and the Military Department during the war and was diverted to the civil court near my house, till I ended up in the kibbutz in Israel peeling potatoes in the kitchen.

Anyway, the Government Service had advantages for a woman in my position. The pay was low (my mother earned more in the Ferry and Transport), but the salaries were the same for men and women, if it was the same position. Promotions were all according to the number of years of service, and you can get a pension if you work twenty-five years. There were quite a few young women like myself working as teachers and lower clerks. Their families just hoped they could pass the matriculation and get work, to bring some food into the house. I heard one man saying, "Only when the daughters of the house went to work we got something to eat in the house." The sons would spend their earnings on their own pleasures, not to help the family. We came from families that haven't got the money to send their daughters to university. For higher positions you must have higher education. If I had stayed on in India, after years and years I might have been able to be a head clerk. That would be as high as I could go without a B.A.

WORKING AS A TEACHER

I started working as a teacher with no training. That was the fashion: finish the matriculation and apply for a job first, in time to get into the Government Service before the age bar. Then there was a Jew Town girls' school, and the Jewish girls got into that school. For the others it was a privilege. But for me no.

First of all, the headmistress of that school of course was a lady, and they often have a prejudice. They think, If I can do it why can't you? Moreover that headmistress was an Anglo-Indian who went to college with me. Though she learned in another college, we went to Ernakulam together in the same boat for years and we were friends. Now I had to be under her.

But some funny things happened with the pupils. I was teaching in the first standard with forty children, most of them from the Conganies, a caste of people from the north who don't speak Malayalam well. They sent their children to school just to get rid of them for a few hours from the house. So they admitted children of four years instead of five years. These children did not know when to go to the loo [toilet], and they had running noses which the teacher has to clean. When I taught them to say, "How old are you?" one little girl got up and said, "I am twenty-eight years old, Teacher." Then another little one got up and asked her, "Then have you got married?"

At one time I was teaching in the third class, all boys of eight and nine years old. They were so mischievous. One Jewish boy annoyed me so much I asked him to stand up on the bench. As soon as he got up all the rest of the boys as one got up upon the bench and wouldn't get down in spite of my coaxings. I was so embarrassed I had to plead with them to get down. That boy is living in Israel now with children and grandchildren. God bless him.

Anyway, I soon knew that teaching was not the career for me. Mother went and requested that I get a transfer to a clerical job, and fortunately her effort was successful.

LIVING IN TRICHUR

Every three or six months we got thrown out of a position when the workers came back from leave to their permanent place of work. Sometimes I was sent to work in other places, and then I had to find a place to stay. This was not easy for a young woman in those days.

Three different times I was posted in Trichur, which is a big town about two hours away from Cochin by train. I remember the first time I was sent to Trichur to work in the Registry Office. When I arrived there, one of the elderly clerks was very helpful to me. After some time he asked me if I am the daughter of Daniel Hai of Cochin Jew Town, since my surname was also Daniel. He said that when he was working in Cochin many years before, Daniel Hai was his friend, so that is the reason he went out of his way to help me. Actually his friend Daniel Hai was my cousin, who had gone away to Bombay when I was small and died there.

Anyway, this gentleman took me to the YWCA. Since the schools had vacation, the place was closed. But he took me to the president's house and had me admitted in the hostel. There we found only a woman who looked after the girls when they are there and an old servant woman and a few girls. From that time on, I always stayed at the YWCA when I worked in Trichur.

The first time I came into contact with girls of my own age was when I lived at the YWCA hostel. There were a few Christian girls from rich and good families staying there. I felt at home with them, so I was happy. Some were nurses and some learning needlework, and so on.

I was the first Jewess they had ever come across. They thought I know a lot. I heard some elderly ladies from their families came to visit them. One of them told the girls, "You know the Jewish ladies know a lot of needlework. I have seen Jewish women dancing with slippers which they got from Japan and Burma, with velvet of different colors and some embroidered work for the top of the slippers. Why have you wasted the time with her? You should have learnt from her." In fact I knew next to nothing of needlework. I was so lazy Aunty Seema had to fix even a button for me. I learnt a little bit of embroidery only from these friends there in Trichur.

At eight o'clock at night we had to go upstairs, where we slept on mats on the floor. How can one sleep at eight o'clock? So the girls used to come and sit around me and ask me to tell a story. I always like to read books about crimes, but I would forget one story when I read the next. So I used to tell them stories my grandmother told me when I was small. They roared with laughter and said, "Oh! It is lies, lies!" Then what is a story if it is not a lie?

That is the time when Miss Mani comes up the staircase. She was the woman who took care of the hostel, and she was always afraid for us. Because sometimes there were a few boys from the YMCA parading in front of the YWCA, with hooting and whistling as boys usually do. Anyway, as soon as we hear her steps on the staircase, all run to their beds as if nothing happened. Then when Miss Mani goes down, all the girls are back again on my mat. Miss Mani will come up two or three times every night. She will shout, but who cares?

The nurses were working in the hospital, which was next to a Hindu temple. One night there was supposed to be an *ulsavam* there—a celebration and a competition between the temples of two communities. It was said there will be a hundred and one elephants. The nurses took me with them to see it. That time there were only thirty elephants—fifteen from each temple—but still it was a grand sight. The elephants stood fifteen on one side and fifteen on the other side, facing each other. On their backs people were sitting with silk umbrellas of different textures with broad chains of silver and gold hung around the umbrellas. Some carried round fans made out of peacock feathers (*alavatham*) and the white feathers of ostriches (*venchamaram*). In addition to that, there was the music and drumming from all kinds of bands and tom-toms.

I heard from these girls at the YWCA some stories about how women or girls were treated in their places. If a girl gets pregnant before marriage, they told me, either she is killed or driven out of the house and she runs away to save her life. They told me about the cruelty of some rich and proud Christian women and how they treated their servants. One woman they heard about had poured boiling oil on the girl who was working for her, because the onion she was frying got burnt. Another put the hand of a servant's young son into the fire for doing some mischief.

Some things I learned in the Registry Office also shocked me. Once I had to copy a document. I read it and was surprised to read about a woman who was the wife of two or three men at the same time. When I asked the people working with me what was it all about, they told me there was a caste where the eldest son in the family gets married, and she is the woman for all the brothers.

Working in the Courts

When I was young my father was well-known to all the clerks of the law courts, because he used to write documents. My grandfather also went often to the courts, because he was the agent of some rich people who were all the time in a hurry to go to the law courts. I remember Grandfather and his friends carrying halakhah books with them, since the Judgment for the Jews was according to the Jewish Law. I was small and used to wonder what they are always going to the court for. I hated the court because I missed Father and Grandfather in the house. The irony of it was when I grew up I worked in the Judicial Department for more than ten years! I worked in both Ernakulam and Cochin, in the High Court and the District Court and the Munsiff Court.

All the heads of the department were men and only a few girls working as clerks. The men were usually helpful, not like the women teachers and headmistress who had given me trouble in the past. Among the clerks, if somebody happened to make a mistake, the others hushed it up and corrected it without letting the heads of the department know about it. In all the offices I worked I was friendly with everybody and all liked me. I used to make fun of them and joke with them, not like their girls who were quiet. But I was privileged as a Jew, as I was the only Jewess there then.

In Ernakulam, the Treasury Office was next to the court where I worked. There was only a partition of iron bars. There were only men working there, so they joked at women, but anything they say I used to answer back. Just to hear from me they would say things so I had to reply. One day I was quiet and did not listen to what they said. So one of them asked, "What has happened? Ruby is not working today?" In fact I don't know any of them by sight. Everybody knew me. So I went from department to department.

After some time working in this court we had to pass an exam from a book called *Huzur Office Manual*, about a hundred pages. A Muslim boy named Muhammed, who was working with me, lent me his book. He had failed the exam the previous year and was not going for it that year. I read the book a few times and as usual I forgot many things but I had a certain idea. We were a few girls working in government offices going together in the steamboat to cross the harbor to Ernakulam for the examination. They were still reading the book on the boat, some trying to learn by heart, and some were ones who had gone for the exam the previous year and failed. Some girls asked me what is this and that from the book. To tell you the truth I did not know the answers to their questions. I told them I don't know. They won't believe that and thought I did not want to tell them.

For the examination we had to answer questions from the manual and we

A "trio" of friends—Christian, Jewish and Hindu—working together in the Munsiff
Court, Cochin; (*left to right*) E. C. Tressia, Ruby Daniel, and Sarojini, late 1940s.
(*Collection of Ruby Daniel*)

had dictation in English and Malayalam as well as a handwriting and speed test. Anyway the result came in the government gazette [official newspaper announcement of appointments], so I went to the court to look. That Muslim boy Muhammed was sitting there with the gazette and told me, "Buy *laddus* (a kind of sweets). You have passed." I said I won't believe unless I see the gazette. So he gave it to me but I could not find my name in the second and third classes. So I shouted at him that he was making fun of me. He said, "Look on the top." Then I saw my name among the eight people who passed first-class. I was surprised myself. It was during the summer vacation, but there were a few advocates and court attendants on duty, so I had to buy *laddus* for all of them, which is the custom on such an occasion. Muhammed said he was not sorry he lent me his book.

At this time I was in Habonim, a Zionist youth organization. There was one white Jewish boy—a lawyer who was working in the auditing office. He also had passed this above-mentioned test, the previous year before I took it, and he also passed first-class. When we came down from the Habonim meeting, people went and congratulated him for it. But when I passed the same test first class there was no one in Jew Town to congratulate me. This Jewish boy said, "Of course your test must have been a different one." Ours must have been different? After all it is only the same *Huzur Office Manual*! It was another example of their jealousy.

Some of the clerks used to leave arrears of the week, specially Muhammed. So during the holidays the judge would call me and ask if I am going anywhere for the summer vacation. Then he will ask me if I can come and finish the arrears because the others are living far away and my house is three minutes' walk from the court. So I went and finished it. Once he left three hundred files. Then Jew Town people were wondering why I was going to court when they had holiday.

A VISIT TO BOMBAY

Though Kerala is a small country and a poor country, at least I had a good job. In other places women didn't have as much chance for work. In Bombay and other cities, they would have been happy with a job like mine. I learned about the situation there when my cousins invited me to visit them in Bombay. I found my relatives there living in crowded conditions, with wives and children and grandparents and their unmarried children all living together, and they were lucky if they had two rooms.

My cousin Joseph's father was working in the mills. They had a white Jew also working there as head of the department. When my uncle took me to see the mills, he took me to him. And he thought I was trying to find some man or something. That's how it happens. I had another relative whose uncle was looking for a wife and he wanted a Cochin wife. The man from the mill told my uncle, "She's a good-looking girl. Why doesn't he marry her?" And my uncle replied, "She didn't come here looking for a man to marry. She is working in the High Court in our country." My relatives were so proud. They have never seen a Cochin woman working like that. The women in Bombay go to work in the mills, just cleaning the cotton mill or work like that, like a sweeper's job. Compared to them I had a good situation.

A young man who came to tutor my cousin once read my palm. He said that he saw in my palm that there would be a break in my Government Service. This was a long, long time before the break came.

Chapter 7

THE TIME OF WORLD WAR II

A few years before World War II broke out, a German cruiser named *Emden* came to our shore for a friendly visit. The sailors went on shore for excursions into every nook and corner. At the time my uncle Daniel was getting married in Rangoon. As Grandmother (his mother) was living with us, we made a dinner party in Cochin on the night of his wedding. It is the custom for the bridegroom's family to make a party, even without the bridegroom. If you put a few lights in the house, everyone in Jew Town became curious, because the houses were facing the public road. So many people who passed came up on the veranda and looked inside through the doors and windows. Two of these German sailors also came to look.

One of our relations, an old woman with poor eyesight, thought they were the sons of Mr. Koder, who were also very tall and fair skinned. So she went out and caught hold of their hands and said, "Son, come in! Why do you stand outside?" So of course they came in. All our community of white Jews were sitting at the table, so they were also asked to sit at the same time. Only when they came in, she found out her mistake. She went to my grandmother and said, "Ahi, Docho! What did I do? I made a mistake!" Grandmother said, "So what? We have food enough for two more."

But what those white Jewish men did! They removed all the cutlery and threw them under the table, so the Germans had to eat with their hands. The Jews always hated the Germans, but that was the only punishment they could give them. Afterwards the sailors congratulated my grandmother and went away.

A few days later the ship left. At that time they played their military band. The German band was very famous, and to my ears it was fantastic. Many people went to the beach in Fort Cochin to see the flags and the sailors standing at attention—fair and pink faced in their smart white uniforms—as the ship sailed through the channel and out to sea. Such a thing very seldom happens in our part of India. I was so thrilled, I ran from one end of the beach to the other till I no longer could hear the music. Then I told my mother, "You know, if I were a boy I would have been with them now." At that time, long before the war, I didn't think about if they were Germans; I only thought about the uniforms and the band.

After some time we heard a rumor that these sailors, when they visited the interior villages, were given coconut water from the tender coconuts and other nice things to eat, as the people of Malabar always do to strangers. Then the soldiers gave the villagers small flags, and they told them that someday the Germans will come back and capture this place, but they will do no harm to you if you show them these flags.

It was about eight or nine years later that the World War broke out. The British were involved in the war, so we knew there would be war in India too. Of course in the meantime we learned about what was going on in Europe, with the rise of Nazism and what the Germans were doing there to the Jews. We always read the papers in our family. Grandfather used to get Hebrew magazines from America and other places, and he would tell us what he read. Then my mother always bought the newspaper too, every day. She was so interested in the news, she would take an atlas, and whenever there were some places bombed she looked in the atlas to see where it was, and she would explain it all to us and to the other women in the neighborhood too. Even when she came to Israel and lived on the kibbutz, she used to read the English paper every day.

WARTIME IN COCHIN

During the wartime there was a scarcity of everything. One thing we could not get was pencils. My sister Royal saw that a classmate of hers had a nice pencil with different colors on the wood, so she asked her where she bought it from. She said her father bought it for her, so Royal requested her to ask her father to get one for her and she will pay for it. It was rather expensive. Her classmate brought her the pencil but she wouldn't take any money from her. Her father told her not to take the money from Royal. It seems he was an advocate and knew my father very well when he was alive, and he told his daughter what a nice man he was and all the good deeds he had done during his lifetime. It was another example of how the people of Cochin are friendly and grateful for even a small good deed done to them. This man was a high-caste Hindu, a Brahmin.

Sometimes people made jokes at my mother during the war, saying that Hitler is coming to kill the Jews. Once this Brahmin gentleman happened to be there. He said to them, "Don't make fun. Salvation is coming for the Jews. It is time for them to get their country back. If there is any nation to be called innocent it is the Jewish nation. Any country coming to their ruination, they always fall upon the Jews. Then that nation will disappear and the Jews will be present at their funeral."

At one point during the war, the Japanese bombed Chittagong in the northeast of India. The first time this happened, our government of Cochin told the people that it was expedient for those living in the port cities to evacuate and go inland. But they did not help the people to do this, just put the fear into all the people by making the announcement. After all Chittagong was five days away from Cochin by train—as if the Japanese had no other big ports to bomb, so that they have to come all the way down to the remotest part of India. I wonder if the Japanese knew there was such a place as Cochin!

There were many poor people who were affected by this advice of the government. Some who had only a cow for a living sold their cow, and some sold their crockery and whatever they could dispose of, and they escaped as if the Japanese were at their doorsteps. There was a blackout from sunset to sunrise. All these people stayed away as long as the money lasted. When they came back they were worse than paupers. The scare just ruined these people.

Well! The white Jews ran away to Alwaye, where the rich people had two or three houses, and they all stayed there. The other Jews went inland to villages such as Parur and Chendamangalam, where they had relatives. My mother took Grandmother and the rest of the family to Chendamangalam. There she rented a small house in Paliath, the property of the rich and famous Paliam *tarwad*. My sister Royal still talks about that house, because the countryside all around it was peaceful as well as green and beautiful. They became friendly with the people in the neighboring house, who were from the royal Paliam family, and there they heard many of the stories I have told about Paliath Achan, etc. My mother herself had to stay back in Cochin because of her job at the Ferry and Transport office, and my brother stayed with her because she was alone. I was not working in Cochin at the time, I was working in Trichur. When I came back home, Jew Town itself was empty. It was *Pesah* time, so even my mother and my brother were gone away on leave for Passover, so I had to stay with my aunt Dolly in Fort Cochin.

The Jewish men who had to stay back in Jew Town because of their work stayed together in one house. One of them cooked for the whole group. Once it happened he had no oil for cooking so he looked here and there and found a bottle of oil, which he cooked with till it was finished. When the family who lived in that house came back, the lady of the house was looking for that bottle of oil, which she had put somewhere, but the boy who was cooking had used it all up. It seems it was a special oil prepared from frogs and earthworms, which she used for massaging her child because he was very thin and weak.

RELATIVES IN BURMA

We were very worried when we learned that the Japanese had invaded Burma, because there were many Jews from Cochin living there. Of course there was my uncle Daniel, who went to Burma looking for work when he was eighteen and got married there. His wife's family was from Calcutta. By this time he and his wife had two children and another one on the way. There were many men from the Kadavumbagam community who went to Rangoon because they could earn money there and send it to their families. My cousin Ezzie had an uncle named David, who had lived in Burma so many years, so that if anyone went from Cochin, they would go to his house and he helped them to get work. David had ten children, and many of them died in the Japanese bombing. We didn't hear from them afterwards. The situation in Burma was very dangerous. One Jew who spoke against the Japanese was taken away from the synagogue; they killed him and cut him into pieces and put him in the coffin and threw it at the synagogue door.

When the Japanese were invading Burma in 1942, all the people from India tried to go back, to escape to safety. Those who left early had ships and planes to take them, but those who came later had to walk through forests and jungles which human beings have never penetrated. There were thousands of people trying to escape. In some places there were no footpaths, and people had to cross rivers infested with crocodiles. They tied ropes across and people had to wade through. Many died on the way of cholera. Every drop of drinking water had to be boiled. Hundreds fell on the way and there was no one to bury them.

My uncle Daniel and his family had moved from Rangoon to Mandalay, where he worked with a British jewelry firm, Coombes and Company. He left Mandalay when the first bomb fell, only ten days after his third child, Molly, was born. The family couldn't leave earlier because his wife was about to give birth. So he had to take his wife and three small children by foot, along with his mother-in-law and four other sisters and brothers of his wife. The children were too small to walk, so he had to hire palanquins to carry them, paying a lot of money. The jewelry firm had given him a certificate and some money when he left.

After walking twelve miles, the people came to a place where they were given a little rice and some cooked dal and salt. After eating it they had to walk another twelve miles to come to a stop to get the next ration. Sometimes there will be only dal and sometimes only salt left. After walking for 32 days like this through the jungle they finally arrived in Calcutta. The whole family were taken to the hospital with acute malaria, with blood coming out of the pores in their skin.

By this time my uncle had no money, only the certificate from his company. Anyway he found a jewellers, Hamilton and Company. At once he was hired and given five hundred rupees in advance, and they said come on Monday to start work.

After a little while my uncle's wife and children came to Cochin to stay with us for a few months. Once when we went to the beach, I remember there were a few small ships called LCTs sailing, which made a great noise. Those children started screaming in fright, because it sounded like the noise they heard when the bombers came in their homeland. The family stayed in Fort Cochin in a house which Gladys's father gave them, because our house was too small to accommodate them.

I went there sometimes to stay with them in Fort Cochin, before they returned to Calcutta. I was the only person the mother, Seema, could talk to. We used to sit up in the night. She said she can't sleep because she is thinking about all the things that happened. And she was all the time smoking, smoking. Then she used to give me a cigarette now and then, and little by little I started smoking too. My mother said, "You are going to spoil her with this bad habit." But my aunt said, "She should have at least one bad habit." I didn't smoke very much. When you are going to work you can't smoke. I stopped for a while, but afterwards people came asking for cigarettes and I would give them, and then I started up again. People thought it was such a disgrace for a young woman to smoke. I remember one day I was standing on the veranda smoking and my brother came and said to me, "You are going to spoil all the girls in the Town!" I didn't say a word: I just went inside.

I JOIN THE ROYAL INDIAN NAVY

I think it was late in 1942 that they started recruiting women into the armed services in India, and I decided that I wanted to join. At that time I was working in the High Court, but those who left the government service to join the army were assured of their place of work when they came back. The people in Jew Town were afraid that girls would get spoiled if they joined the services, but my mother didn't object. I was grown up, thirty years old, and she knew I wouldn't listen to her, so she kept quiet. My Aunty Seema didn't want it—she was so fond of me—but what could she do? Also they knew I would get better pay there. It took some time to get my security clearance, because the police office was transferred somewhere and they lost my papers. In the meantime my cousin Matty joined the army, in the General Services where she had to stay in the camps and all. I was feeling very impatient to join.

So finally at the beginning of 1944, I joined the Women's Royal Indian Navy (WRIN). Not long after I joined, I had to go to Bombay for training. My cousin Matty also went along. There we stayed in a marble hall, which had been taken over by the army. It was a three-story building all made of marble. The staircase curved around, and the railing of this staircase rests on black marble, all the sides carved, and a white marble handrail. It was beautiful! We stayed in that building maybe two weeks. We slept there, ate there, had the training there and everything. Sometimes we went out to visit our relatives.

There were many women at the training, from all parts of India. There they examine you to find if you are qualified for such-and-such a work. We had to learn about all the insignias and other matters about the army, and we had parade every day. When I went to Bombay I was not yet wearing a uniform, just a white sari with a blue border like the other girls. I was feeling shy in the Town to start wearing a frock. But I went from Bombay back to Cochin in uniform. It was a white dress for the navy, and a round cap. If we are wearing the cap, we must salute when we saw the insignia of an officer—a gold anchor or whatever it was. Sometimes I didn't wear my cap. I would take it in my hand or in my bag, because if I wear the cap, I have to salute. And those officers started complaining. I was the only woman who had a cap, because the others wore a sari and no cap, except for one or two Anglo-Indians and of course the English women who were officers. I have a photo of myself in the uniform, but without a cap. It's a pity I lost the one where I was wearing the cap.

Back in Cochin I worked in the naval base on Willingdon Island, coming home every evening by ferryboat. At first I worked in the platoon commander's office with the rank of a leading hand. I did secretarial work in that office, sending details about all the workers to the head office. After some time the Confidential Books (CB) officer requested a "responsible worker" for his office. My platoon commander, who was an Englishwoman, recommended me for the position. Well I had been working ten years in government offices, so I had to be responsible.

That was how I came to the CB office, where the work was more interesting. There they kept many different books, all in code. There were girls who decoded messages in the Port Security Office, and every day the codes were changed. Then when we got the messages we had to correct all the codes in all these books. Tomorrow's message would be in a different code, so there was always plenty of work. When the officers used to come from the

(*Top*) Petty Officer Ruby Daniel in uniform, Women's Royal Indian Navy, 1944. (*Collection of Ruby Daniel*); (*bottom*) Ruby enjoying the same photo on display at the museum of Moshav Nevatim in Israel, 1993. (*Photo, Barbara Johnson*)

warships and take the various books, we had to give them the correct books and take their signatures. When I first got there everything was in a big jumble, because all the papers had been put in one place for such a long time, without being filed properly. So I had to arrange and file all the papers. That was my first responsibility—to straighten everything out. The officer was very pleased. He was a Muslim from the Punjab, and he used to be nice to all of us in the office. After one or two months I was promoted to the rank of petty officer, equal to a sergeant.

Then there was another Jewish girl who wanted to join up. In spite of all the objections of her relations, she came with me to the base and I took her to the naval recruiting office. She was put to work in the office of the Port Signal Officer (PSO), who was an Englishman. This girl was tall and fair and very beautiful, and the officer lost his head over her. He wanted to give her a grade, but at that time there was no place for her. So he went to the platoon commander, and then I have had it. My officer was away on leave, and there was nobody to speak up for me.

One day the platoon commander called me and she spoke as if they wanted to give me a better place. She said they are sending me to the Royal Naval Department to work in the post office. But then I would have to give up my grade. After I learn the work, which will take six months, only then I will get back the rank of leading hand. Then I realized that the PSO intended to put this white Jewish girl in my place, with my rank. Then, fortunately, my officer came back and I told him what is happening. He lost his temper and went to the naval secretary, who was also a Punjabi. I don't know exactly what happened then, but my officer came and told me, "Miss Daniels"—that is how he called me—"You are not going anywhere. You are staying here." The Punjabis were also fed up with the color prejudice of the British.

The PSO was crazy for that white Jewish girl, and as it happened, this Punjabi officer was crazy for me. He had two wives and fourteen children. (Punjabis had no objection in marrying more than one wife.) He still wanted someone who would go about with him while he was in Cochin! He was a big man. Once he told me, "I am not as old as I look." He did not realize it won't work with me. But he behaved correctly toward me. We were all girls working in his office, and we had a good laugh at the craze of these men.

Then came some Australian soldiers, very wild and misbehaved. As soon as one person sees a soldier in our Town, we all ran inside and closed the doors. Once one of them just kicked at our door. There were complaints about it; then Jew Town was made out-of-bounds for the military. Occasionally one or two Jewish soldiers visited the Town, for Yom Kippur or some Festival. At Passover time the women in Jew Town made so many matzot to send to Jewish soldiers in other places.

One of the biggest adventures that happened to me began when I was told I had to go for a course in the northern province of Bihar. I did not know how to go there. I was told, "Find your own way." In my house as usual, everyone was worrying about me. First I thought I have to go to Calcutta and from there to change to Jamshedpur. My uncle was in Calcutta, so Mother sent a telegram to him to meet me at the train. But from Madras I met some WRIN girls who were going to the same course. As it turned out we did not have to go as far as Calcutta. The place for the training was in a jungle. The lorry [motortruck] came to the railway station and took us there. The course after all was for three days only, but getting there by rail and lorry took four days.

Of course as soon as I arrived at the training camp I wrote home. I knew that my uncle would go to meet me at the station in Calcutta and that he would not find me. A telegram from him went back home to Cochin that I did not arrive. So telegrams went back and forth. I knew what will be going on in the house. Aunty Seema was abusing my mother for sending me. "Where the hell do you think you are sending your daughter? For the sake of money?" Aunty loved me the most. After the course, those who want to visit Calcutta were told they can go next morning when there is a transport to the railway station. So I jumped at the opportunity.

When we arrived in Calcutta there was a Hindu-Muslim riot going on. There was a mother and daughter going with me, so we took a taxi. I was not sure of my uncle's address. Anyway, they wanted to see me safe in the house, so they waited until I found the place, saying that if I could not find the house they will take me with them to their relations' house and not to worry.

All the people were behind locked doors, being afraid of the riot. No one would open the door when I knocked to ask for the correct address. Finally I found the house. As I was shouting my name, my uncle's mother-in-law opened the door. "Where have you been?" was her first greetings.

I stayed in Calcutta for three days. When it was time to leave I went to the railway station, and the one who was arranging places in the train said, "If you want to stay for another week, I can arrange and give you a letter saying that there was no place in the train." But I said no, because I was sure my mother and aunt will be worried to death until I reach home.

I had to change the train halfway to Cochin. The trains were so packed that you cannot open the door. Suddenly I heard somebody calling me: "Teacher! Teacher! Come here!" The door of one compartment opened and there were two Muslim boys from Cochin. A long time before, I was teaching for just a short while in the school where they were learning, but they remembered me and pulled me into the compartment. There was no place to sit at all. All the benches were occupied, and they said they were sitting on the armrest of the bench for three days, coming back from Delhi.

When the train was coming near the station in Cochin someone said, "Here is a relation of yours." Whom did I see? My brother Bingley, with a few books under his arm, walking down towards the train. He took half a day off from the college to come and meet me. I asked him how did he know that I am arriving just then, and he answered, "It is just a calculation." When I arrived home I was sitting at the table when the postman brought the letter I had written from the training camp ten days before! Usually letters take three or four days only. Altogether I had been away from home only two weeks.

LADY EZRA'S HOSPITALITY

Later, while I was still in the WRIN, I made another visit to Calcutta, along with my cousin Matty. During that time I had the chance to visit the home of the famous Lady Ezra. She was from the Sassoon family, who first came to Bombay from Iraq. They had some money and built a few cotton mills in Bombay. By the end they had thirty mills in Bombay. Whatever this family touched turned into gold. I have heard that Lady Ezra got a whole street in Calcutta as her dowry when she married Sir David Ezra. She had so many houses besides, she was not allowed to buy any more houses in Calcutta. They had something like a zoo in the backyard of their house, with animals that were collected on excursions to different parts of the world.

This Lady Ezra was famous for the help she gave to others. She did a great deal to help the refugees who arrived in India from Burma, fleeing from the Japanese invasion. She made a big hostel somewhere along the Indian border, and every refugee who arrived from Burma, with no difference between caste, color and creed, could stay there with all expenses met till they could make other arrangements. She also gave tea parties in her home twice a week for the service people in Calcutta. Anybody can go. There was no difference between officers and ratings in that house. Those Jews who wanted to keep Shabbat could go to her house without invitation. After the war, the Indian government presented her with the greatest honor they can give—a Kaesari Hind medal (meaning "Lion of India").

I had heard all about the Sassoons and the Ezras from some of my relatives and neighbors who worked for them in Bombay and in Calcutta, so I was happy for the chance to visit. It happened like this. My friend Gladys Koder's mother was living in the Ezras' house in Calcutta at that time, and Gladys had given me a few embroidered handkerchiefs to give to her. During the war, clothes were rationed, and one could not send any clothes at all by parcel. My uncle and I stopped by the Ezras' house on our way to somewhere, but there was nobody in the house, so my uncle gave the parcel to the guard. The next day Lady Ezra phoned my uncle asking him to bring us to dinner one night. My cousin Matty was feeling shy, so for two days we did not go. When would we get another chance to visit such a place? Again Lady Ezra phoned my uncle, asking why we did not go and telling him to bring us. They knew my uncle because he was working in the Jewellers Company. She even said, "Tell them to come in their uniforms. They don't have to dress up. The dinner is private." So we had to go.

The front room was decorated with all the trophies that the Ezras got in Derbies etc., and many of their collections. Sir David Ezra was eighty years old then. He told us the story of all his collections. The only thing he did not remember was the engagement ring he gave to his wife, Rachel Ezra, or at least that is what he said when she showed it to him. It was a big ruby. He has to be given concession for his age, or maybe it was a joke. I am not sure.

At the table, Sir David said the blessing on the bread and the blessing after the meal. They sat with us for two or three hours. Afterwards Lady Ezra said they are having an "At Home" or open house twice every week and asked us to go. "Come early," she said. But we came late, as is usual with my family.

When we arrived, we saw the house was full. Hundreds of people were there. Almost all were service people, black and white officers and soldiers and ratings. Lady Ezra saw us from far, and she came to us and said, "You are so late!" She called a man and said to prepare a table for the four of us— my Uncle and his wife and Matty and myself. Afterwards she called a boy and asked him to show us her garden. The things we saw there were really fantastic. So many kinds of peacocks and crocodiles and snakes. It was the first time I saw green snakes, deer, and many other animals. When we came back she said, "It is a pity you could not see my birds. They all are sleeping now." Afterwards they had singing and dancing upstairs. And that old man Sir David stayed on with them and was still there when we left.

I don't understand why Lady Ezra was so kind to us. Perhaps that is why I am writing about them now, to explain how selfless and kind they were. Gladys's mother, Mrs. Rachel David, was also loved by many. She could talk and attract people. All the big shots I saw there shook hands with Lady Ezra but kissed Rachel. Well! That is my experience with them.

On our way back from Calcutta, Matty and I had planned to travel by way of Delhi and Agra to see the Taj Mahal and some of the other famous sights. But suddenly we received word that Matty's father had died, so of course we had to come back to Cochin. I never had a chance to go back to North India again. During the war we could travel free during our vacations, but after that we didn't have the money to go.

Chapter 8

FAREWELL TO COCHIN

During the war, government servants who joined the military service were granted leave for the duration of the service, and then we could go back to the civil service where we had been working. When I left the WRIN, I was given a permanent job as clerk, with a promotion, and after being transferred from the remote village of Wadakancherry, I began working in the Sub Court of Cochin, just five minutes away from my home. The six years I worked there was the best period of my career in the civil service.

I enjoyed working in the Cochin court, and after my time in the army, I used to talk and be more forward compared to the other women. I sat there in my office wearing a sari and sometimes a little lipstick—which nobody used then in Cochin. Anybody who passes by, they think I am somebody. They say, "Salaam, Missy. Salaam, Missy." On one side is the Registrar Office, on another side the Magistrate's Court, and this side is our court. I am sitting by the window and a thousand people are passing by. They see me all the time sitting there. From the outside I was something, but on the inside, nobody knows the story.

With the passing of time, things had become more comfortable at home. With Mother and myself both working, we had repaired the house, and Bingley started to work in the Tata Oil Company. But I was always unhappy in the house. Though they tried to make me comfortable according to their way, it was not what I wanted. From the age of eight or nine I had wanted to get out of the house, only there was nowhere to go and no cash to set up in life. I had visited my relations in Bombay, and I knew that their standard was not for me.

I was torn between two worlds. All the time the idea to leave the house

"A willing and efficient clerk." Discharge certificate, releasing Ruby Daniel from naval service, 1946. (*Collection of Ruby Daniel*)

lurked in me. My father had died, leaving the family "on my shoulders," as he said, and I still felt the responsibility as a burden on my heart. No one inquired how I lived or if I am hungry. I denied myself many things. I won't request, I won't complain. It was below my dignity. People say I am a proud woman. Maybe they are right. If I think there is a place where I won't get the respect due to me, I won't go to such a place. My grandmother used to say "Royal birth and fortune of the broom," meaning our behavior and character were like privileged people but we had no money or luck.

Why did I hate the house of my grandfather, where I was born I am sure without my consent? As I have written, there was the belief that it was haunted by the spirits of those who were deprived of their share in the house. I began to think that if the spirits and ghosts cannot leave the house, let them all go to hell with their house; I would leave it myself. The second reason was that too many people lived there. There was no privacy. Quarrels among my mother and her sisters, and shouting and screaming were usual in such a close family setup. But we cousins never quarreled with one another and we still love one another. Though I hated the house, I loved its inmates.

I think I should have seen a psychiatrist, but such a thing was not very popular then. Now I am using this paper to talk.

Anyway, I came to the limit of my patience. *Dai*. Enough. I wanted to get out of the whole setup. Maybe I was foolish. I did not try to make friends in the Town. Among the Jews, in my opinion then, there were not many who came up to my standard. With the exception of my friend Seema Eliyahu, girls from Kadavumbagam and the other Jewish communities did not study. They got married young and had children, and we had no interests in common. The other girls I liked were the ones I had studied with, the daughters of rich people, fair and good-looking, who I think ignored me when they were in the limelight. If I went out for a walk with them the people would make a lot of them while I waited like a dog. So I stopped going out even to the beach for a walk. Their parents said I am haughty and too proud even to accompany their daughters. The real reason I did not tell anybody except now. In my generation I was different. I wanted to be respected.

At that same time, around 1950, there was a lot of tension in Jew Town because of the marriage of Mr. Salem's son Balfour to one of the white Jewish women, Seema (Baby) Koder. The white Jews of course opposed the marriage, and they did not allow them to marry in the Paradesi Synagogue, so they had the wedding in Bombay. Then there was a lot of conflict in the Town about it, and I hated to hear all the insults against my relatives. Mr. Salem could stand it. They said he has thick skin like an elephant, but I am just the opposite. On the last Simḥat Torah which I spent in Cochin, all the men were drinking—as they usually do on that holiday—and some of them came into the place where we used to sit in the Synagogue. Some of them began to insult my aunt. Well! When I lose my temper I lose my temper. I abused them. I abused their fathers and their grandfathers, all the way back to Shelomi Mudaliar, saying, "It won't work with us. It worked with your great-grandfather, but not with us." Everyone heard and no one said a thing. They were just quiet. Two of my friends took me from the synagogue to their house and gave me something to eat. They didn't say anything about my outburst; they just took me away so I would stop.

In the past we depended on the white Jews for everything. But from that time I said, "I will not stay in this country."

ZIONISM IN COCHIN

As I was waiting for an opportunity to extricate myself from all my problems, there came the founding of the State of Israel. Cochin Jews had always dreamed of Zion. Even before the founding of the state, we sang about Israel in this Malayalam song, which was written by the late Isaac Moseh Roby (nicknamed "Kakicha"). It is a popular song with the Cochin Jewish women even today:

LOKAM IRUBHAGANGALIL

(Kakicha's Song)

When the national spirit of the Jews
Living in both hemispheres of the earth
Revives toward God,
Zion will be protected.

The hope we have had since ancient times
To return to the land
Given to us by the One God
Has not faded.

Brethren of the Diaspora,
Listen to the song of our future.
As long as Jews are alive
Our hope will endure.

The House of Jacob will again reside there,
Through the sacred love of God.
By the grace of the Almighty God
The Raja *Mashiaḥ* will rule over her.

The city of Jerusalem
Will be rejuvenated like the *nesher**
And remain in splendor and renown.

The hope you have given us
May you be pleased to fulfill,
And may you protect those who sing
In praise of your worship.

Our ancient hope,
The hope of returning to our ancient abode
Where David resided,
Has not faded away.

In Cochin we had been following all the news about Israel, in the newspapers and from visitors who came to the Town. Satto Koder had started the Habonim, a Zionist youth group, in Cochin, and we called it *Gedud Shingly*

*A mythical, immortal bird.

(Shingly Battalion), after the original Jews of Cranganore or Shingly. For the roll call when someone said, "*Gedud Shingly*" the reply was, "*Anshei Shingly Hai*" ("The people of Shingly is alive"). There was a Baghdadi Jew named Jack Japheth, who would come to Cochin for several months at a time. He had been a Habonim leader in Bombay, and he taught us Hebrew songs and something about the way they wrote Hebrew in Israel.

When Lord Mountbatten, the last British viceroy of India, came to Cochin, our Habonim group put up a guard of honor for him in front of the Paradesi Synagogue.

When Gandhiji was killed, there was a large public meeting in which people from the various communities in Cochin made speeches and sang songs and all. One of the Jewish men named Abraham Hai offered to sing a Hebrew song, and we were all wondering what he would do. He sang one of the songs which we had learned in Habonim, about how Joseph Trumpeldor died in a battle with the Arabs, but whenever the words should have been "*Gibor Joseph nafal*" ("The brave hero Joseph fell"), he sang, "*Gibor Gandhi nafal.*" Only the Jews knew what he was doing!

When we came to know about the war that was being fought in Palestine, everyone was very worried. The Jews started early morning prayers and fasting. That was the only way they could help their brethren. There was a synagogue in Ernakulam and there was a mosque on the opposite side of the road. When the Moslems came to know that the Jews are praying for the Jews of Palestine, they also started praying for the Arabs. The rest of the people—Christians and Hindus passing through the street—could hear prayers from both the synagogue and the mosque at an unusual time. They asked for the cause and it was explained to them: that one is praying for the Jews and the other for the Arabs. They said both these people are praying to the same God; now let us wait and see whom He is going to favor.

During the Israeli War of Independence, the Muslims in Cochin were very excited. They did not know what they can do to help their brethren in Palestine. The Jews of Cochin, I mean those who lived in Jew Town, were surrounded by many thousands of Muslims. On both sides of the town lived Muslims—in Kochangadi in the south and Mattancherry in the north. There were a few educated people and very rich people among the Muslims who controlled the mob. If any trouble ever happens from them, the government told the rich Muslims that if they do not stop the mob, they will be the ones to be punished. A word from them and the troubles stop.

So this time also it happened that way. The Muslims decided to have a great meeting in Mattancherry side. Many important Muslims had to come from other cities to Cochin to give lectures on the situation in Palestine. The Jews in Cochin were frightened that the mob might get out of control. The day

set for the meeting was a Friday and the time was five o'clock in the afternoon, when the Jews were getting ready to go to the synagogue.

Mr. Satto Koder, the leader of the Cochin Jews, lifted his phone and informed the secretary of the government what was happening in Cochin. The
Jews were asked to stay indoors at that time, because the Muslims going for
the meeting passed through Jew Town, though there is another way to go to
the meeting place. I remember we all got inside the house and locked the
doors and peeped through the keyholes. The people in thousands were passing the whole breadth of the road full, for half an hour, young and old. I
wonder if they knew anything about what was happening in Palestine except
for the hatred towards the Jews.

After half an hour people started turning back, and the whole mob dwin-
dled away. We were wondering what happened. Only the next day we came
to know. None of the important men supposed to come to lecture had arrived. The Muslims all waited for some time and then went away. The reason
was that the Secretary of the Government phoned to all the important Muslims supposed to come from other cities and told them they should not come
to Cochin on that day. He also said that if even one young Muslim boy throws
a small stone at a Jew, the leaders are the ones who would be held responsible. So nobody arrived and the people who went to the meeting so enthusi-
astically dispersed without a word.

On the day when the independence of the State of Israel was declared, we
were so happy we made a Simḥat Torah celebration in the Paradesi Synagogue. It was the idea of one of the young boys—Sammy Koder—and his
grandfather and the others agreed. I never heard of any other occasion when
the Sefer Torahs were carried around in procession except on Simḥat Torah
itself, but we did it in Cochin. We all went to the synagogue dressed up nicely
and had a grand celebration.

ALIYAH BEGINS

Then came the idea of *aliyah* (emigration to Israel) among the Cochin Jews.
Especially in Ernakulam some youngsters wanted to go to Israel. They also
had Zionist meetings and organizations. In Parur, one of the learned men
named Eliyahu Meyer wrote a song in Malayalam to celebrate the birth of
the state of Israel:

PADUKA PADUKA

Sing sing we all.
While singing praises of God, let us be happy.
Dr. Chaim Weizmann be blessed, be blessed for long.

Mr. David Ben-Gurion be blessed, be blessed for long.
For two thousand years we were like slaves.
After two thousand years we have a state.

Jews from all over the world,
All the sacrifices to go to Israel have to be suffered.
If we are born we must die;
Within our lifetime we have to succeed.
We should be ready to go to Israel.
Let this day of liberty be enjoyed in thundering happiness.
Let us enjoy by singing songs.
Let the one God be praised.
Let the one God be praised.

Why were the Cochin Jews eager to go to Israel? It was certainly not because they were persecuted in India, as the Jews were in so many other places in the world. But, for them, Israel was *kadosh* (holy); that was the first reason. Then for some, there was the chance to improve their situation. Some were living in poverty without work. Some wouldn't work for non-Jews, because they didn't want to work on Shabbat and Festivals, but they didn't earn much working on their own. Many were afraid to send their children outside for education, especially the girls, for fear they might go away from the caste and get converted or something. There were others who had good positions—not rich, but they had work and were eating three times a day. There were a few families that were very rich, with much land and money. In some families the sons wanted to go, or the brothers or the father wanted to go. Then they saw all their relations were going, and they knew they had no future there.

It was mostly the Jews from the other Cochin communities who left in the beginning. In the Paradesi community it was different. Most of the white Jews did not decide to leave Cochin till much later, in the 1970s. They thought in Israel there was nothing then, nothing but a lot of hard work. Why should they leave their comfortable life and come to Israel? I would have thought the same thing if I had the same chances they had and if not for this trouble between us.

But I was caught in the middle, and I was in middle age too. A little later and it will be too late. My brother Bingley had started working and then I had some peace of mind, knowing there was somebody to look after my mother. I knew if I don't do it now it will never be done, so I started to make my plans. Then my sister Royal wanted to come with me, and I had to wait another year for her to get the passport. Bingley saw that I am delaying. He said, "You want to go to Israel? Either *you* go or *I* am going. If you are staying, I am going." I said, "No, no, if I stay and you go, all the burden will be on my head again." So I decided to leave.

Then came some *shelihim* (emissaries) from Israel—representatives of the Jewish Agency, who made false promises that they will take all of the Cochin Jews to Israel by Rosh Hashanah. One of these men took money from the synagogues for their passage, and people were getting ready to leave. They resigned from work, sold the houses and property they had, and waited. This man was sitting in his Bombay office. Two years passed and still there was no reply from him. They ate away the money they had, leaving them with no food to eat and no house to live in. Many families of Ernakulam went to the interior and built huts near a new road there called the seventy-feet road. Some of the young boys went to Bombay and after a long time of trouble managed to get to Israel. When I came to Bombay in 1951 on my way to Israel, I went to the office of this man. He said my sister and I had to pay for our own passage. We paid and then I asked him how he could promise those people that he will bring a ship to Cochin to take them. "Where is the ship?" I asked, and he said to me, "It is in the air." I felt like spitting at his face.

One excuse given for the delay by the Jewish Agency was that some of the Cochin Jews were suffering from filariasis or elephantiasis, and they had to establish that it was not contagious. Finally the Cochin Jews sent Mr. A. B. Salem to Israel as their *shaliah* (emissary), and he was instrumental in starting the large wave of immigration in 1954. But I left before then.

The last *shaliah* who came to Cochin while I was there was Aryeh Levy, who came to get people for the kibbutzim in the Galilee, in northern Israel. Anyway, I had decided to go to a kibbutz and live a quiet life without having to depend on relations. I thought it would be a good situation for a single person, so I went and talked to him in the Koders' house and told him, "I want to go to a kibbutz. Can you make arrangements?" and he told me that he could.

My sister Royal was quite young, and she left the college because she could not leave me. The judge I was working with called me and said that he is sorry I am going to a strange country. "Well," he said, "you are an elderly woman. But why do you take a young girl with you? You have no idea what a responsibility it is. Listen to me," he said. How right he was!

LAST DAYS IN COCHIN

When I think about my last days in Cochin, I am in duty bound to record more examples of the friendliness of the people of Malabar. When my sister and I applied for passports, they sent me a few forms to be filled up. I filled them out to the best of my ability and sent it as required to the police commissioner. But it came back after some time. It was not filled out correctly. A second time also it came back. The third time I wrote and said I did not understand what they wanted. After a couple of days I got a letter from the

Ruby Daniel's passport photo, 1949. (*Collection of Ruby Daniel*)

police commissioner. He was coming to camp to a place which is quite near to where I lived and asked me to go to his office. When I arrived he brought me a chair and asked me to sit down. Then he called his clerk and asked him to fill up the forms as needed. I only had to sign it. In a couple of weeks the passport arrived. It is important to note that this commissioner who was so helpful to me was a Muslim. That was a time right after Indian independence, when the Indian government, which had been so friendly to the Jews, also now had to lean on the side of the Arabs. They were afraid to issue a passport to Israel. So I was given a separate passport to Israel with instructions that it should not be shown in any Arab country.

When I was leaving for Israel the people I was working with in the Sub Court were very sorry. They made a farewell party for me and had a group photo taken. We always used to make a farewell party and sometimes had a photo taken of the whole staff if anyone retires. Now I have this photo hanging on the wall of my apartment in the kibbutz.

Staff of the Munsiff Court, Cochin, at their farewell party for Ruby Daniel, 1949. In the first row center is the judge, with Ruby seated on his left. First on the left in the second row is the bench clerk, Krishnan, who saved Ruby from embarrassment. (*Collection of Ruby Daniel*)

What I want to stress is the consideration of these people not to hurt one's feelings. A few days before I left, I invited the staff of this court for a tea party to my house. I went to the court and invited them in person. But I did not invite the judge, as I thought he may not come. On the afternoon of the party, the bench clerk, whose name was Krishnan, requested the judge to dismiss the court a little early. The judge asked for the reason and he told him that Ruby invited them for a party at five o'clock that day. So the judge asked why Ruby did not invite him.

I don't know what I would have told him in my perplexity if I was in that man's shoes. I don't know how it got into his head that very moment. Of course he was a B.A. graduate who was working as a bench clerk in the court amongst advocates for many years. It was years later that I thought of this man Krishnan who did it for me. I wrote at once to one of my friends in Cochin asking her about him, and her reply came saying that he died a year earlier. I put the question to a few friends here to find out what they would have done in his position if that question was put to them. One woman said that she would have told him that, he being a great man, I thought that he would not accept my invitation. In fact that was my thought at the time, but I would not have told him so then. Now after living for so many years in Israel—and in a kibbutz at that, where people are very outspoken—I might express that. Perhaps. But this bench clerk saved us both from embarrassment by telling a white lie.

Krishnan told the judge that Ruby went there to the court to invite him, but she could not get to him because he was in session. She had no time to wait. She said that she will come back later or send the invitation in writing. Then Krishnan went out and dispatched one of the clerks posthaste to my house to tell me what happened and ask me to go at once or send a letter. So I at once wrote to the judge all the same lies and requested him to honor me with his presence in the party. Of course he accepted it. He came walking at the head of the whole staff. People in the neighborhood were wondering what was happening. Is he going to arrest someone or confiscate the property in person or something? When they entered my house, all the neighbors were out at the entrance. It was an honor for me. Was not Krishnan a great man? I think that he was. May his soul rest in peace.

Before I left Cochin, Aunty Seema told me that I should go to the graves of my father and my grandfather to say goodbye to them. They were dead for I don't know how many years. What was I going to tell them? They can't help me, they can't give me money or anything to help me go. What is the point of going to the cemetery? Are they still there to hear me? If they can hear me there, they can hear me anywhere. But Aunty Seema forced me to go. While I was standing there I remembered what Grandfather had told us, many years before he died. "After I am gone you should go away from this country," he had said to us. Just then I thought of that and so I said, "You wanted us to leave. I am leaving." Then I came back and told Aunty, "I talked to them and they are not answering me." She complained to my mother, "Before she even left this place, she is already spoiled."

Aunty Seema was so sad I was leaving, it was as if I was taking her *neshamah* (soul) with me, she was so fond of me. When I came away to Israel she went to live next door with Aunty Sippora's daughter. They had a Christian girl named Thressy working in the house, who used to wash Aunty Seema's clothes. After some time, that girl left Cochin and went to work for Aunty Sippora, who was living in Bombay. One night she dreamt that Aunty Seema came flying through the window with two angels on both sides and called out, "Thressy, you don't have to wash Aunty's clothes any more. I am going." She told the dream in the morning, and in the afternoon they had a telegram saying that Aunty Seema had died that day.

On Our Way to Israel

On the way to Israel my sister and I had to stay a long time in Bombay, waiting to get a plane. First we went to that man from the Sokhnut (Jewish Agency) who took our money for the ticket, and then there was no plane. We waited three months, staying with our relatives, and I finished all my money. At that time another man from the Sokhnut was in Cochin. He had been there the year before, and he had promised to help me then. Gladys's father and the Koders all knew that I was waiting in Bombay, so they shouted at him, "You promised to take her to Israel." So he said, "Write to her and tell her to come and see me in the Taj Mahal Hotel when I return to Bombay." Well, I went there to meet him. It is the most expensive hotel in India. He told me to go downstairs and book my passage in the Dutch KLM agency downstairs. So I went and made the arrangements and went to take back my money from that first fellow, and he gave me a hundred rupees less than I had given him! At first I didn't look, but there was another man working in that place who told me he found 100 rupees difference. When I went again to take it, the first man said, "Give it for charity." I said, "I cannot give charity because I have no money." I had learned not to have any faith in those Sokhnut people. My intention was to go to a kibbutz, as Aryeh Levy had arranged.

On the way to Israel we had to pass a night in Karachi, in Pakistan. It was in 1951 right after the partition of the subcontinent, when Pakistan and India were at loggerheads. Pakistan was a new Muslim state. They used to murder the Hindus, pack the trains with their dead bodies, and send the trains to India. Almost all of Pakistan's Jews fled. Everything was in chaos. So I got down from the plane with a heavy heart. When I passed the Passport Control my passport was not returned. When I asked for it, the officer said that I will get it when I board the plane, and if anybody inquires, to say that it is with the Karachi police inspector. My God! What has the police got to do with my passport? My heart went pit-a-pat. Then we had checking of the luggage to go through. How am I to do the repacking? My cousins in Bombay had done all the packing for me!

I saw a big officer in full uniform, and a Muslim at that. He asked me from where I am coming and to where I am going. So I had to say I am going to Lydda Airport in Israel and that we are coming from Bombay. But it suddenly came from my tongue to say, "But we are from Malabar." Then he asked if we are from Cochin. He was so happy to hear that I am from Cochin. He said he was also from Cochin, that his family was in Karachi with him, that it was a pity he was on duty or he could have taken us to them; they would have been very pleased to talk the same language, that it was very seldom they now see a countryman, and so on. He asked me where my luggage was and wrote on it, "Passed, passed, passed," without asking to open a single one of our bags. He also reassured me about our passports.

Afterwards we were escorted to an airport hall by two guardsmen. Our flight to Israel was not until twelve o'clock at night. We had to wait half a day. Those two guards were fully armed, with swords in their belts, guns on their shoulders and chains of cartridges. That was the first time I saw an armed soldier. "What do they want from us!" we whispered to each other. Wherever we turned they were there. I think now that they were guarding us. We had a shower and for the first time we found out that saltwater can come out of a shower bath. Our flight to Israel left at midnight. We were escorted back to the airport and boarded a KLM plane. Only when it took off did my heartbeat become normal.

On the other hand, when we arrived at Lydda Airport I myself had to struggle to carry my luggage. The inspectors pulled out all the contents and pushed them back. The Israeli porters sat down and laughed at me. My first taste of Israeli friendliness!

When I arrived in Israel, I didn't know where I am going, or what I am going to see. All the feelings were going inside me: Where to go? What will happen if nobody comes to get me? Then as I was getting down from the plane, suddenly I heard somebody calling me: "Ruby, Ruby!" It was such a feeling of relief, like cool water on a burning fire.

The man who was calling me was Abraham Hai, a friend of my cousin. They were living in a *moshav* (village) in the south. My cousin couldn't come to meet me because he has no time. All the men from that *moshav* work in Sodom, way in the south, building roads from Sunday to Friday. This Abraham Hai was not feeling well, so he didn't go to work that week and he was free to come to the airport. I told him, somebody is supposed to come from the kibbutz to take us, but they are not to be found. Then he waited while he got some sugarless tea like water, and a slice of bread with a piece of salt fish, but how long can you wait? So he took us to the *moshav*—to his house and then to my cousin Joseph's house.

Then after we left the airport somebody came from the kibbutz, and they said we had gone to the *moshav*. When they came there to get us, my cousin's wife said, "No, they are tired, they will stay with me a few days and then come." We stayed there two weeks, till we found somebody to bring us here to the kibbutz, with all our luggage.

Chapter 9

LIFE IN THE KIBBUTZ

Well, we came to the kibbutz. Neot Mordecai is situated in Upper Galilee near to the Lebanon and Syrian borders. This side of Israel has more greenery and more water than the south, but it was a young kibbutz of five years old when we came in 1951. There was no grass even. The whole place was mud, with only thornbushes growing, and full of jackals, as was written in the Bible: that the Land of Israel will be given to jackals and owls until the Jews come back again. There was scarcely any green.

The first settlers here in 1946 had lived in tents. They then worked fourteen and sixteen hours a day when they started the building, sometimes sleeping out under the stars on a blanket spread on the ground with stones poking up every few inches, with a gun at their sides. They did not look at the watch, but who had a watch then? By the time we came just a few years later there were wooden huts, with two or three families living in one hut. There were not many children then, but there was a separate house for the children. I stayed in one hut with my sister Royal, who was now called Raḥel, and I was called Rivka. Sometimes some of the other Cochin women stayed with us. During summer it was so hot and in winter it was cold. There was no heating equipment and no cooling apparatus.

Kibbutzim are in isolated places, many of them near the borders. In the beginning, when people were coming to Israel from all over the world, where can they put them? The government had no money. We had to do something about security. Enemies are all around, so people were asked to make a settlement on the borders. Nobody can come into a kibbutz from the outside without being known.

Before we came to Neot Mordecai there were no paved highways in this

"The whole place was mud . . . there were wooden huts, with two or three families living in one hut"; Kibbutz Neot Mordecai in 1949. (*Photo, Gad Livni*)

area and no bridges over the Jordan River, which runs across the kibbutz. So people had to cross it in small boats to go to the next kibbutz or if one had to travel anyplace out of the kibbutz. Even when a woman wanted to give birth there was no transport to take her to the hospital in Safed. One lady told me she had to travel at the back of an open wagon. Some gave birth before they could reach the hospital, waiting for a lift. It was the case in all the kibbutzim which are at the borders far from any big cities. When we came here in 1951, they had built a wooden bridge over the Jordan River and there were buses coming twice a day. The nearest town was Kiryat Shemonah, which in those days was just a small settlement of tin huts with a clinic, some shops, and the central bus station.

On a kibbutz, you live together, you eat together, you work together. Everything is equal. All the money is pooled and you are given according to your wants. If I have any money, I can't keep it in my name, it has to be given to the kibbutz. Even people who get reparations money from Germany, they have to give it to the kibbutz. It is all given for some common use for everybody. There are a lot of expenses: lighting, water, to keep the place clean, food, construction and repairs—all must come from the pool. Everybody is equal. If you have four children, your children will be fed, and if I have no children, I am feeding your children. Many of the people coming to Israel at that time had no choice. They came from Europe after all the troubles, and they worked hard, very very hard.

The clothes we got were from the used clothes Americans or someone else sent to the kibbutz. Olives, white cheese, and salt fish was the common food, with bread and once in a while an egg. Everything was rationed except, as they said, bread and air. We ate in plastic plates, sometimes on the aluminum covers of cooking dishes. For glasses and cups we used the small, empty bottles of "Anchovy Teatime Paste." Coffee and sugar were out of the question. We put saccharin on the table to add to the light tea. I hated saccharin then as I do even now, so I did not drink any tea. We are not used to drinking plain tea. In every tea shop in India, when you ask for a cup of tea they give tea, milk, and sugar mixed together.

Coming from Cochin, we did not eat meat for a few years because it was not kosher. Neot Mordecai is not a religious kibbutz. Once in a while somebody shot a wild boar, or a donkey died by accident, or an old horse was shot and brought to the kitchen. Anyway, Indians won't eat such food. Even the few times when there was chicken, we didn't eat because the kitchen was not kosher. There was nothing else to replace it. So instead of meat we were given white cheese. And of course there was no rice, which we were accustomed to eat every day in Cochin.

When people got married in the early days, sometimes for the four poles of the ḥupah (marriage canopy) they used brooms and spades with a handle. Everyone could not afford a ring, so one ring went around for a few couples. Sometimes the bridegroom would be away and he could not get a transport to come in time, so he would ask one of his friends to go to the ḥupah instead. The same with women. The rabbi, who came to the kibbutz just for this occasion, never asked questions. Whether he knew or not I don't know. "Just let them get married" was his attitude.

When I think of those early days, the worst part of it was the lavatory. It had holes covered with planks and enclosed with some tin sheets. But in two or three years' time, everything was changed. Then flush systems were made in all the houses and wooden huts. What a relief it was! Well, we knew many people were living in worse conditions—in tin huts in Kiryat Shemonah and tents in transit camps.

Imagine the experience of someone coming to the kibbutz from an environment of ghosts and devils in Cochin! It is said that there are no such spirits in the Land of Israel, because King Solomon drove them all away, but how could we be sure? At times I had to work alone at night in the kitchen, and the only company was the cry of the jackals. In the early days I also worked at night, drying clothes in the steam house. This was before we had a dryer in the laundry. The clothes all had to be hung out on lines. But during winter it was impossible, as children's clothes had to be washed and dried every day. So after washing in the machine, we carried them to the steam house and hung those clothes on a screen in front of the machines so the hot air would dry them. The steam house was far away from the living quarters. Anyway, the living quarters were just a few wooden huts here and there.

When the moon comes up it reminds me of the graveyard. No graves, but it was vast and empty, and you won't see a single soul except for the night guard who patrols the kibbutz and who would come in every few hours to put water in the steam machine. The road across was so muddy that if you walk even with the gum boots they will get stuck, and if you pull your leg, the leg will come out and the boot will be stuck there. In case you have to run, you cannot. To make matters worse, I always like to read books which frighten me, like the story about a man diving to find a sunken ship. The inside of the ship was so dark that all he could see was eyes all around him. They were octopuses, and once he suddenly felt someone tapping on his shoulder. I tried not to think about such things, but they would be at the back of my mind.

Anyway, I was the one put to work there in the steam house at night. My sister and another young Indian girl who were working with me said they were afraid, so they won't go there at night. I was older and how can I say that I am afraid, even though I was more afraid than they were? One of the guards, an American boy named Mordecai, had a dog which always came before him, so I would know when to expect him. One night the dog did not appear. I was standing putting clothes on the screen in front of the machine, which makes such a deafening noise one won't hear anything else. Suddenly I felt a soft tap on my shoulder. I just got frozen. I couldn't move until Mordecai asked, "Did I frighten you? I called out to you so many times and you could not hear, so I tapped your shoulder." Just that night he hadn't brought his dog.

Unexpected Discrimination

Before coming here I knew all about the conditions of Israel. I did not expect anything much different, but what I did not expect was the behavior of the people. Most of the members were from Europe. There were a few boys and girls from Cochin here, so I thought we can get on. But we did not get a good treatment. They thought we have come from some jungle. Everywhere we felt discrimination, and I still do. No one came forward to help and talk to me. There was an American who was looking after the interests of the

Cochinis, many of whom did not know English. But he did not talk to me or ask what I am doing here. Afterward I came to know that was because nobody introduced me to him. What did we know about introductions? That is the reason he did not do anything about us. He thought I could fend for myself. Afterwards a single word did not pass between us.

The first few weeks, I worked in the fields, digging carrots and potatoes. Then I was put to work in the kitchen. There were two women there who spoke English who were good to me. So it was bearable. The others would be speaking in German or Czechoslovakian, and I couldn't understand them.

The behavior of many kibbutz members we did not like. We said between us, "They are like animals." Excuse the expression, but that is how we felt. We are altogether different in color and culture from the Europeans, who think they are superior to the Orientals and look down upon others. They did not know anything of our background and did not try to understand us. The Indians were not demanding and shouting. It is a disgrace for us to do so. We kept our self-respect. Once I heard a lady boasting, "We have the Central European culture." Then I said in my mind, "If that is culture, God save me from culture."

The straw that broke the camel's back was, one day pork was served in the dining hall and the Cochin people were given it without their knowing it. From that time the Cochinis did not go to the dining hall. Then the kibbutz gave us a separate place to cook, but it is not the same. They wanted me to be the cook. It was not a success. I got fed up—one person cooking for fifteen people and not only cooking, also cleaning and all, three times a day. And with our own kitchen we were separate altogether. Then came the Festivals. Here there is no Rosh Hashanah, no Yom Kippur, no synagogue. During Passover they ate bread.

The worst thing for the girls from Cochin was the public bathroom, where all the women bathed naked. One girl did not take off her underwear. So a woman pulled it off her. Our own mothers have not seen our body after we came of age. You go to a doctor here, the first thing he said was, "Take off your clothes." Damn him! Which doctor had ever asked us that? In case one had to be examined in India, the nurse covered the body with a cloth and the doctor then came to examine the part that needed to be examined.

The Cochin people would talk among themselves, saying, "This is not a place for us. We can't mix with others, because others don't want to mix with us. The culture is completely different. Why stay and work and slog for them? For what?" Well, they bided their time and when it was certain there will be *aliyah* of their relations, all of the boys joined the army. When their relations finally arrived from India, all of them left and went to *moshavim*, villages where they could have their own houses and earn money and work more independently. There they led their own life and prospered as agriculturists, government service workers, and military men. Now there are several *moshavim* with large populations from Cochin, such as Mesillat Zion and Taoz near Jerusalem, Nevatim in the south, and Kefar Yuval in the north. Kefar Yuval is the only one nearby, just a few miles from our kibbutz.

There are scarcely any Cochin Jews in the kibbutzim now. When the big Cochin *aliyah* came in 1954, the secretary of one kibbutz went to the Sha'ar Aliyah (transit camp) and promised to give them anything they need, and they brought a whole community of Cochin people to that kibbutz. They were given a kosher kitchen with their own people to work there, and they were given a place for prayer too. But they put some boys to work in the pig sty. Then the boys started eating bread during Passover with the other kibbutz members, saying matzot don't give them satisfaction so they cannot work hard and so on and so forth. Within two or three years all left except a couple of families. They went to a *moshav* and set up a life of their own and are living happily. Another big set of boys and girls came from Calcutta to the neighboring kibbutz near us, and within two or three years all except one family left, some to England, America, or Australia. They cannot stay with those bossy people, as they said.

So my sister and I were left alone. I had a great problem. I was not used to the life of those Cochin Jews from Ernakulam and other places. I scarcely knew any of them before I came to Israel and sometimes I could not agree with their behavior. At first some of them came to the kibbutz to inquire if I want to marry somebody. As if I am looking for a man! I didn't even know these people, and I didn't know what they wanted from me. If you feel like marrying or if you want a man, it's different. But I am so independent minded. I said, "I'll stay here." I did not want to go with them to a *moshav*, and where else could I go? I was a single woman without any profession to show. Where could I find work? If I go to a city, I have no relatives to live with. I am tired from all the worries, and I don't want to be a rich woman. I just want to spend my life quietly, not bother about anything. In a kibbutz you can live like an ordinary person.

I was thirty-eight or thirty-nine years old when I came, and they will not take you in a kibbutz after forty. If I go to some other kibbutz I have got to stay a year before they decide to take me, and then I'll be over age, going from pillar to post. All the kibbutzim are the same. Whatever I suffer, I've got a house, I've got food. What else do I want? So I decided to stay. It did not make a difference to me whether it is the Indians or Europeans I stay with. There will be the same problems. My own people were left behind in Jew Town.

After all the other Cochin people left, the kibbutz members said to me,

"You can work in the kitchen and whatever you want to make for yourself, you can also make it," so that was good for me. Eventually we could get rice and other kinds of food, and I started eating a bit of chicken—even though it wasn't kosher—because I was getting ill.

I worked in the kitchen for ten years. We were all women working there, and some of us became friendly with each other. I used to make the salads. The mothers would go home and see to the children. I was working as the assistant, the slogger, but when the cook was not there I would do her work. Then they asked me to go for a cooking course, and then they would give me more responsibility, because I knew to cook, more than them. I was waiting and waiting to go, and they suddenly sent somebody else. The next year they wanted to send me again. This time I'm standing waiting with the suitcase, and suddenly I see they are sending somebody else. Again I felt that discrimination. Some of the others also felt it was unfair, and they also didn't want to work under that woman who was sent for the course. Such a mouth and such a tongue she had! The first time she came into the kitchen she said, "I'll teach you all to work," and I thought no, she won't teach me. And then they sent her for the course. I said, "I should be under that woman? She will stand there until everything is ready. That is her idea."

After some time, all the women who were working in the kitchen left. I saw most of them are working in the *maḥsan* (laundry storeroom), sitting down and quietly folding clothes or mending or ironing, so I said to the work coordinator, "Why not put me there in the *maḥsan*?" He did, and from that day twenty-six years ago I am working there. After retirement age we do not have to work, but I volunteer in the mornings.

FAMILY MATTERS

In 1954, when all of the people from Kadavumbagam Synagogue in Cochin came to Israel on *aliyah*, my mother and Bingley came along with them. At first they were living in Sha'ar Aliyah, a transit camp where they had to stand in a queue to get the food, which they would then bring home and cook it again so they could eat it. My mother can't stand this. She was old and she had high blood pressure. She didn't want to come to the kibbutz, but where else could she go? She couldn't stay with Bingley, as he had no place for her.

I didn't want Bingley to come to the kibbutz, and he also didn't want to come. I wanted to be sure he had a chance for himself. First I sent him for a Hebrew course in Jerusalem. Then he heard about a job at the Weizmann Institute in Rehovot. He had learned chemistry in school and had worked in the Tata Oil mills in Ernakulam, so he was interested. But they wanted references, and from where can a new immigrant get references? Fortunately,

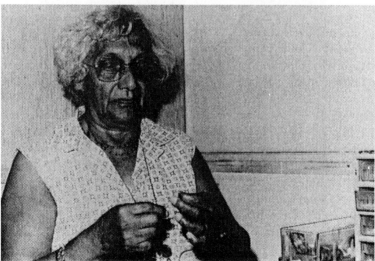

(*Top*) "After retirement age we do not have to work, but I volunteer in the mornings." Ruby folding clothes in the laundry storeroom of her kibbutz, 1990. (*Photo, Barbara Johnson*); *(bottom)* Ruby mending clothes for the kibbutz laundry. (*Photo, Dan Kala*)

Dr. Immanuel Olsvanger appeared on the scene. He was a professor from Israel who had visited Cochin a number of times, and he was very fond of the Cochin people. When I talked to Olsvanger and requested him to help, he wrote a recommendation for him. Bingley got the job and moved to Rishon LeZion, where he met his wife Daizy, who was from Iraq. Later he found work in Arad in the south, and they moved to Dimona with their five children.

The kibbutz was willing to take the parents of members, so I brought Mother here to live at Neot Mordecai. They gave her a room of her own, and she worked in her house sticking on labels from the shoe factory. I would bring the labels to her in her room. Now I realize I made a mistake when I said I wouldn't let her go to the factory or somewhere else to work. Then she would have had some contact with others. She was not like me; she was forward and all. But when you think of these things, it will be too late.

It was not always easy for Rahel and myself, because Mother was very strong and very stubborn. She would never eat in the dining hall. Everything we had to do like in her house in Cochin. She would never eat chicken from the kibbutz. How can she eat when she sees them bring the chicken and kill it with an axe? I had to go every Thursday to Kiryat Shemonah and stand there with hundreds of people waiting to buy chicken. I hate the smell of the chicken and the place where they clean it, and I hate all the *shohetim* there too. They had three or four knives, but I never saw them examining the knife as a *shohet* should. My grandfather used to sharpen the knife and put it on his tongue to find out if there is any flaw.

For Passover we used to have our own seder, in my mother's house. I bought everything from Kiryat Shemonah and cooked it on the small kerosene stove. Bingley used to come from Dimona, when his children were small, and we had some guests too. Everyone ate. Mother knew the whole Haggadah and she would read it out in a strong voice with all the tunes. The kibbutz had a seder for everyone in the dining hall, with a choir and all, and we would have our seder early so we could go to the dining hall too. We would go and sit there, but not eat. For the week of *Pesah*, I won't eat in the dining hall. Nowadays I go to Dimona to my brother's house for the whole week.

At the beginning, Mother used to mix some with other people. At that time there were many older people—parents of the first members. They used to put a table outside and she would sit with them in the evening. I made sometimes cakes or other refreshments, and they used to invite her for every party. But she couldn't talk their language and they didn't know English. After some time she didn't want to go out anymore. The fact that people saw her as "just an old woman from the Orient" wounded her, and she always wanted to go back to Cochin, as she said, "to my castle."

"Mother knew the whole Haggadah, and she would read it out in a strong voice." Ruby's mother, Leah Daniel, reads from the Passover Haggadah at a family seder, Kibbutz Neot Mordecai, 1976. (*Photo, Dan Kala*)

Even with all this she was happy with her grandchildren. My sister got married to a kibbutz member, and when her first child, Shula, was born, I also went crazy after her and forgot all other troubles and disappointments. I was all the time with her. I used to stand near her bed and just look at her, I loved her so much. She lived first in the baby house, then the toddler house, then with the older children according to age. Everyone finishes work at three o'clock and has a rest; then at five o'clock the parents will go and pick up their children to take them to their own house until it is time for bed. I would go and pick up Shula before Raḥel came to take her. Her mother would say, "Where is my child?" I used to carry her all the time. Children like to be carried in the hand, not in the carriage.

Sometimes I had to do guard duty at night, looking after the children. It was only for one week at a time, once in every three or four months, and there would be two of us women watching together in the children's house. What I liked about it was that it was early in the morning when all the children awoke. The babies start twittering at the same time with the birds outside, about 5:30, at dawn. Then the little bigger children start talking to one another in their own language. When you go out, if it is springtime, you feel the lovely smell of blossoming flowers with the cool and clean breeze.

When Shula was in the toddlers' class, she used to come home straightaway from the school, and I would be lying down on the bed, resting after the day's work. One day she came and I didn't want to get up. She said, "Get up, get up!" and she removed my blanket. That is the one thing that I hate! I remember in Cochin when I was lying down with the blanket, my mother used to come and take out the blanket, and I would get wild. So I scolded Shula, saying, "Go out, go to your mother." And she gave me a hit on the face. She hurt me, so I shouted at her. Then suddenly she felt what she was doing and started to cry: "You don't want me? You don't want me?" I said, "No I don't want you. Go out." Then she said, "If you don't want me I will not go to my mother, I will not go to my father, I will not go to my *safta* (grandmother). I will go to my toddlers' house. I don't care!" So I had pity on her and took her into my bed. Now, when I tell her this story she doesn't remember. "Did I *HIT* you?" she asks.

Raḥel also has two sons—Ari and Daniel—and they also are very fond of me. I remember when Ari was small, every time I go to see him in the toddlers' house he won't leave me. Finally I would say, "Now I have to go to work." He understood about responsibility, so he would allow me to go. Even on Shabbat if I said, "I have to go to work," it was all right. When their mother went away on holiday, I would sit with the children until they fell asleep at night. Ari would just hold my hand until he slept. One time when Raḥel was away, I was sitting with him, and suddenly she came back. She took him up, and he saw me standing there still. He didn't want to tell me to go away, so he just told me, "*Dodah* (Aunty), you are working."

Daniel always wants me to cook for him. I know when he comes to me, he always expects to have food. He always used to come home with my mother too. He would sit with his *safta* and sing Shabbat songs with her. Raḥel asked him if he would like to have a Bar Mitzvah when he was old enough and he said yes. There is one man in the kibbutz who leads prayers on Shabbat and holidays for a small group of people, and he taught Daniel. We made a big party for the Bar Mitzvah on Sukkot in 1976, and the Cochin people came from many places, in addition to our relations from England. My uncle Daniel and his daughters had left Calcutta for England many years before, and he had not seen his sisters for about thirty years, so we were happy that they came to Daniel's Bar Mitzvah.

Shula got married to an American and now they live in Minnesota. When Mother was still living and Shula would bring her daughter Tal back to the kibbutz, it was amusing to see how Mother and Tal teased each other—the grandmother laughing and the great-granddaughter completely serious.

Mother reached a good old age and breathed her last on her ninetieth birthday in 1982. She was the first daughter of India to be buried in Neot Mordecai.

TIMES OF WAR

Sometimes I go to Kefar Yuval, which is only a few miles to the north of us, on the Lebanon border. Kefar Yuval is a *moshav* of the Cochin Jews, mostly from Ernakulam. They have a synagogue, and there was a *hazzan* until last year, when he died suddenly. I had a friend there, who always invited me. She said, "Come whenever you want," so I used to go especially for Rosh Hashanah and Yom Kippur. Now that she is no more, I still visit her daughter Rachel.

For the 1973 war I was in Kefar Yuval. It started on Yom Kippur. I was in the synagogue and we were just taking the Sefer Torah for the *Minhah* (afternoon service) and suddenly we heard the noise. We didn't know what was happening. Then we could see from the windows four planes with fire—two of theirs and two of ours chasing them back over the border. All the children were out. All the mothers started screaming. We didn't know until later: their planes had come to bomb Rosh Pinah (to the south of us), till our planes went to chase them. They were running away, going back over the border. Our planes didn't want to shoot them down, because where would they fall? So they just chased them out.

In a few minutes there came all the soldiers. "Go down to the shelters," we were told. But the *hazzan*, he will not leave there. He was just going to take the Sefer Torah. All the others went, except the *hazzan's* sister-in-law. She said, "If something happens to the synagogue, we will die there. We won't leave." I stayed there for some time but there were no prayers, so I also went down to the shelter. We came back after two or three hours and finished the prayers. The *hazzan* was there all the time.

Just after we finished the synagogue, people went home. They had no time

Ruby holding her grand-niece Tal Foley, Kibbutz Neot Mordecai, 1977. (*Photo, Dan Kala*)

to eat something. Then came the lorries from the military, taking all the men. They are sitting near the television to hear their number being called. I said to my friend's son, "You eat something, put something in your mouth." He couldn't, he was just waiting. Within an hour the village was cleared of men. There was one woman whose son was not called, but he wanted to go. As he was going, someone said, "You are not called. Why do you want to go?" On the way, he was hit, poor thing.

So I was there in Kefar Yuval. I couldn't come back to Neot Mordecai, as there were no buses and nobody came to fetch me. Till the eve of Simhat Torah, two weeks I was there. On Yom Kippur, my mother and Rahel were with our relatives in Haifa. They took the first bus back to the kibbutz the next morning; then a few moments later there were no more buses. But in

Haifa they didn't feel as we felt it here, where we could see the airplanes and the shooting.

Fortunately it was good for me in Kefar Yuval, better than here in the kibbutz. Here when there is a siren, we can't get out of the shelters. There we were asked to sit in the shelter all the time, but who has time to sit in the shelter? There were all the chickens to be attended to and the food for the people who were sitting down in the shelters. The women are always out. Then when sirens come they will go inside for a minute, and then they go out again, so I didn't feel it so much as we felt here. Those people would look after me if I don't go out, and if I like I can go, because the shelter is just opposite their house.

One night there was a lecture from Golda Meir at nine o'clock on the television, so we wanted to hear. Rachel and her sister and I sat down in the house; we didn't go to the shelter. Then just a few minutes later the *katyusha* rockets started falling! You can hear the noise, as if it is next door, but you don't know where it is. Fortunately, it was after Kippur, so the moon was bright, just like day. When they started falling, we didn't know where to hide. We were asked to sit under the beds, but the beds are so low you can't go under them. For two hours we couldn't move from the house. We didn't know what to do. No *katyushas* fell in the village, only in the fields. But you feel it—oh, what a noise! A lot of flares, then suddenly you see the fire when it explodes.

From where I was standing in Kefar Yuval, I could see nearby, on the top of the mountains, our planes are coming and bombing there just opposite the Kinneret [Sea of Galilee], just before the town of Rosh Pinah. And I was wondering why are they coming there, why don't they go to the Syrian side? Then I came to know that the Syrian troops were there! They just came from their side and they had to stop there to get orders, what to do next. When the Syrians first started coming, there was no resistance. We had only a few soldiers there, and they went into the shelters, because they had nothing to defend. The Syrians came in tanks, right over the shelter, so our soldiers could hear everything. And there was no resistance. Then suddenly the Syrians thought, Oh, there must be an ambush. They didn't know what to do. For everything they had to take orders from home, so they stopped at the place where they were asked to stop, waiting for their orders. They thought, It will take two hours to arrive at that place. But they came one hour before because there was no resistance. And while they stopped there for an hour, within that hour we had to prepare.

People said what they saw. They said, "We were just looking up, and the Syrian army was coming and they stopped there." They just had to cross a little bit! They wanted to cut Galilee into two, so they can just wipe out

Galilee. But they didn't do it. Is it not God's work? My grandfather once said, "We won't see God, but we know how there is a God, by His work. He changes the time." That's how it happens.

So many miracles, people say, but others don't believe. Our soldiers came to Rosh Pinah, and they wanted to go up the mountain on the Golan side. But they couldn't go up, because there was no footpath, and the enemy is standing on the top, shooting from there. But one fellow said he saw a woman standing on the top of the mountain and waving to them, "Come up," and at that time they were able to climb up. Some people felt it was *Ima* Raḥel [Mother Rachel]. Who knows? They saw somebody, a woman standing.

And in Sinai the commander had a girl secretary with him. As they were driving, she suddenly sees there is fire in front of them. She shouted, "Don't go, there is fire, don't go!" There were a lot of enemies there, but there was no fire. He couldn't see any fire. But she sees fire, and so they had to change the course. That saved them.

So many stories we heard at that time, you know. On Yom Kippur, four thousand soldiers fell on one day, at the start of it. So many soldiers they had, ten times more than we had. How could we stand that? Whose strength? Is it my strength, is it your strength? The enemy just simply was afraid and ran away. I don't know what they saw.

In Yesod HaMa'alah, a *moshav* not far from here where some Cochin people are living, they could see the fire from one side hitting the other side of the mountain. Syrians were on the one side, and in the morning they can shoot very well. In the afternoon the sun is on our side. In the morning the Israelis can't see them because of the sun. My friend Nissim's house got hit. So many years ago, in World War II, some of these same people ran away from Cochin because bombs fell on Chittagong! And here they were— standing, watching the cannonballs passing from one side of the valley to the other. What can you do? It was either the fire or the sea. The brass cannon cartridges were lying there, all lying in the field in Yesod HaMa'alah. There are so many houses there, but the shell casings were all lying in the field. After the war, people brought them in and polished them and put flowers in them.

Neot Mordecai was hit only once by *katyusha* rockets, during the Lebanon War. Twelve of them fell in the open spaces between the dining hall and other buildings. I was not here then, as I was staying with my relatives near Haifa. So many *katyushas* have fallen on Kiryat Shemonah. A school was hit, but the children were not hurt. One house was hit, but the people of that house were somewhere else that day. So many wonderful things happened, when you think about it. You can say the enemy made a mistake, but why did they make a mistake?

Living here, of course we all feel the tension. Everybody is afraid, but what can we do? At night, before the Lebanon War, we couldn't sleep, because we were supposed to keep our things ready. As soon as the siren goes we must go to the shelter. Every day! Before and during the war. That's why we started the war, because we couldn't sleep in Galilee. But it is going on anyway, so what's the use of being frightened? Where can you go? During the war the men are away. Lots of people went from here, and during the Six-Day War all of them came back without being hurt. During the 1973 war we lost three men. At Beit Axi, our kibbutz clubhouse, you can see their photos.

CHANGING VALUES

When I arrived in Israel, the country was a desert. People were arriving from many parts of the world with their own culture and language. At first it was very difficult to adjust with one another. We the pampered Jews from India could not understand the behavior of those who had suffered so much in their homeland. Some had nightmares which kept sleep at bay or made them wake up screaming. Some who escaped from Babi Yar and from the concentration camps, with numbers tattooed on their arms—I am not going to judge these people whatever they do. We were the only people who came from a country where we did not have to look back when we are on the road.

There was a time when nobody on the kibbutz had anything, and I hear people say they were happier then. Now we have everything that is needed but no luxury. Now I have an apartment with my own kitchen, where I can cook Cochin-style dishes whenever I want, for friends and relatives who come to visit. Before we had only pocket money, but now we are given a certain amount for dress, a certain amount for shoes, and so on. We can adjust and use it for something else we want. Now the kibbutz children live with the parents instead of in the children's house. Once in twenty years we get the chance to travel, so I visited my cousins in England.

But it seems that now people on the kibbutz are not satisfied. When I sit with a few people the only conversation I hear is about how many times one traveled abroad, how one arranged the house, how much one works—only criticisms. It is like the English say: "Familiarity breeds contempt." At the same time, in dire need people help one another.

The families are closed up among themselves, as now people have children and grandchildren and television. They have no time for outsiders. Single people have no rights for anything and nobody cares, as if we are not human. As if our needs should be quite limited. People don't seem to realize that though the bed is small it needs four legs.

Now the things and people are changed. Either they changed or we

Ruby in front of her apartment building, Kibbutz Neot Mordecai, 1990. (*Photo, Barbara Johnson*)

changed. The kibbutz is changed. Many old members are dissatisfied. But it is too late to do anything. Those who come to join the kibbutz now are those who have problems at home, which the kibbutz solves for them. A few members who were born and bred here and married with children are leaving. Maybe they are looking for better pastures or just want to be on their own. The old ideology is gone. I wonder if there is a necessity for the kibbutzim anymore. Everybody wants to be independent, as it is happening all over the world. If the youngsters leave, there is no survival for the kibbutz. Only the oldsters are sorry, because the system they built up with some pains would not survive and all their efforts would be wasted.

On her three-wheeled cycle, Ruby travels throughout the kibbutz. (*Photo, Nicky Morris*)

COCHIN COMMUNITY IN ISRAEL

After many years, most of the Paradesi community came to Israel from Jew Town, including my relations. They are living in many places, working in offices and banks and factories, and some of them as doctors. All are spread out and there is no more communal life like the life we enjoyed in Cochin. At that time we thought it a nuisance living together too long, but now we miss it. We are trying to find any excuse to flock together. For a holiday or a child's birthday or a wedding or Bar Mitzvah, all the people of this community from wherever they are will join together. Somehow we find a place for everyone to sleep one or two nights. On the bed or on the floor or a couch does not make any difference; we just spread quilts or blankets on the floor and sleep one next to the other. Sometimes it reminds me of the Victoria Terminus Railway Station in Bombay. Once my cousin from England came to visit and asked me if the walls of my house are made of elastic!

Some people write that the Cochin community of Jews is dying. They don't realize that a root from that tree is shooting up in Israel and starting to blossom. As long as we keep up some of our traditions, I hope that this community will never die.

Part Two

THE PAMPERED JEWS
OF MALABAR

Chapter 10

MORE TALES FROM COCHIN
JEWISH HISTORY

W̲e always hear about the Jews being ill treated all over the world in one way or other. The so-called "enlightened" world—England, Russia, Germany, France, Poland, Portugal, Spain, not to speak about Rome and Greece—all had their share of persecuting the Jews. Christians call themselves humanitarians, but they would burn all those who don't believe in Christianity, if they could. They believe if they convert one Jew they will go to heaven, even if he is a dead man.* Then come the Muslims. They also want everyone to believe what they do, or they must murder the unbelievers. So everyone is happy to kill a Jew.

The Muslims and Christians as well as the Jews have stamped the Hindus as idolaters. But if you want to know what is humanitarianism you must go to them. You must look at a group of Jews who lived under the regime of these Hindu rajas for the last two thousand years without knowing discrimination. The Hindu rulers protected them when they came under attack by the Portuguese and Muslim rulers. In his petition to Oliver Cromwell before 1655 for the resettlement of Jews in England—from where they were driven away in 1290—Manasseh Ben Israel pleaded and gave the example of the tolerance enjoyed by the Jews of Cochin under the Hindu regime. The Jews of Cochin should be grateful to those Hindu rajas and the people of Cochin for their very existence as Jews in their country forever and ever.

---

*It happened in Cochin that a Jewish man was very ill in the hospital, and one night when he was very bad, unable to open his eyes even, a priest came to him and put a cross on his lips. He jumped up from the bed shouting, "Get away from me!" and he didn't die that night. I heard this from his granddaughter.

PALUR AND THE PALIATH ACHANS

There were synagogues in Palur and Muttath which were destroyed long ago. The Jewish women of Mala have a song about the building of their synagogue, which says that the first Jews arrived in Palur, and then they had to flee to Cranganore. Some of the Jews from Palur found peace only when they came to Cochin, where the maharaja took them under his wing. Perhaps the families who formed the Kochangadi Synagogue (the first synagogue in Cochin) came from Palur after that colony was destroyed.

In recent memory there were no Jews living in Palur, but there is a *rimon* (a type of ornament) from Palur used for a Sefer Torah in the Nevatim Synagogue in Israel today. This *rimon* was extricated from Palur Synagogue long ago and brought to the Parur Synagogue. Ernakulam Synagogue bought it from Parur, and now it came to Israel.

Palur is mentioned in two other Malayalam folk songs of the Cochin Jews. One is sung by the women of the Kadavumbagam Synagogue in Cochin, who sing it as they clap their hands and dance in a circle. It tells the story of a bird who flew away to escape the hunter, and it is said that the bird refers to the Jews who fled from Palur to some place of safety. This song does not appear in the books of the white Jews.

SONG ABOUT PALUR

Milk with banana shall be given,   —*Ayaya*
To you lovely bird.   —*Ayaya*
The fruit from the branch I shall   —*Ayaya*
Pluck, and I shall give to you.   —*Ayaya*
Telling a good news,   —*Ayaya*
I shall pluck and give to you, parrot.   —*Ayaya*
Like this, at one time   —*Ayaya*
Birds did not arrive.   —*Ayaya*
Seeing the coming of the birds,   —*Ayaya*
A hunter came and interfered.   —*Ayaya*
Seeing the coming of the hunter,   —*Ayaya*
The bird lost its color.   —*Ayaya*
With the stick of the hunter   —*Ayaya*
They leapt up with palpitation.   —*Ayaya*
How can one forget?   —*Ayaya*
Another place was not found.   —*Ayaya*
To an elevated place   —*Ayaya*
The bird flew and perched   —*Ayaya*
Near the seashore of Palur.   —*Ayaya*
It saw the trees   —*Ayaya*

Near the seashore of Palur. —*Ayaya*
The birds flew and perched —*Ayaya*
Near the seashore of Palur. —*Ayaya*
The bird went and bathed —*Ayaya*
Near the seashore of Palur. —*Ayaya*
Listen to the wicked thing that happened to the bird! —*Ayaya*
A palace of green stone, —*Ayaya*
God! make an umbrella of the precious stones over us.* —*Ayaya*
Gather all of us together —*Ayaya*
To fly and perch there. —*Ayaya*

In another Malayalam folk song, special praise is sung to one Komar Achan of the Paliam family of Palur, as a man who was just to refugees who came to sojourn in the country under his jurisdiction:

Who are they that are going with tom-toms
    and making such noise?
It is the commander of the twelve thousand,
    the Nayar brigade and bodyguards.
People who come as refugees and mere foreigners
    are given presents and charity by this Paliath Achan,
The handsome Paliath Achan of Palur,
    the Komar Achan of Paliam,
Is the only one who could do it.

This song is a precious record of past history which I have not found in any of the notebooks of old songs copied by the women of our community. My mother was the only one who knew it. She must have learned it when she was a young girl, because such songs are sung by the children when they play and dance. It suddenly came to her head when her great-granddaughter Tal was here in Israel. That is the first time I heard it, when she sang it to the child. Catching the words "Palur" and "Paliath Achan," I made her sing again and copied it. I don't know if there were more verses, as that was all she remembered.

I would like to say something about this Paliam family mentioned in the song. This family is very special. They were known for their valor and for their hospitality toward strangers who came among them. These people were fond of the Jews. They were also very, very rich and highly cultured and had high positions in the government. Usually the prime ministers of Cochin were nominated from their family. Their male members are referred to as Paliath Achan.

---

*It is said that at the time of salvation, when the Jews are gathered, an angel (Michael or Gabriel) will go and sit on the planet Noga (Venus) and rain down green diamonds on those Jews and make an umbrella over them. This I heard from my mother.

They have much treasure hidden away underground. The storehouse of the Paliam dynasty contains diamonds, rubies, green diamonds, and other precious gems in small containers. There are replicas made from solid gold of all kinds of vegetables and fruits that grow in the country and household equipments—even brooms—also the bloodstained clothes of those who had fought and died in wars.

I came to know of this from a Jew named Kochu Vavu, who came from Chendamangalam. When Shunmukan Chetty came as the *dewan* (prime minister) of Cochin, he wanted to dig up all the rich people's treasures, so with one or two of the trusted members of his staff he went to find out. One of the men who went with the Chetty was this Kochu Vavu. Once when our family was staying in Alwaye, a health resort, Kochu Vavu came to visit us, and I heard him telling this news to my mother. He also said that this Chetty, the *dewan*, took ten or twelve of these green stones, saying he wanted to find out the value of these gems. But Kochu Vavu did not know whether they were returned or not. As my grandmother used to say, "Whoever puts his hand into the pot of jaggery, there is no one who will not lick his fingers."

A number of years after we met Kochu Vavu in Alwaye, we went to stay in Chendamangalam during World War II, and we happened to stay in the property of this Paliam *tarwad*. There was a young couple from the *tarwad* living next door. My mother asked them about this treasure, and the lady smiled and told a story:

Once upon a time, she said, one king or chieftain conquered a territory where there were many Jews. All these treasures belonging to their synagogue were taken away by the conquerors as booty. After some time, the people of the Paliam family went to war with that other chieftain, defeated him, and brought these Jewish treasures back to the Paliam storehouse as booty. They are not using it; they are just guarding it. She told my mother that her ancestors used to say that all these riches were the property of the Jews and that a day will come when it will go back to the Jews. Well! That was her story.

When I started thinking about all these things, I very much wanted to contact Kochu Vavu, but I did not even know where he was living in Israel. A few weeks before writing this, I was waiting for a bus in Kiryat Shemonah. Suddenly I thought of him. There I met a couple of my friends from Kefar Yuval. They said that they were going to visit a friend in the Safed hospital and then to a funeral, and this funeral happened to be that of this Kochu Vavu. A pity.

PARUR AND TIPPU SULTAN

When I was young there were still a few wealthy Jewish families living in Chendamangalam and in Parur, along with other Jews who were not so rich.

Formerly, Parur had a very thriving community of Jews. There were four streets, the synagogue in the middle, and forty *rabbanim*. There is a story about these *rabbanim* of Parur. Once there was a great epidemic that could not be stopped. So these *rabbanim* were so bold that they burned *ketoret* (incense) like the Israelites did in the wilderness of Sinai when they were affected by an epidemic. But the *rabbanim* could not get all the ingredients mentioned for this ritual in the Bible. They did not know exactly what they were. So they used whatever was available instead. As soon as the incense was lit, hundreds of people died. They should have heeded the warning which is read twice every morning in the *Shaharit* service: "If any ingredient is missing, it will be death."

Many more Jewish deaths in Parur were caused by Tippu Sultan, the Muslim ruler of Mysore, a kingdom far to the northeast of Malabar. He was a very cruel man and is known as the Tiger of Mysore. His father, Hyder Ali, was the commander in chief of a Hindu raja by the name of Krishna. Hyder Ali murdered the king and took his place. But even he did not like his son Tippu because of his cruelty.

This Hyder Ali had a bosom friend who was a Jew. It so happened one day that Tippu, who was only a boy then, did some very cruel deed, which did not please his father. Hyder Ali drew his sword to kill Tippu, but his Jewish friend intervened and begged him to spare the life of the boy, who had to take his place one day. Hyder Ali could not resist the pleadings of his friend. He spared the life of his son because of him, but he warned the Jew that his death would be at the hands of Tippu, and so it happened. When Hyder Ali died and Tippu became the sultan, he found some fault with this Jew and ordered him to be put to death. He was shut up in an iron cage and paraded through the city on the way to his execution. He stopped at every corner and told this story to the people.

Wherever he went, Tippu spread murder and arson. He converted to Islam by force many Hindus of the places he conquered. Those who resisted were killed. He sent his soldiers all around with a cap in one hand and a sword in the other. They called out, "Choose cap or sword! Either the cap on your head or your head into the cap"—wearing a cap is a symbol of identity for the Muslims as for the Jews. Out of fear for their lives, many Hindus converted to Islam. Some were forced to eat beef, so they got polluted and they had no choice but to convert. There is a class of Muslims who keep away from other Muslims even today. They say that they were high-caste Hindus who were forcibly converted by Tippu Sultan. They still don't eat beef, and they keep some Hindu customs. This group is called Naina.

When Tippu Sultan invaded South India, he set fire to the synagogue in Parur and killed many Jews. Of those who escaped, some ran away and many got converted to Christianity. When Tippu destroyed the Parur Jewish community, he expressed a wish that he wanted to brew his coffee on the breast of Jewish women. Before he could realize his dream he was called back home, as his father was dying.

After the destruction, the community of Parur did not prosper much, though they did rebuild the synagogue. Till recently it was a practice for Cochin Jews from all the communities to make vows to contribute money or oil to light lamps at the Parur Synagogue or to take a child for whom the vow was made to Parur to do it. They would give a small party at the time. Now that all the Cochin Jews left for Israel, only one Jewish family lives in Parur. That lady still lights the eternal lamp in that synagogue.

KOCHANGADI SYNAGOGUE IN COCHIN

I have also heard some stories concerning the Kochangadi Synagogue in Cochin, the one south of Jew Town which was destroyed long before I was born.

There was once a Jewish widow living in Kochangadi. One evening an old beggar came to her door and requested her to give him a pot to cook the rice which he got by begging. This kind hearted lady gave him a new clay pot with a cover. The women in Cochin usually cooked their food in clay pots, and some still do, though not everyone. The old man took the pot gratefully and went away.

Next morning this lady got out of the house to sweep the backyard of the house. There she found the pot which she had given to the beggar the previous night, standing on three stones. The pot and the stones were all turned to gold! She called the people and showed them. They found that all round the pot, a foundation was laid for a synagogue. From the money they realized from selling the gold, they built the Kochangadi Synagogue.

Later, some Muslims started living nearby Kochangadi and became a nuisance to the Jews. They threw stones into the synagogue in the times of prayer, which broke the lamps and made the place dirty. There is a story about a Muslim boy who always came and urinated in front of the synagogue. The Jews went to the *rab* and complained about it. He told them to tell the boy not to do it again because the *rab* said so. But he did not listen. So they went to the *rab* again. Then the *rab* said to tell him to continue urinating. When he started doing it, he could not stop until he collapsed. Then his parents and relatives went to the *rab* and begged his pardon. Then the *rab* told them to tell him to stop, and finally he was able to do so.

Anyway, the Jews found it difficult to stay there any longer. So they left the place. Only a piece of wall was left standing in that compound. I have heard that sometimes they would light a lamp there. A Muslim woman who lived nearby swept and kept the place around it clean. It was worth her while. I have seen that piece of wall years ago, but I don't know if it still stands today.

KADAVUMBAGAM SYNAGOGUE

After they left Kochangadi, the Jews built the Kadavumbagam Synagogue at the southern end of Jew Town. In front of the synagogue site is a landing place for boats traveling southward, especially for fishing boats. (In Malayalam *kadavu* means landing place and *bagam* means side.)

A space was kept open between the synagogue and the river. In the days before cars or trains, the maharaja used to travel by boat from his palace at the northern end of Jew Town. In order to travel south, he would pass by this site. Whenever he was about to pass by, the Jews of this synagogue were informed ahead of time. They would then open the doors of the synagogue, and they would also open the *heykhal*—the ark where the Torah scrolls are kept. The maharaja's boat would stop at the synagogue landing, and he would stand up and then prostrate himself toward the synagogue. This was the practice as long as the maharaja's residence was in Cochin. In fact, even after the Royal Residence was transferred to a palace in Ernakulam, the landing place by the Kadavumbagam Synagogue in Cochin was still kept open.

Many miracles have been attributed to the Cochin Kadavumbagam Synagogue. Therefore if anyone became ill, or was embarking on a dangerous journey, or lost something and wanted to recover it—or when a woman was soon to give birth—it was customary to bring a gift or donation to this synagogue and to pray for one's well-being. People even prayed for intercession in the name of that synagogue for answers to their prayers, as they do in the names of Rabbi Meyer and Rabbi Shimon Bar Yohai. Also, the gentile people living nearby had a firm belief in the miracles associated with this synagogue. They usually would bring a glass of oil for the synagogue's eternal light, as a gift.

Once, it seems, a thief entered the Cochin Kadavumbagam Synagogue in the middle of the night when he thought it would be safe to steal its valuables. He tried to approach the *heykhal*, but whenever he did so, he heard the cracking of a whip in front of the *heykhal*. This so frightened him that he could not control himself, soiled the place, and fainted. He was apprehended in the morning.

Years ago there was a great earthquake near Quetta, in Afghanistan, when the earth opened its mouth and swallowed up whatever was nearby. One Bene-Israel boy perished in this way. It was to the Cochin Kadavumbagam Synagogue that the father of this boy sent some money so that every year on his son's death anniversary the boy's name could be remembered. The fame of the Kadavumbagam Synagogue had spread so far through a member named Mosheh Madai, who was a *hazzan* for the synagogue in Karachi.

When I was young, in the early 1920s, this synagogue had to undergo some repairs. Learned men from the various Jewish communities were present when they broke down the wall of the *heykhal*; among them was their own *Moreh* (Teacher) Eliyahu and my grandfather Eliyahu Japheth. Amidst the rubble were found some writings (not holy writings), some in Hebrew, some in Malayalam, some on scrolls, and some on copper plates, and also some large stones with writing on them. After they had been read, some were reburied in the same spot and then paved over. Others were brought to the Paradesi Synagogue. Even those stones which are now used as stepping-stones in the vicinity should be closely examined. Maybe things from this site might reveal information of historical value.

In two old songbooks which have been collected from women in the Paradesi community, I found copies of a song about the building of the Kadavumbagam Synagogue. Never having heard it sung, I asked many elderly people from Kadavumbagam about this song, but they also do not know the words or the tune either. Some of the words are difficult to understand, but this is my rough translation:

SONG ABOUT KADAVUMBAGAM SYNAGOGUE OF COCHIN

1

An important land in the world is Cochin.
The honorable Jews of Kadavumbagam are there.
All the Kadavumbagam people joined together
And raised up carefully a synagogue.
Important people gathered and said the blessings,
The elders and the young people together.

2

Saying the blessings the foundation was laid.
Gold and pearls were put in the middle,
And they raised the synagogue over the pearls.
The place where God's Eminence is seated
Is on the western side.
The *heykhal* was established like pure silver.
There were two doors.

3

The pillars were bent and made into an arch with two rooms.
The Torah that was created before two thousand years,
The Light of the Lord of the World,
It is there for a fact.

It has brightness like the sun and the moon,
Under the tiled roof.

4

Beautifully ten and five sections were divided into fifteen.*
At a height of five and a quarter *koles*,† there stood pillars.
On this the platform was made at a length of five *koles*.
A staircase was put there to climb up,
And a place for the ladies (the ones who cover their heads)
To sit and pray to God.
To see and hear the prayers being conducted, there were three doors.

5

They made very red crests and engravings,
Beautiful lotus flowers too.
In the middle a beautiful *tebah* was made, with legs of wood.
By the grace of God, bring near the good years.
Please bring the nation who are Your children
To the noblest land of the world.

KURUKKAN‡

In all the world, one of the best ports is Cochin.
The famous Jews have come there also.
God, who reigns in sound and light,
We are Your slaves, praying to You
To save us also.
David and Eliyahu will come.
Then the shofar will blow
Eight hundred people will pray.
Help us, God, forever.

When virtually the entire congregation of the Cochin Kadavumbagam Synagogue left for Israel, they sadly had to sell their synagogue. Muslims wanted
to buy it in order to turn it into a mosque, but the Jews refused their offer,
saying that it is forbidden to sell a synagogue for holding prayers of another

---

*This is the description of the ceiling, which is divided by beams into fifteen sections, with a carved
lotus flower in the center of each section.
†A *kol* is a unit of measurement, equivalent to an English rod (16.5 feet). The maximum height of a
coconut tree is 100 koles.
‡*Kurukkan* is the term for a short chorus or song at the end of a longer Malayalam Jewish song, often continuing the same theme. *Kuruk* means "short."

religion. The synagogue was sold to people who used it for storing merchandise such as areca nuts, ropes and dried shrimps. But the people who bought the building did not prosper. One purchaser suddenly lost two of his sons. Thereafter he did not want any part of that place. No one else prospered there either. People were sorry about the fate of that synagogue, including myself, although I was not a member of that community.

Now I am surprised and delighted to learn that the inside of the Cochin Kadavumbagam Synagogue has been carefully dismantled and brought to Israel, to be reconstructed for permanent display at the Israel Museum in Jerusalem. I wish all success, long life, and prosperity to all who are involved in this project. It would be wonderful if its own *heykhal* and Torah scrolls and other items, which are now located elsewhere, would be returned to it, to be on display at its new site. When that happens I, with all former members of that community, will be satisfied. I hope to live to see that day.

THE COPPER PLATES

The copper plates which were given to the Jews from Cheraman Perumal are at present in the possession of the Paradesi Synagogue in Cochin. On the plates it is clearly stated that they were presented to one Joseph Rabban in 1000 C.E., long before the Paradesi Synagogue was built. Some people are wondering how the copper plates came into the possession of the Paradesi community rather than the original Jews, who had been in Malabar for a much longer time.

In this connection I have to mention what I have heard from my grandparents. I am not sure in which community these copper plates were preserved after Joseph Rabban. But when the Paradesis arrived, they kept away from the Jews who had lived there for ages. They built their own synagogue and found favor in the eyes of the native rulers as well as the Portuguese, the Dutch, and finally the English colonial rulers of the area. During the time of the white man's rule, these people were the only other white people in the locality, so they were made much of by the white rulers and of course by the British, who were notorious for their color prejudices. So the foreigners' contact was only with the white Jews.

All of the foreign officials who visited the Palace of the Maharaja, which is next door to Jew Town, came to see the historical Paradesi Synagogue. I doubt very much if these officials ever knew about the existence of the other synagogues in Cochin State, several of which were founded earlier than the Paradesi Synagogue.

It was told me that when Lord Curzon, one of the British viceroys of India, came to visit Cochin, the arrangement was made also to visit the Cochin

Kadavumbagam Synagogue at the other end of Jew Street. That community had made all the preparations for his reception and waited for him in their synagogue. But when a Kadavumbagam leader went to accompany him, he found that he was being kept back in the Paradesi Synagogue with the excuse that the other synagogue was very far away, when in reality the whole of Jew Town is not more than a couple of furlongs in length. So this gentleman, who was well versed in the English language, went straight up to the viceroy and told him that his community was waiting to honor him in the other synagogue as it was scheduled, and his refusal to visit their synagogue would be taken as a great disgrace to them. So the viceroy went to the Kadavumbagam Synagogue on foot. I wonder what he thought of the long-distance scare! When the prayer for the royalty was read—as is usual when a ruler visits any of the Cochin Synagogues—his wife said, "Aamen," as the Jews say, and the viceroy said, "Amen," as the British say. But she insisted that it should be said "Aamen," and he agreed.

Non-Paradesi Jews will tell you that when officials visited the Paradesi Synagogue it was the custom to borrow the copper plates from the other Jewish community to show off, as if the copper plates actually belonged to the Paradesis. Thus it happened when one British officer visited the Paradesi Synagogue, he was shown the copper plates as usual. But this fellow, unlike the others, took a great interest in them and would not hand them back. He said that such things of historical value should be under the direct protection of the government. He wanted the plates to be taken to London. When the Paradesis protested, he said that he would make a copy of them and send the original back. But the big sahib (Englishman) did not keep his word. The true owners of the plates started pressing the Paradesis, and in turn they pressed the sahib, till at last he sent the copy to them and kept the original, which he said is in a museum in London. When the Paradesis gave the copy to the owners, the latter refused to accept the copy and insisted on the original, which the Paradesi people could not obtain. So the Paradesis kept the copy while the true owners were left with nothing—neither the original nor the copy. In the course of time the whole affair was forgotten, and the copper plates stayed in the Paradesi Synagogue and no one challenged their authenticity or which community was the legitimate owner of the original copper plates.

Something to this effect was published in the book *From Cochin to the Land of Israel* by the people of Nevatim Moshav, when they celebrated the thirtieth anniversary of their immigration to Israel.* I heard a protest from a Paradesi family here in Israel. They said that the official who was mentioned did not take the copper plates away with him and that what they have got now

*BJ: Shalva Weil, ed. *MiCochin leEretz Israel* (Jerusalem, 1984).

in the Paradesi Synagogue in Cochin is the original, and the copper plates originally belonged to the Paradesis. If there is anyone who really cares to know the truth, I suggest they go and check.

THE COCHIN MAHARAJA AND THE JEWS

The Cochin Jews have always had a special relationship with the maharaja of Cochin. The whole of Jew Town was given by the maharaja to the Jews, and most of our houses were tax free. The property was given to the Jews to possess it, as the dried palm-leaf documents of the time said: "To him [each Jewish owner], his family and all his generations forever and ever." Even if one sells a piece of property, his son can claim it because this property can never be sold. I think other people, if they knew it, would not have bought those houses. The palm-leaf documents do not exist any more. Moreover the government is changed, and of course all the rulings of the maharajas are no longer valid.

The Paradesi Synagogue is situated next to the maharaja's palace in Mattancherry. These two are divided by only a wall. Immediately next to the wall on the palace side is a small Hindu temple. They also have a feast every year during the time of the Jews' feasts between Rosh Hashanah and Yom Kippur. We in the synagogue were a little disturbed by their songs and drums, specially during the Kippur service. But the Jews kept quiet.

The Deity and statues of the Hindu temple were kept exactly near the dividing wall closest to the synagogue. One year during the *Musaf* Prayer on Yom Kippur, when the Jews prostrate and say the prayer "*Barukh Shem*," all these Hindu statues fell down. When it was brought to the notice of the raja he decided to remove the synagogue to a place further away. That night he had a dream. A big peacock came and started pecking at him from head to foot. Three times he dreamt the same dream. He was worried, so he called his astrologers and told them about the dream. Their interpretation was that the peacock is the vehicle of Subramanian, one of the saints in Hindu mythology. He did not approve the raja's idea of removing the synagogue from its place. So he sent his vehicle to convey his disapproval. So the raja canceled his decision. Instead he ordered all the statues to be placed on the opposite side of the wall, and they did not fall again.

This story was told to the Sassoon Hallegua family by an elderly gentleman who came to their house for a visit. He heard it from his parents or grandparents. When Mrs. Ruby Hallegua came to Israel, I asked her about it, and she confirmed that the man did tell such a story. Then suddenly her sister Essie Ashkenazi said that she had heard the same story from her grandmother. Also a Hindu woman who came to Israel from Cochin to work for a family here said that she heard the same story from her grandmother.

In Cochin the maharajas followed the custom by which the sons do not inherit from the father. Like some of the other high-caste Hindus, their inheritance goes to the sister's children because of their marriage custom which is called *marumakathayam*. With inheritance by nephews in this fashion, there are many claimants to the throne and a long wait. Often when the rulers finally come to the throne, they are old men with only five or six years left to rule. I have heard that the Jews once helped a young boy who came from a poor branch of the royal family. They gave him a lot of money and made him rich, and that is how he came to the throne. He and his descendants formed the Perumpadappu dynasty. I don't know if that is true, but the Jews were in fact very friendly with this dynasty, which became the Rulers of Cochin for many generations.* When any need arose the Jews were ready to help the rajas.

Once the Cochin raja visited the Travancore raja, who ruled the kingdom south of Cochin. He was received with great pomp. They even tied his boat with silver chains. The Travancore rajas were very rich. When the time came for the Travancore maharaja to visit Cochin, the Cochin maharaja was not rich enough to receive him as he was accustomed in Travancore. So the Cochin maharaja called the Jews and told them the story. The Jews said to him, "Don't worry, Your Highness. If he tied your boat with a silver chain, we will tie his boat with a golden chain," and so they did.

MACAULAY SAHIB AND THE JEWS

There was one occasion when the Cochin Jews helped a British governor called Macaulay, rather than the raja.† There was some misunderstanding between this Sahib and the maharaja. It was a serious matter. At last it became a matter of life and death, and the raja wanted to kill him. So he always sent policemen to try to catch him whenever possible. The raja had no right to arrest anyone in Fort Cochin where Macaulay lived, because it was under British jurisdiction. But this Englishman also had an office in Jew Town and he used to go there to work.

Once when the raja was informed that Macaulay was in Jew Town he sent his policemen. Macaulay suddenly found himself surrounded by police with no way of escape. He had a box full of gold coins on the table. He just threw

*BJ: According to Hebrew documents written in Cochin, David Rahaby I (1646–1726) was instrumental in settling a dispute over succession to the Cochin throne in 1690, winning the loyalty of the rajas who descended from the victorious faction of this Perumpaddapu dynasty. See "Ḥidushim Shel Kadmoniyot" (c. 1800, Sassoon ms. 1023b) pp. 34–38; Naphthali E. Roby, "Toldot Beit Rahabi be-Cochin" (1939, photocopy in Judah Magnes Museum Library, Berkeley, CA), pp. 3–5.
†BJ: See Walter Fischel, "Cochin and Some Prominent Jewish Personalities," in *The Joshua Bloch Memorial Volume*, Abraham Berger, ed. (New York: New York Public Library, 1960), pp. 162–164, for written sources in Hebrew and English about Colonel Macaulay. See also T. K. Vijayamohan, "Col. Macaulay, the Political Resident of Travancore (1800–1810)", *Journal of Kerala Studies*, vol. 6:287–291.

the box of gold on the floor, and all the coins spread over the floor. These policemen, who had never seen a gold coin, forgot Macaulay and started picking up the coins. In the confusion, Macaulay ran away but there was no place to hide. So some of the Jews took him to the lavatory. The lavatory at that time was a pit dug in the ground surrounded by walls and covered with wooden planks with a hole. They pulled out some planks, put a chair inside, made the sahib sit on it, and put the planks back. He had to sit there till the coast was clear. Drunk with the glut of gold, the policemen did not see what happened to Macaulay. One put his cap on and another put his coat on and danced as if he was Macaulay Sahib. When the gold picking was done, they found that he had escaped, so they left. Macaulay, sitting in the lav, made a vow to the God of the Jews that if God will save him from the hands of the raja, he would make an offering.

Anyway, he escaped, but he was not safe in Cochin. So he escaped to Travancore, where he became the *dewan*. He told this story to the raja of Travancore, and that raja made a crown of gold with stones of different colors and sent it to the Paradesi Synagogue, where it is still used as the crown for one of the Torah scrolls, the "*Sefer Rishon*."

THE STORY OF A "BELL THIEF"

The Ernakulam Jews, too, have their rights and property because of the Cochin maharaja. Once it happened the raja had a quarrel with a foreign Governor. He lived three miles away from Cochin Jew Town in Fort Cochin, a territory which was under the direct jurisdiction of that foreign power. (I am not sure whether it was the Portuguese, the Dutch, or the British at that time.) That territory is still called Fort Cochin, because it used to be surrounded by a fort. The gate of the fort was opened in the mornings and closed in the evenings. Those who entered the fort during the day had to leave before the gates were closed for the night. Some Ernakulam Jews had dealings with the governor's house, as they were the suppliers of chicken and eggs for his household. They carried these things in big baskets on their heads.

It so happened once that the governor insulted the raja, and the raja, in his anger, swore that he would pull out the governor's tongue for that. He did not realize at the time the seriousness of his outburst. But he had to keep his word. The governor would not put out his tongue to be pulled out. So the raja decided to pull out the tongue of the great bell that was hung on a high pillar on the hilltop where the governor's bungalow was. Underneath is the sea; that was the only unguarded entry.

At that time, also, the Jews came to the aid of the raja, who requested them to help him keep his word. The Jews who brought chicken and eggs had admission to the governor's mansion without being searched. One day they took a short boy in a basket, along with a thick and long rope and some cotton wool, and put some chickens on top to cover him. They went to the governor's palace, gave them the merchandise, and returned in the evening, conveniently forgetting the basket with the boy inside and leaving it at the bottom of the pillar where the bell was. In the middle of the night, two of these Jews went in a small fishing boat by the sea and waited at the bottom of the hill.

As they waited, this boy climbed up on the pillar, covered the tongue of the bell with cotton wool, removed the entire bell, tied one end of the rope, and threw the other end into the sea. The boatmen caught the end of the rope, and the bell was slipped noiselessly to the boatmen's hands. They took the rope and the bell and paddled away with all speed. The boy climbed down and hid himself in the basket as before. Early next morning the Jews came in, took the basket with the boy, and rushed away. By the time people realized that the bell did not ring, the adventure was completed and the bell rang in the raja's palace instead.

In gratitude for this, a whole street was given to that Jewish community as a freehold; that is the Jews Street in Ernakulam. The natives still call the Jews "bell thieves" (*manikallar*).

In Cochin itself there is a group of Hindus called Conganies. They were the ones who pestered the Jews more than anyone else with this epithet. Once it happened that this group of Hindus had to steal their own Deity. They had lent their Deity to another temple as usual for a celebration, but this time the other temple refused to return it. So the right owners had to bribe the priests of the other temple to rob it and bring it to them. So it was done. From that time, when the Conganies called the Jews *manikallar*, the Jews called them back *devankallar*, which means "God thief." So they stopped calling the Jews *manikallar*.

In this connection there was a funny development, though it has no connection with the Jews. When the theft of the Deity was discovered, those people filed a suit that the Deity belonged to them, and it was decreed that the statue should be returned, but the defendants refused. Then the case went to the Appeal Court, where it was decreed that the British governor himself should go and take the statue from the temple and return it to the appellants. But the defendants were not strong enough to stand against such a judgment. So they found a means to protest. They decided to commit mass suicide if the governor sahib touched the wall of the temple, which would have polluted the temple. So they took pieces of rope, made a loop at one end, and tied the other end to the branches of trees that were around the temple, and all of them climbed upon the trees and sat and waited with the loops in their hands for the sahib. As soon as the governor and his retinue touched the temple wall, everyone was to put the loop over his head and jump down. It was arranged so quietly that no one else knew it. So it happened the governor and his people arrived at the appointed time. As they were approaching the temple they heard shouting and screaming overhead, making a terrible sound. The sahib looked up at the moment they were putting on the loops. He was shocked and asked what they were doing there. When it was explained to him, he made a right about-face turn and retreated as quickly as possible with his men, and never bothered them again.

CORONATION CUSTOMS

Long long before I was born, the maharaja had moved his residence from the palace in Mattancherry to Ernakulam. Every time a new raja was crowned, he had to go to New Delhi—the seat of the viceroy (the British governor-general) for confirmation. The rajas usually traveled by train. A special carriage painted white was attached to the train specially for the raja. On his way back home he had to go across the Jew Town of Ernakulam to reach his palace. I have heard from some of my Ernakulam friends that the Jews of that Town would then request five minutes of his time to stop in front of the synagogue. They made a decorated canopy for the raja. The whole town would be decorated with bunches of bananas and bunches of orange-colored coconuts.

When the raja arrived, the elderly men of the Jewish community went out from the synagogue in their festive dress and blessed him, the eldest man raising his right hand over his head. Whether he touched his head or not I don't know, because the rajas are not to be touched by other castes. Then the elder would read the special prayer for the royalty from the prayer book, which starts with the words "*Hanoten teshua lemelakhim*" ("The One who gives salvation to the kings"). They would have a translation made with the name of that particular raja and present it to him in a gilded frame. Then he was garlanded with jasmine flowers. All the people that gathered were sprinkled with rose water from a bottle specially made for that purpose. The whole ceremony lasted about twenty minutes and not five. But the raja was gratified and everybody was happy. This kind of affair used to take place every five or six years.

SPECIAL PRIVILEGES

As long as the raja ruled in Cochin, the Jews had their own jurisdiction. In case of any litigation within the community, the decree was according to halakhah. All the minor complaints among them were settled by the five oldest men of the community who were fully versed in halakhah. In any serious cases, the senior members of the seven Jewish communities met and decided things. They had the approval of the Chief Rabbi to settle cases of marriage, divorce, etc. There were few litigations and practically no criminal cases among the Jews. So one or two cases that did happen were excused by the government.

One case happened in this way. It must have been less than one hundred and fifty years ago, in the time when Eliya Roby was leader of the Paradesi Jews. He belonged to the great family of Rahabis, descendants of Ezekiel Rahabi, who came to Cochin a long time before.

At this time a crazy fellow from one of the other Jewish communities got into a Christian church, pulled out a statue, and dragged it along the public road. When he was nearly caught, he put it into the fire on which food was being cooked for the death anniversary of someone. The food became polluted under the Jewish law and had to be thrown away. All the Christians of the state joined together and filed a suit for permission to retaliate by acting in the same way toward the synagogue. The case went to the High Court of Appeals and then to the *dewan*.

The *dewan* was a friend of Eliya Roby, who was a famous and popular man. Eliya Roby took the criminal to the *dewan*'s office. When he arrived by boat in Ernakulam from Cochin, there was no place for him to pass. The whole place from one end to the other end was filled with Christians just waiting for the word from the *dewan*'s office to start the riot. When they heard that Eliya Roby is come, they just moved apart to make room for him to pass through to the *dewan*'s court. As soon as he entered the *dewan*'s office, Eliya Roby asked him if there was a war in the palace and told him to look out of his window. When the *dewan* looked, he found a human flood. He got wild and sent out the order for the whole lot to get out of Ernakulam. Only two members from each Christian community were to stay. At this command, all fled.

Then Eliya Roby argued, "If one crazy man did a criminal act, why should the others be punished? You can kill him for his offense. If *you* don't kill him, *I* will kill him in front of you." So saying, he pulled out the slipper from the *dewan*'s foot and hit the fellow mercilessly till the *dewan* felt pity for him and stopped the beating. And so the case was settled without bloodshed.

When a Jew had to see any official, he never had to wait in line. Once it was brought to the official's notice that a Jew was waiting outside to see him, the prompt answer was, "Show him in," and most often the Jew did not come out empty-handed. Jews in government service did not have to work on Saturdays or on Jewish holidays. When there was a public examination on a Sabbath for matriculation or universities, the Jews were allowed to answer the paper on the night after the Sabbath. They were closeted in a room during the Sabbath day. The Jews and Muslims and those who came under the section of "backward classes" had to pay only half fees for the school.

But this state of affairs came to an end with the coming of Shunmukam Chetty as the *dewan* of Cochin. He was a foreigner from some other part of India. At that time, in 1930s, the *dewans* were sent by the central British government in Madras, instead of being appointed directly by the raja. The ruler of Cochin at that time was a weak raja. The new *dewan*'s argument was that he found the Jews all over Europe working on Saturdays and going to school on Saturdays, and he could not see why a small group of dark-skinned Jews in Cochin should be given all these privileges. The Jews' school fees were doubled and other privileges were taken away. Some people who could not do otherwise started working on Saturdays, and others resigned from their government jobs.

At about the same time, Mr. A. B. Salem, who was the first Jewish advocate in Cochin, was instrumental in the establishment of a State Legislative Council in Cochin. There were always one or two Jewish members in this council. Whenever there was a state dinner, kosher food was prepared for all.

Once when there was such a dinner, Mr. Salem took with him fifty skullcaps like the caps the Cochin Jewish men are accustomed to wear. Mr. Salem always wore one at meals. At that time people were wondering in Jew Town as to why Mr. Salem wanted so many caps, because he asked all the Jewish ladies in the Town to make a cap for him. So when everybody was seated at the dinner table, he took out a cap from his bundle and put it on his head. Then he took another one and put it on the head of the *dewan*, Shunmukam Chetty. When the others saw it, they all asked for one, and soon there were fifty members of the State Legislative Council sitting at the dinner table and eating, gleefully wearing Jewish skull caps. Then one of the members called out and said, "When Tippu Sultan wanted to convert Hindus to Islam he had to send his soldiers with a cap in one hand and a sword in the other. They called out, 'Either the cap on your head or your head in the cap.' So out of fear many Hindus converted to Islam. But when Mr. Salem wanted fifty people to put on the cap, he managed without instilling fear of death."

AFTER THE MAHARAJAS

After 1947 when India achieved independence from the British raj, all the maharajas were removed as rulers throughout India. In Kerala, their titles, their money, and their palaces were confiscated by the communist-minded people. A nominal pension was granted for life to the ruler who was the last in power.

Today there are hardly any Jews remaining in Kerala, as almost all have emmigrated to Israel. Only about thirty are still living in Jew Town Cochin.

Very recently the Cochin municipality wanted to join the main road in front of the old maharaja's palace with the main road at the back of it. So they decided to cut this road across the palace ground in the space between the palace and the wall separating the synagogue ground. But again the Hindu astrologers interfered. They said if such a road is made there will be a separation between the synagogue and the palace. They existed together for ages and if such a separation is made, some calamity will befall. The project was dropped.

When the Jews started emigrating to Israel, one of the Christian priests used to preach every Sunday in the church not to send all the Jews away and that if all the Jews leave, a calamity will befall the country. This reminded me of what happened in Fort Cochin over a hundred years ago, when a group of Jews went to live there near the sea and at the same time the sea went back and a beautiful beach was formed where there was no beach before. The people of that time believed that it was the Jews who brought this miracle. It may be a coincidence, but when nearly all of the Jews left Kerala, the sea rose up and that beach in Fort Cochin no longer remained. I have heard a similar thing about the health resort in Alwaye, where the Jews used to have houses on the hilltops. The Jews sold their houses and went away, and now it seems the water has nearly dried up, and what water remains is polluted and dirty. It is said that the whole land of Malabar rose up from the sea when King Parasurama threw his hatchet. If it ever happens that that piece of land sinks into the sea as it rose up, I suppose the Jews again will be seen as the culprits!

After most of the Jews came to Israel from Cochin, their property was bought by Muslim merchants. So these merchants requested the municipality to change the name Jew Town into Muslim Town. But the municipality refused, saying that the name Jew Town will remain forever as a symbol that the Jews were staying here for so many hundreds of years.

Part Three

OUR TUNES ARE VERY SACRED TO US: SONGS AND CELEBRATIONS OF THE COCHIN JEWS

Chapter 11

JEWISH FESTIVALS IN COCHIN

When I think about my childhood, I like to remember the way we celebrated all the Jewish Festivals. For Feasts and Shabbat we had everything on the table, and we were very happy. When my grandfather was living in Fort Cochin, teaching Hebrew to the Koder children and working as the *shoḥet* there, sometimes he could come to Jew Town only for Festivals and other special occasions. How happy we would all be when he arrived! For us, that was when the Festival began. People in the neighborhood said, "When we see Eliyahu Kaka [Uncle] getting down from the rickshaw, then the whole Town has the Festival feeling."

We celebrated our Feasts and Sabbaths and other ceremonies with great freedom. The Jews got on well with Hindus, Muslims, and Christians, one helping the other in case of emergency. One never interfered with the religious practice of the other. The women lent to one another jewelry for weddings and Feasts. On Sabbath days and Feast days, no outsider was allowed to come into Jew Town carrying an umbrella, because the Jews did not use an umbrella on a Sabbath or on a Feast day, rain or shine.

All the Festivals were celebrated two days, as is customary for Jews in the Diaspora. It was the Sephardi prayer books that we used, imported from Livorno, Amsterdam, and other places. All these books have been with us for more than a hundred years. The tunes for a given prayer vary for different Feasts. Unless people hear the correct tune, they don't feel as if they are celebrating that particular Feast.

The Jews of Cochin enjoyed full freedom inside Jew Town. They did not go out to other parts of the city to show off how they were celebrating, unlike the Christians and Muslims, who went out in processions carrying their statues of saints on the backs of elephants, with music and bands. The Jews knew their place and kept it honorably, I think.

ḤANUKKAH*

Ḥanukkah, the Feast of Lights, is celebrated for eight days and nights. Each night we light oil lamps, not candles. Our family had a big brass lamp with spoon-shaped sections, where we put the wicks to light. It was a very nice lamp, decorated at the back with engraving, but the engravings were worn from so much cleaning. Some families used glasses with oil floating on top of water. The lamp would be put away and brought out only for Ḥanukkah.

When I was small, Grandfather used to light the Ḥanukkah lamp. I remember he would hold me on his arm and make me light it with him. After the eight days I will start crying, "I want to light again!" I will cry and cry. So on the next night after Ḥanukkah, he would put all the remaining wicks together in one place and let me light them.

At the time of Ḥanukkah we have good weather in Cochin—not very hot and not very cold. That's the time people like to get married, because there will be no rain.

Every night during Ḥanukkah a few people would join together and have a party in one house or another in the Town, a different house every night. People shared the expenses and made some snacks—such as a small roasted fish stuffed with onions and chilies—and toddy and other things too. This was the time the ladies would sing and dance around in a circle clapping their hands and keeping time with their feet. The ladies and girls from Kadavumbagam Synagogue particularly enjoyed these songs and dances, and we liked to join in their parties. On such occasions we sang many of the Malayalam Jewish songs, all the ladies and girls bringing their songbooks to the party. As I have written, my birthday was on the first of the month of Tebet during Ḥanukkah, so in our house we always had a party on the seventh night.

There was a learned man years ago in Cochin named Nehemiah Motha, who died on the first day of Ḥanukkah. The Jews from Kadavumbagam and Tekkumbagam celebrate his death anniversary on that day with a large Feast, at the expense of the synagogue or at the expense of someone who made a vow. It was believed by many that he had some power of wonderwork. He came from Yemen, and he composed the hymn "Norah," which is sung in Cochin during Yom Kippur prayers.

*BJ: Ruby Daniel begins her account of the Jewish holidays in Cochin with Ḥanukkah rather than Rosh Hashanah, the New Year. When the JPS editor questioned this, I phoned Ruby in Israel to ask why. "I suppose because I was born at Ḥanukkah. Before that I didn't know any holidays," she replied with a smile in her voice. "But I don't mind if you change it." I told her that I like the way her arrangement builds up to the celebration of Simḥat Torah as the high point of the year, and she added, "Yes, if you begin with Rosh Hashanah, you must end with Tisha b'Ab!" So we will begin with Ḥanukkah.

The occasion on which he composed "Norah" was when his teacher died. His teacher was a very learned man called "Valiya Achan" (Big Master), who belonged to the Paradesi community. He and Nehemiah Motha had a falling out, due to some disagreement. Nehemiah Motha had divorced his wife because she disobeyed his instructions, but since her disobedience came through a misunderstanding, the teacher thought she was not to be blamed and tried to stop Motha from the divorce procedure. But he did not obey Valiya Achan. Then the teacher gave instructions that this pupil of his should not be allowed to touch his body even when he died. When Valiya Achan died, Nehemiah Motha was very grieved, so he composed this hymn and followed the funeral of his teacher, reading this lamentation.

Nehemiah Motha's tomb is the only one that still stands in the old Cochin cemetery. When someone is very sick, people make vows to paint the tomb and light a lamp there if the person is healed. Even the gentiles believe in his power, so this tomb is spared and preserved till this day. This cemetery is about seven hundred years old, and all the other tombs near it are razed to the ground.

PURIM

The whole week of Purim had a festive feeling in Jew Town. Every evening the Jewish boys would cut branches of trees and carry them in a procession from the Paradesi Synagogue at one end of the Town to the Kadavumbagam Synagogue at the other end. Three times they would go, and at the end of the third procession they would beat the branches on the steps of the synagogue. Whatever day of the week Purim comes, from the previous Saturday evening they would start these processions. On their way through the Town they sang loudly, one group singing "*Ale falleso*" and the others answering "*Aleso!*"—or so it sounded to me when I was young. I thought the song meant "All the enemies of Israel should fall, as did Haman." In later years nobody knew what this custom was all about. They said "*Alipiliso aliso*" instead and called out the names of people in the Town, as a joke. My grandfather said that the correct words were "*Ale falleso*," but he also was not sure what they meant.

The families would send sweets to one another. My father used to give me a small plate with fruits to give to a few families. And people would sometimes give presents of money to the children. Mr. Salem used to give new coins from the bank to the children in every house.

One time years ago, the people in the Town made a drama in Hebrew about Purim. It was a success. But it seems the one who acted as Esther became a leper soon after, and the one who acted as Haman became mad and stood with folded hands as he had stood before the hangman's rope. The one who acted as Ahashverosh became a drunkard. What other things happened to them I don't know.

On the eve of Purim we would read the Megillat Esther (the scroll of Esther) in our house. My grandfather, his friends Nissim and Barak, my father, and my uncle were there, at the time that I remember. All the grandchildren and the neighbors' children came and sat round with all kinds of instruments—they said to kill Haman. Everyone wanted something which would make more noise than their friends, to obliterate the name of Haman. We would go on hitting—some on the floor, some on the table or chair—wherever it would make more noise. It was enough to dim the names of Haman, Ahashverosh, Mordecai, Vashti, *and* Esther. In fact, the whole *megillah*!

My grandfather himself wrote the *megillah* from which he read on Purim. He prepared the leather himself—perhaps from a goat which he killed—and sewed all the pieces together, then wrote it all in big letters so it was easy to read. That same *megillah* is here on the kibbutz now. After he died, my uncle Daniel took it away with him. When my uncle visited us here in the kibbutz for the Bar Mitzvah of my nephew Daniel, he saw that there were a few people here praying regularly, so he sent it back to the kibbutz, in memory of his father.

I remember how the Muslim gentleman next door to us in Cochin enjoyed our celebration of Purim. He sat at the veranda of his house, from where he could see what was going on in our house. After my grandfather died, we did not read the *megillah* in the house. It so happened that there was always sickness in the house that year. So that Muslim gentleman said to my mother, "Soon after that old man died you stopped celebrating the Feast. Why did you not make Purim in the house this year? Do you see all the sickness in the house?" Perhaps he must have thought that we had been exorcising devils from the house by making all that noise.

On Purim day itself, an intruder could not complain, whatever happened to him in Jew Town at the hands of the Jews. On that day the Jews got drunk till they could not distinguish between Haman and Mordecai. If nothing else, they poured red paint to symbolize Haman's blood on everyone passing the street, Jew or gentile.

It happened one Purim day, some years ago, when the Jews were celebrating the Feast of Esther, that an Anglo-Indian came into the town. The Anglo-Indians also like to drink and sing and dance. He was welcomed by the people, given food and drink, and made happy. As he was leaving, one of the mischievous boys took his hat, filled it with all good food, and handed it to him to take home for his family. It was a great insult to him. So he went straight to the magistrate and complained that the Jews had disgraced him. The magistrate, who was well acquainted with their pranks and who very often was their guest, sent the Anglo-Indian away, saying that first of all he had

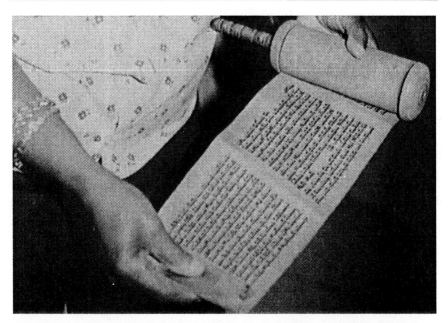

The *Megillat Esther* (Purim scroll) made and written by Ruby's grandfather, Eliyahu Japheth. (*Photo, Barbara Johnson*)

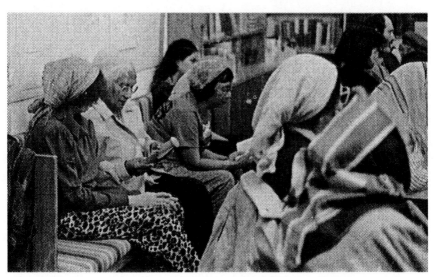

Purim, 1990, Kibbutz Neot Mordecai. Ruby reading from her grandfather's *megillah*. To her right, Lillian David; to her left, Raḥel Kala. (*Photo, Barbara Johnson*)

Ruby rewinding the *megillah*, with the help of Lillian David, Purim, 1990.
(*Photo, Barbara Johnson*)

Purim celebration, Israeli style. Ruby with her nephew, Ari Kala, and his wife, Dina, in costume; Kibbutz Neot Mordecai, 1990. (*Photo, Barbara Johnson*)

no business there. But anyway, since he had enjoyed the Jews' food and drinks, he had to take their jokes too.

There is a Malayalam song which the women would sing to recount the story of Esther and Mordecai:

AHASHVEROSHINDA PATTU

1
The One who knows all from the beginning—
During the reign of Ahashverosh this happened.
The cursed Haman and the righteous Mordecai
Went to fight in someone's country.

All the money was wasted by Haman.
When the money was finished, more money was requested from many
   people.
Nobody gave it to the cursed Haman.
It was requested from the righteous Mordecai.

2

"If you sign a bond of slavery, the money shall be given," said
   Mordecai.
The bond was put in writing and Haman got the money.
The cursed Haman nurtured his anger against Mordecai.
The cursed Haman went to Ahashverosh.
"A certain nation should be humiliated one day.
For this I will give ten thousand gidhal* of silver," said Haman.
Consent was given by Ahashverosh.
The decree was announced in writing by the cursed Haman.

3

Letters, written on *ola* [palm leaf], were sent to each place.
The letter for one particular place went to another place.
The cursed Haman was outwitted.
In sleep a *ḥalom* [dream] came to the righteous Mordecai.
Shaken, he awoke, sitting up in pain.
He put on sackcloth and besmeared himself with ashes.
He fell on the earth crying.
Eliyahu Hanabi appeared in the garden.
Mordecai got up and wished him "Shalom."

4

He inquired about what was going on in heaven,
And what judgment had been decided upon there.
"Is the decree signed in mud or in blood?"†
The judgment was signed in mud.
At once Mordecai sent for Queen Esther.
She came painfully, in distress.
"What is the reason for summoning me?"
"There wasn't any reason to call for you," he said.

5

"Your nation is doomed to be killed," said Mordecai.
"What can I do about it?" asked Esther.

*The meaning is unknown. Perhaps a gidhal was the currency of Persia at the time.
†If it was signed in mud, it could be changed.

"In haste you have to go to the king," said Mordecai.
"How can I go when it is not my time to do so?" asked Esther.
Mordecai did not care.
Young men, women, and children prostrated in prayer and fasted
    three days.

6

With her hair arranged beautifully, wearing the golden crown,
Queen Esther went.
While walking up and down in the garden,
She came in sight of King Ahashverosh.
He waved the scepter and called out:
"Beautiful Esther, melting in beauty, have you come? Who told you to
    come?"
"It was not because anyone told me that I came," she said.

7

"Haman and his children should be given a dinner," she said.
"Do all that you wish, Esther," said Ahashverosh.
At once she went and prepared for the dinner.
While preparing for the dinner, Haman was invited.
Haman and his children came to the dinner.
"Haman and his children who dined with us today
Should come tomorrow also to dinner," said Esther.
Then Zeresh (Haman's wife) started to worry, thinking,
"There is some reason for this dinner!"

8

The next day they also went to dine.
After eating and drinking, the beautiful couch was arranged.
On that beautiful bed Haman lay down.
The proof of this was attested and signed by Queen Esther, who reflected
    thus:
"In the past he ordered Vashti to be killed.
Now did he order to kill me too?"

9

The right of power over them should be given into her hands.
Authority was given.
Haman had shrewdly built many houses.
All the houses he built went to Mordecai,

All those houses which Haman had hoped to have for himself.
But Haman forgot the One God.
The gallows for hanging Mordecai, which were built by Haman, can be
    seen.
Haman was hung on them.
Blessed be God forever and ever.

PASSOVER

When I was a child, the Feast of *Pesaḥ*, or Passover, was an elaborate affair, starting with the cleaning up right after Purim. During *Pesaḥ* the Jews
could not eat any food which was *ḥametz* (leavened). This meant that we had
to clean the entire house and any utensils which were to be used for *Pesaḥ*.
Any *ḥametz* remaining in the house had to be removed. Many families have
a separate set of utensils, from plates to pots, for Passover. We had a smaller
house, separate from the one where we usually stayed. After Purim we lived
in that house, so grandmother had a free hand to do what she wanted, with
the help of servants and the older girls of the family. We children had the an-
nual examination in the schools about that time, so when I was in school I
was safe from this manual labor.

Grandmother would buy whole coffee, spices for cooking, coconut, and of
course rice paddy with the skin on. All of this had to be cleaned so there was
no *ḥametz* in it. The coffee was washed, dried, then baked and powdered.
Spices like coriander, chilies, and turmeric had to be washed, dried, broiled,
and ground. To prepare salt, we had to wash pieces of salt and keep it for
one or two days, till all the mud sinks to the bottom, and then we filter the
salt off the top and cook it into granules. One *Pesaḥ* my aunt did all this and
put the salt on the roof to dry in a bamboo sieve. In the evening she forgot
to take it, and the whole night it was raining! The next morning, when she
looked, there was no salt at all, so she had to do all the work again. Then
when she went up to take the salt, there was wheat on top of it, maybe brought
by the wind or by a crow, so she had to throw it out again. The third time
she did it, it was all right.

Then came the process of cleaning the rice. All this was done with the help
of a mortar and pestle, kept separate for Passover. We had a big stone, thick
and high, with a cavity in the middle. The pestle was made of a thick and
long piece of wood. One end had an iron cap and on the other an iron ring.
The former one was used for grinding and the latter for separating the rice
from the husk and polishing. Fortunately, the Cochin Jews eat rice during
Passover, so we would keep all this rice flour ready for making cakes and all
kinds of pastries during *Pesaḥ*.

Each family had to clean their well for *Pesaḥ*. Two people go down into the well to draw the water out; then they cover it with a bamboo mat so no *ḥametz* will fall in. My Dolly Aunty was the one to get down in the well, while the others would stand on the side, and she would pass the bucket up. Our well was a little bit small and very deep. I would be the last person to go down into that well! (The well is used as a *mikveh* or ritual bath, for the bride, and I told my mother, "If I ever get married, don't ask me to go in the well.") One of the Muslim girls living in the next house was so mischievous. She knew we don't eat sugar for *Pesaḥ*, so one year she brought sugar and threw it in the well. Then we had to clean the well again.

Special preparations had to be made for the unleavened bread (matzot), which is eaten during the eight days of Passover. Some Jews went to the fields and reaped the wheat harvest themselves and preserved it till the next *Pesaḥ*. Then they sold it for making the unleavened bread. For the seder plate we made special cakes from this *shemorah* (guarded) wheat. These matzot, called *sedarim* because they were used for the seder meal on the first two nights, were made separately from the regular matzot, and every *shemorah* cake was made from a quarter kilogram of flour.

Some days before the making of matzot and *shemorah*, the wheat was sorted out and ground in a grinding stone. The grinding stone was put on a white cloth, and two men sat on both sides to turn the stone. I remember my grandmother stood with a towel in her hand to wipe off the perspiration from their faces, and she would not allow them to open their mouths to talk, fearing that their perspiration or their spittle might fall into the flour. If any moisture touched the flour, it could not be used for making matzot. Grandma and other ladies then separated the husk with the help of a tray made of thin bamboo mat. Then they separated semolina from the flour. The semolina would be separated into two kinds—fine and thick. They usually made the seder cakes with fine semolina. From the rest they made matzot.

Regular matzot were made the week before *Pesaḥ*, but the six cakes for two nights of the seder were made only on the day before Passover after the burning of whatever *ḥametz* was found at the end of the cleaning. While making the *sedarim*, some people blew the shofar and sang parts of the Haggadah, commemorating the Exodus from Egypt. At least it was done so in my house by my grandparents from both sides. All this was a prolonged affair in our house, because people who were unable to take all the trouble at home brought their flour to our house to make their *shemorah* matzot there. The water was kept in a clay pot overnight to make the dough.

Six women would make the *shemorah* matzot. First these ladies washed themselves and put on clean clothes. As far back as I can remember, Grandfather made the dough with just enough water. He divided it into six por-

Women making matzot for Passover in Jew Town, Cochin, 1981; (*from left*) Gladys
Koder, Abigail Joseph Hai, Fiona Hallegua. (*Photo, Barbara Johnson*)

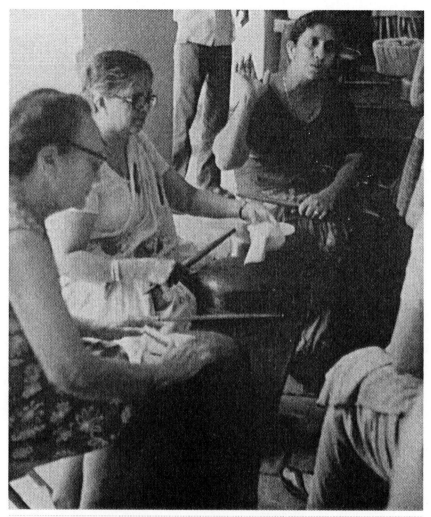

Women rolling matzot for Passover with brass rollers, 1981; (*from left*) Lily Koder, Saru Elias, Abigail Joseph Hai. (*Photo, Barbara Johnson*)

tions or seven. Before it was divided, a lady said a blessing, removed a handful the size of an egg from it (called *ḥallah*) and burned it in the fire. The six women stood near a board made of copper plated with zinc, each with a rolling pin made of brass with tinkling brass bells inside. When they rolled the matzot, the bells made a beautiful sound like music. (I still have one of these brass rolling pins from my house. They were used only for *Pesaḥ*.)

Each portion was given to one of the women, and together they finished the six. Then because these *shemorah* matzot should not be burnt or broken, as a precaution they made an extra one.

Grandmother did the finishing touches. First of all, she made sure that all cakes were of the same size; then she pierced them with a fork but not making any holes. Then she made lines on each one like a diamond shape. On the first she put two small lines on the side, on the next three lines, and then on the next four lines, standing for Cohen, Levi, and Israel. These three cakes were to be put on the seder plate in that order. Before the service starts, the middle one—Levi—is broken into two pieces, and one piece is kept away for the *afikoman* (dessert matzah) which is eaten after the meals in remembrance of the paschal lamb. For our house the *shemorah* for the seder plate had to be made double—twelve instead of six—because we put two seder plates on the table, one at each end. Not only were we a big family, we also had a number of guests.

The children were not allowed to touch the dough. I was small so my job was to stand there with a tray made of bamboo mat covered with a white cloth. If they bought a new piece of cloth, it had to be washed and dried before use. When one cake was finished, Grandma put it on the tray and covered it with one end of the cloth so the sun wouldn't come on it when it was carried to the kitchen, which was a few steps away from the house. I was so proud to carry it to the kitchen. My father and Aunty Seema were there to bake it. Aunty was very fair, and I remember how her face would be red from the heat.

Six clay pots were made hot beforehand, and as soon as the cake arrived it was put on the hot tray. These clay pots were specially ordered with flat bottoms from the potters. Those who baked the cake had a small bundle of cloth with which they pushed down any bubbles that might appear on the cake. After the baking, each cake was carefully examined to see if all the parts around were done well. Then it was spread on a table to cool and then put away.

How they did all this work! After making the *shemorah* matzot on the eve of Passover, then they had to clean everything and dry it and put it away. The utensils are all *ḥametz* afterwards. (They won't use them for *Pesaḥ*.) Only then would Grandmother start cooking for the evening, for the seder meal.

From the time I can remember, our house is full for *Pesaḥ*. Our relatives would come, along with in-laws and neighbors who had no men in the house to conduct the seder. The table was very long, to accommodate all of them. Grandfather sat at one end, my father at the other end, both dressed nicely in white shirts. And my grandmother dressed as she would for the synagogue, with a white blouse with tinsel on the sides and neck, and a scarf on her head. Until she comes to stand by him, Grandfather will not start the seder. That is what I remember.

A Passover seder held by Ruby's family at Kibbutz Neot Mordecai in the 1970s, with Bingley Daniel presiding. (*Photo, Dan Kala*)

Ḥag HaShavuot: The Feast of Pentecost

After the Feast of Passover, the Feast of Pentecost, or *Shavuot*, seems obscure, though it is a very important Feast as the day of receiving the Torah. Usually people start preparing for Passover just after Purim, which falls a month before, worrying about cleaning up, getting rid of *hametz*, making matzot, and all the rest of the work. But for Ḥag HaShavuot there is no such

Ruby's nephew Daniel Kala and her sister, Raḥel, read from the Passover Haggadah at a family seder, Kibbutz Neot Mordecai, 1973. (*Photo, Dan Kala*)

excitement. It starts in the evening and finishes by next evening here in Israel, and two days in Cochin, as elsewhere in the Diaspora.

In Malabar this is the rainy season and the season for the jackfruit, a huge fruit with many small sections, very sweet and tasty. Most of the families used to buy this fruit, and they would throw out the thick skins. I remember the skins floating in the rainwater on the sides of the road. Very often, when the Jews go to the synagogue for *Shavuot*, they go in the rain. As they never carried an umbrella on Shabbat or Feast days, so most of the people took a blanket or something to cover the head and body. Raincoats were not in fashion then.

In the synagogue they read the *Pesukim*, which is the six hundred and thirteen commandments. The first part is the commandments one has to do and the next part is the commandments one should not do. Usually the young boys read them, three or two sentences in turn, and if anyone makes a mistake they call him all the way home "*kuthukolle*," meaning "the one who made a mistake." The boys were so ashamed to be called this, so they tried their best not to make a mistake.

When the prayers are over and they start singing "*Ein k'Eloheinu*" with a nice tune, at that time they throw sweets all around for the children, and everybody picks them up. In the Paradesi Synagogue, they used to get big pieces of sugar candy and big pieces of other sweets, and they threw it from above and from downstairs. They are quite wild. Finally, they hurt people, and they broke some lamps in the synagogue, so they stopped it in the Paradesi Synagogue, but in the other communities they still did it.

After the afternoon *minḥah* prayers, they read the Book of Ruth, half of it on the first day and the next half on the second day. It is a happy holiday. In Kefar Yuval, the Cochin village near my kibbutz, they still throw sweets on *Ḥag HaShavuot*, so I always buy some sweets and take them whenever I go there for the Feast.

THE FAST OF THE NINTH OF AB

The ninth day of the month of Ab is a day of twenty-five hours of fasting and lamenting in memory of the destruction of both the First and the Second Temples of worship in Jerusalem and the dispersion of the Jews. For some unknown reason, the Cochin Jews called that day "*Seerya*."

In Cochin the first nine days of the month of Ab are days of mourning. We did not eat meat on those days. The *shoḥet* puts away his knife till the end of the ninth day. People did not dress well, and no weddings or any other celebration took place. Those nine days were considered to be a bad time for the Jews. It was said that you should not go to dangerous places or leave the children alone, or an old man called "*Seeriya Mutha*" would come after you.

The Jews had special games for that season, at the beginning of Ab. The men used to gamble with a special kind of coconut. It had a thick shell, small and oblong in size. They threw it up and when it fell down it was broken into pieces. They count the pieces and if the number is according to that they specified beforehand, they win. Or they put the coconut on a stone and guess how many pieces it will be broken into. They keep one palm on the back of the other palm and hit the coconut with both hands. Sometimes the coconut is broken into very small pieces and they count them. I think it is a show of strength. They say that it is showing how the Jews fought with one another, and their heads rolled.

One rich family gave small coconuts to children to play with. Another family sent to all the Jewish families of the Town a sort of porridge made of rice, coconut, and a kind of red beans, which would be eaten only during the first nine days of Ab.

The ladies and girls usually played a game called *aasha* during that season. We made circles on a piece of plank, something like the game called *damka*. *Aasha* is played with twelve small shells for each of the two players. You throw five larger cowrie shells with one of them broken on the back, and you move the shells according to the number you get from the throw.

We did not take this game very seriously then. It was just a board game like many other board games. But recently Mr. Koder of Cochin gave an old *aasha* board to someone from the Israel Museum in Jerusalem. They put it in their catalog, which came to the attention of Dr. Irving Finkel, an Assyriologist from the British Museum in London. The British Museum has collected a number of game boards from archaeological sites all over the world. One of these game boards which was found in Ur Kasdin (the country where Father Abraham was born) had some similarity to this Cochin game of *aasha*. Though the boards were found, no rules were found.

Dr. Finkel thought that this royal game from Ur must have gone with the Jews who escaped to South India from Babylon. By looking for someone who knows how to play this game of *aasha*, they found me in Israel. I left Cochin forty-one years ago, and nobody has played this game since! There are only two or three of us left now from the old generation. So I gave all the rules of the above game to Dr. Finkel for the book he is writing of all the games they found.

In those days we used to say that the twelve shells for *aasha* represent the twelve tribes of Israel, who fought each other, and the five shells represent the fifth month of the Hebrew calendar, which is the month of Ab. But recently I was reading the story of King Shaul and King David. When Shaul died in the war with the Philistines, the kingdom should go to his son, but there were others who wanted it to be given to David. So Shaul's commander in chief—Abner—and Yoab—the commander in chief of David—stood up for their masters. Both these men were helped by twelve great men each, and there was a great fight between these two sides when many people died. Perhaps this game of twelve killing each other is in memory of that. I am not sure.

In Cochin the Jews would begin their fast on the eve of *Seerya*, the Ninth of Ab, and fast for twenty-five hours, as on Yom Kippur. My grandfather, who used to sleep on a bed with double mattress, slept that night on the floor on a mat and a piece of stone as the headrest.

In the synagogue they put a black curtain for the *heykhal*, the Ark where the Torah scrolls are kept. It was removed only at ten o'clock in the morning after the morning prayers. They read *Kinot* (Lamentations) in the synagogue in the evening and again in the morning. Some of the people used to shed tears when they read the Lamentations. They deserved to see the creation of Israel more than we.

None of us wore shoes on that day. Those people who are not used to walking barefoot did not go home from the synagogue till evening. They stayed in the synagogue reading the book of Job. They did not sleep or read anything else during that time. In our house we sat on mats on the floor, and the house was swept only in the evening.

After the morning prayers, people in Jew Town brought sacks of rice with the husk on and threw rice from the upstairs onto the courtyard of the synagogue, where the native poor people collected it. I wonder why they spread it then instead of handing it to the poor, as was usually done.

For breaking the fast, we made something special. Rice flour dough is spread on a kind of leaf. They put coconut cooked in jaggery on the dough and fold the leaves, and then it is steamed. Jaggery is unrefined sugar, brown in color, whereas for happy occasions we used white sugar only.

But even at this solemn season, there were people in Jew Town ready to make a joke. Many years ago this happened. There was a man who had a servant called Shomron, an ignorant and innocent boy. On the Ninth of Ab the men divided the portions of *Kinot* to be read in the synagogue by each person, and it fell to this master's turn to read the *Kinah* which started with the word "Shomron." Some of the mischievous boys in the Town thought this was a good chance to play a trick on that servant boy named Shomron.

They called the boy aside and told him, "Did you see, your master is starving since the night, and in the morning at about nine o'clock he will call out to you to bring him something to eat and drink. So better be ready with coffee and wait in the *azarah* (the entrance room of the synagogue). As soon as he calls out to you, run to him with the coffee. Otherwise, he will be very angry with you, because he is starving."

Those men were so religious and devoted, when they read the *Kinot*, they used to cry and scream. This poor servant boy did as he was told and waited outside. Suddenly he heard his master calling out his name screaming, "Shomron!" So he took the coffee and ran inside, saying, "Oh Sir! Here is coffee ready! Don't scream, drink it!" The whole synagogue burst out in laughter, forgetting their grief.

SELIḤOT

Beginning on the first day of the month of Elul we prepared for Rosh Hashanah (New Year) and Yom Kippur (Day of Atonement) with forty days of *Seliḥot*, special prayers which were said in the night. Every night (with the exception of Sabbath nights and Rosh Hashanah) we would get up at three o'clock and read the *seliḥot* prayers. I remember hearing the *shamash* of the synagogue as he went from house to house in the street calling out the names of the older men to wake them and call them to the synagogue. The young- sters wanted to hear their names called too, so sometimes a boy would give the *shamash* a bit of money, asking him to also call out his name for *seliḥot*.

The synagogue was a little far away, so the women prayed in the house. My grandmother's tunes and the way she read was much better than a *haz- zan*. So we the grandchildren liked it, and all of us got up with her at three A.M. and read the prayers with her in a high pitch.

ROSH HASHANAH

This New Years Day is supposed by the Jews to be a day of reckoning, and unlike the gentile New Year, it is celebrated religiously. One should not sleep on that day, as the spirit will then go to heaven and sign the document of the reckoning of one's sins. Then it would be impossible to change it and will be an established fact. The Cochin Jews referred to this day as *Yom Ha-din*, the Day of Judgment. Grandmother used to drive us mad saying, "Rosh Hashanah is coming. *Yom Ha-din*. Take care of the children, that they don't get sick." As if God is coming or something, *Yom Ha-din* is coming. She makes the whole Town shiver.

On the eve of Rosh Hashanah after the blessing on the wine, we sat at the table and recited blessings on all kinds of fruits, fish, and on the head of a lamb. Then we read the rules of Rosh Hashanah. After the meal the men read the Psalms before they went to bed. Then we got up at three A.M. and read the *bakashot* prayers. One can hear this coming out of every Jewish house in the Town. As early as 5:30 we went to the synagogue for the morning prayers.

The *musaf* prayer for Rosh Hashanah is a long one with protracted tunes and the blowing of the shofar. The morning prayers end with the blowing of the shofar a hundred and one times. After lunch we would sit reading the Psalms, either in the house or at the synagogue. If there is a house where someone had died that year they invited people and read the Psalms there and they are served a hot drink and cakes. For this day we usually made a special drink instead of coffee and tea. Coriander seeds and cumin seeds are boiled together in water, and a little cardamon, cloves, and cinnamon are added; then it is served hot with sugar. A very good idea—good for health and it is also tasty.

On Rosh Hashanah like all the Feasts, it was permitted to make fire to cook the food but forbidden to put the fire out. If this Feast falls on Friday, usually on that day we kept an *erub*—a piece of bread with a piece of cooked meat—with a blessing and then it was permitted to cook the food for Shabbat on Friday.

The clothes we wore on Rosh Hashanah were mostly white with a little sprinkling of other colors, specially red. We did not usually enter the prayer hall with sandals on. But shoes are allowed, as it is a sign of respect because the rulers wore shoes.

Yom Kippur

The days between the New Year and Yom Kippur are supposed to be days of repentance (*Yeme Teshuvah*). On the morning of Yom Kippur eve the men go to the synagogue for a ceremony called *Malkot Arbaim* (forty blows), in which they would be hit on the back with leather thongs in a certain way, perhaps forty times, for repentance. Some men take a ritual bath before going to the synagogue in the evening. Also before going to the synagogue, people would go to one another's house in the neighborhood and kiss the hands or bend to kiss the feet of the elderly or those who are older than themselves, begging to be forgiven.

Everybody dressed themselves in white attire, and women wore white clothes with tinsel work and adorned themselves with jewelry. Some people wore the embroidered white clothes that they had prepared for their death, in which they were to be buried.

On the Eve of Kippur before beginning the twenty-five hours of fasting, we had a sumptuous meal prepared with chicken and rice and other foods, like a Feast day. From that time we would not eat or drink until the next night. Even very old people were carried to the synagogue on their beds, and they also fasted. They bade the people not to give them drink or food, even if they happened to be unconscious and cry for food.

The evening prayers start at 5:30 P.M. and conclude at about eight o'clock. The *Kol Nidrei* prayer was conducted always by the eldest male member of the community. Unless we are in time to hear this prayer we feel as if we did not observe Yom Kippur. If one does not hear that, he is not released from the previous year's vows. After the evening prayers, the women, children, and old men go home. The rest stay in the synagogue reading Psalms and other prayers, some of them all through the night.

All the light in the synagogue came from glass lamps in which flames burned in glasses half-filled or quarter-filled with water and then filled with oil. A wick was made from cotton wool twisted around a kind of thin grass stems, and this wick is pushed into a tripod made of tin or copper and put into the glass with a small part of it above the oil to burn. On Yom Kippur there were a thousand of these lights, and care had to be taken that the lights were not blown out by the wind. They used coconut oil for burning these lights.

For Yom Kippur there also used to be six candlesticks, very thick and tall, stuck into a brass stand. These were lighted in the evening before and lasted till the end of Yom Kippur Day, even after the oil lamps became dim. Those were placed in front of the *bimah* (pulpit) in the synagogue. Sometimes a candle would bend and lose its balance and so fall down. Then they had to fetch the help of gentile servants to put it right. They had the superstitious belief that if one of these candles falls, there will be a death of an elder man in the community that year. Very often it happened. When an old man died they brought these candles and burned them at the head and foot of the bed where the body lay in state. The lighting of candles in the synagogue was stopped when electricity was introduced. A few people died that year, and those who had opposed the abolition of this custom grumbled. These candles were used in the Paradesi Synagogue only. I think that it was copied from some synagogues in Europe.

For Yom Kippur day, the morning prayer starts at five A.M. and continues till one o'clock and people sit reading *pizmonim* (hymns) till two o'clock, when the afternoon prayers start. This ends at seven P.M. There were some people who didn't sit down the whole day. Anyway there was very little time to sit, as most of the prayers should be said while standing.

It is very hot on that day inside the synagogue. The floor around it is paved with granite stones and no trees around, so the heat comes up specially in the afternoon. There were no electric fans till electricity was introduced into the synagogue not very long ago. A gentile servant used to pour water over the granite pavement around the synagogue to keep the heat down the whole afternoon. No snuff or smelling salts were used unless someone felt very faint. It was the custom on Yom Kippur, before the Cohen goes up to recite a blessing during the *mehila* prayers, the Levites poured rose water on the hands of the Cohens. Then some people would wet their handkerchief with the rose water that remains and smell or apply on their forehead.

The five prayers during the day were conducted by five elderly men with two youngsters to help them with those parts recited in tunes. We did not have a hired *hazzan* to sweat it out the whole day, and the prayers are too long for one man to conduct it. We had special tunes for this Feast. Very often the youngsters learn the tunes from the women, who could sing better than the men. The women also sang in high-pitched voices together with the men, though they always sat separate, either upstairs or on a veranda or separate room of the synagogue. If they had been given the green light, these ladies would have confidently climbed up the pulpit to conduct the service.

I remember a European bishop who was posted in Fort Cochin. Every Yom Kippur day as long he was in Cochin he came to the synagogue in the morning and stayed till the evening. I don't think anybody bothered to ask him why he did it.

People used to say that Yom Kippur is also a day of rejoicing. Torah was given the first time on Mount Sinai on that day. It was then the Hebrews worshiped the golden calf and Moses threw down the tablet of the Ten Commandments. It is to atone for that sin that we observe Yom Kippur. I did not hear this explanation anywhere else but in Cochin. A lady living here in Israel, who is a convert, asked me once why every year Jews observe this day. How much have we sinned that every year we have to confess even the sins we have not committed that year? She was satisfied when I explained to her what I had heard, about Moses' throwing down the tablet when he saw the Hebrews worshiping the golden calf, which was the greatest sin against God. To atone for this sin, we have to observe this day forever, I explained to her. She said that then she understood the meaning of this observance.

Some people make a vow to provide wine for the blessing before breaking the fast, which is enough for the whole congregation to quench the thirst. They usually made this wine—called *mai*—by boiling currants in water and filtering it. There is no alcohol in it. Some people would not drink at the synagogue because they want to break the fast from their own provision.

When the prayers were finished, those who were not able to do so the night before would kiss the hands or feet of the elderly people and ask forgiveness, either before they left the synagogue or when visiting the houses after breaking the fast.

Yom Kippur was said to be the day when the dead were wandering about, especially in the synagogue. Many stories are told of ghosts which were seen in the Town at that time. I have heard one story about my grandmother Rivka, my father's mother, who died long before I was born.

The Paradesi Synagogue was a little far away, at the northern end of the Town, while our house was in the middle of the Town. On Yom Kippur eve, everyone was rushing to the synagogue to be in time for the *Kol Nidrei* prayer. After sending the children and the grandchildren, Grandmother was the last to leave, as is usual with the housewives. In those days there were only Jews living in the neighborhood, and all of them had gone to the synagogue. There were a few shops of non-Jews, and during Yom Kippur and Shabbat they had no business, so they closed up earlier and went home. The Town was practically deserted.

It so happened on that particular day, when my grandmother Rivka arrived at the synagogue, she found out that she had forgotten her spectacles. It would be a tragedy if she cannot read the prayers. Then she saw there was time enough to run to the house and get her glasses. So she went in a hurry to the house, opened it, and found her glasses on the table in the hall, where she had put them. She took them and when she turned to go out, she saw a woman in a white dress at the doorway, as if going to kiss the mezuzzah. Grandma was so frightened that she could not even scream. It would not help her anyway. There was no one in the vicinity to hear her. So she collected all her courage and pleaded with the phantom, "If you stand like that how can I go to the synagogue? How can I hear *Kol Nidrei?* It is getting late." Then the woman moved on one side and disappeared, and then Grandma ran back to the synagogue. She did not meet any human beings on the way back.

I was also told about this which happened many years ago. A lady came home from the synagogue after the evening prayers at the close of Yom Kippur. She went upstairs to lay the table. The tables were covered with white cloths in every Jewish house on that day, and an eternal lamp will be burning above it. They used to light the other lamps from this light. As soon as she entered the hall, she saw her brother, who died some time back, standing near the table turned towards it. This lady was very, very fond of her brother. In spite of the shock and fear and love, she went and embraced him with all her strength from the back. But she felt only as if she was holding the air.

A number of times, ghosts were seen in the synagogue itself. On Kippur night the young men stayed in the synagogue reading Psalms and other prayers after the women, children, and old men went home. In the Paradesi Synagogue there are two upstairs rooms, which are connected by a short corridor. The ladies usually sat in that corridor, as well as in the inside room. Late one Kippur night Dr. Simon and another man came out of the lavatory below and saw that this corridor was full of ladies standing in prayer as they always came to the synagogue on Kippur—all dressed in white. He went inside and asked the other men why the ladies did not go home yet. But all the ladies had gone home.

Haim Hallegua had a sister named Dolly, who died when she was a small girl. That year on Yom Kippur day when Haim was standing in prayer and he turned around bending, he saw his sister Dolly standing by his side. He could see her feet and the rim of the dress they made for her shroud.

Another strange thing happened to a man who was visiting in Cochin. Men used to come from Palestine and other places to collect money from the Jews of Cochin for helping the Jews who were living in Jerusalem. Often these ḥakhamim would sleep in the synagogue. One ḥakham was sleeping there on the night after Yom Kippur. Suddenly at the middle of the night he ran out frightened to the door of the neighboring house. He said he heard movements as if the curtains of the Torah were opening, and the sound of praying. So he took his bag of tzitzit and tefillin and ran. The woman of the house listened through an opening, and she heard also the words of the Yom Kippur prayer "*Uneshalema parim sefathenu.*" This lady happened to be my aunt Sarah.

Some people told me that the gentiles who lived around the Jewish cemetery in Cochin used to say that they could not sleep on Kippur night because of the different kinds of noise that came from the graveyard, but other people who lived near that graveyard said they never hear anything like that. Who knows what to believe?

THE FEAST OF *SUKKOT* AND *SIMḤAT TORAH*

The very night after Yom Kippur each family in Jew Town would start building the *sukkah* (booth) for the Feast of Tabernacles, which began four nights later. Just as we were building the *sukkah*, that night or the next there usually was a light shower of rain. This began the second monsoon season, with rain almost every day for a month after the very hot weather of Rosh Hashanah and Yom Kippur. When we read the *parashah* of Noah a few weeks later, it will be raining that week and we say it is Noah's flood.

To make the *sukkah*, the rich people, usually the family of Halleguas, distributed palm fronds throughout the Town, as they had a number of coconut palms in their property. The head of every family made a *lulab* from a tender leaf of the date palm before it opens. Every young boy had a small one made for him. They tie up the *lulab* with knots according to the number of joints of the backbone. A decorated chair was put in each *sukkah* for Eliyahu Hanabi, with a Bible on it. A *sukkah* was not kept in darkness. There will be a light burning throughout the night for each of the eight nights of the Feast. A portion is read from some book on the rules of *Sukkot* every night, and then Hebrew songs are sung. Some people slept in the booth, and all of us had our meals there.

In Cochin one did not have to pay exorbitant prices for the *etrog* (citron) which was essential for Sukkot. Some people had a citron tree in the backyard of their houses. They took care of the fruits so that they would be suitable for blessing—without any blemishes and with a shape like the heart. They distributed them among friends. Some bought from outside. The natives there

Simhat Torah celebrations in the Paradesi Synagogue, Cochin, 1973. Ruby's cousin Morris David (*center*) carries one of the large Sefer Torahs in its silver case. (*Photo, Dan Kala*)

knew when the Jews needed certain things. So they would bring their wares to the Town. They would bring the citron and other fruits with a stem and a few leaves on it to be hung in the booth. The Jews of course paid them a little more on such occasions.

On the seventh night of *Sukkot* is the *Hoshanah Rabbah*. There are overnight prayers and it is concluded with *selihot* prayers and blowing of the shofar. The morning prayers start early and end about eleven o'clock. They have seven *hakafot* (processions) around the Torah scroll with the four species (palm, myrtle, willow, and *etrog*) in their hands. These prayers end with the beating of the *arabah* (willow) on the ground.

Shemini Hag Atzeret starts in the evening. That is the day ladies go looking for silks for veils and different colors of silk and velvet with tinsel work. They adorn themselves like queens, full of jewels and gold bangles. The first day is called *Shemini Hag Atzeret* and the second day is called *Simhat Torah*. The *hakafot* of the Torah are conducted on the second night and the next day.

These two days are the happiest occasion of the whole Festival season. Dur-

Interior of the Paradesi Synagogue decorated with silk hangings and jasmine flowers for Simḥat Torah, 1973. Downstairs is the floor of Chinese tiles, the central brass *bimah* (pulpit), and hanging oil lamps. Upstairs in the back is the women's gallery, and in front of it, the second *bimah*, unique to Kerala synagogue architecture. On the left is Ruby's cousin Morris David. (*Photo, Dan Kala*)

ing this special time, all the Sifrei Torah—the scrolls in their silver cases with silver and gold crowns—stand out of their usual place. They are removed from the *heykhal* and placed on a stand under a *manarah* (canopy) which is made just for the occasion.

Many gentiles come to see the synagogue specially on the first night. The synagogue is decorated with lights and garlands of jasmine. All the walls are covered with *parokhets* (curtains for the *heykhal*) made out of velvet of different colors embroidered with golden thread. A frame of wood in the shape of a cedar tree with oil lights round and round is lighted in front of the synagogue. This kind of light is burnt in front of the other two synagogues too. In Kadavumbagam Synagogue on the front porch of the prayer hall there were lines—hung on the ceiling—of small pieces of tin of different colors. When the wind blows on it there is a sonorous sound, which gives a background music to the songs.

The first day before *minḥah* prayers, the men would sit in the synagogue and read through the whole five books of the Torah, each person reading one

Ruby's cousin Morris David and other men carry the large Sefer Torahs, and a small girl carries the smallest one. Simḥat Torah in the Paradesi Synagogue, Cochin, 1973. (*Photo, Dan Kala*)

portion, all at the same time. This way they finished the whole yearly cycle of reading the Torah and start again the book of Genesis. The second day, the bridegroom (*hatan*) of that year reads the portion *Bereshit* (In the beginning). He is called the *Ḥatan Bereshit*, and his family gives the whole community a treat of light food and drinks.

There are seven *hakafot* at night on *Simḥat Torah* and seven in the morning. The *hakafot* are conducted with songs and prayers in between according to the Cochin songbook called *Kolas*. This songbook contains songs sung by Iraqi and Morocco Jews. Temanim [Yemenite Jews] also sing some of these songs.

There are also three *hakafot* in the next afternoon. This is conducted outside the synagogue in most of the communities in Cochin, and always in the Paradesi Synagogue. They have a handwritten song book for that occasion, with special Cochin tunes, and that is the time they would take the Sifrei Torah out in the courtyard and carry them around the synagogue three times. At the end of these processions everyone goes home.

When they return for evening prayers, they take apart the special stand and the *manarah*, then finally they place the Torah scrolls back in the *heykhal*. *Simḥat Torah* ends with this ceremony. Before they close the doors, a kaddish is read. It is a very long one, which only the Cochin communities say. It is not in the prayer book. Recently one of the rabbis here in Israel asked my brother Bingley where we got that kaddish. He did not know so he asked me, but neither did I know. So I asked Sassoon ("Thachie") Roby. and he said he read that this kaddish is said in only three places: in Cochin and in one of the synagogues in Amsterdam and one of the synagogues in England.

On these two days of *Simḥat Torah* in Cochin, all the men and the ladies, dressed up in gold-embroidered dresses, went from one synagogue to the other to kiss the Torah. There were three synagogues in the Town, and usually the members of one synagogue did not visit the others except on this occasion. My house was somewhere in the middle of the Town, and my father entertained people with *shirbet* (a cool drink) as they came by. In the evening of the second day, Mr. A. B. Salem gave a party for the whole community. Everyone keeps an open house on that day, with tables laden with food and drinks. No invitation is necessary. Drink flows like water.

In no other part of the world is this Feast celebrated so grandly as in Cochin. Usually people visit Cochin specially for *Simḥat Torah*. Those who are in Israel now choose this season to visit their relatives in Cochin, even though there are very few people remaining there.

Chapter 12

BIRTHS AND WEDDINGS

MALAYALAM JEWISH SONGS

The Cochin Jews have many songs in the Malayalam language which were sung only by the women, especially at parties for our weddings and other celebrations. Every woman has her own book of songs, which she copied or maybe someone copied it for her, usually in a composition notebook. Young women go to the elderly people who know the songs, and they sing with them and learn. So if they are going to parties, they carry their books with them.

Some of the songs are very old, maybe three hundred years old or more. They are written in good Malayalam poetry, with some Hebrew words and even some words from Portuguese and Tamil to keep the rhythm and to make the language rich. The songs are very difficult to translate, because the language is so old and there are not many people left who remember them. Though it is not always possible to be sure of the meaning, I have translated a number of these songs from old notebooks, one of which was copied many years ago by my grandmother Docho's great-aunt.

On some occasions in Jew Town, the parties were held just for women, especially during the wedding celebrations. For other parties the men and women would all sit at the table—men on one side, women on the other side—and after the men finish singing Hebrew songs and the *birkat hamazon* (blessings after food), then the ladies start singing these songs in Malayalam. The men know the Malayalam songs by hearing them, but the women are the ones who sing them.

Some of the songs are translations from the Hebrew songs, but the women sing different tunes. One woman must be there—often it was my grandmother—to say what tune to change. For every stanza she had a different tune. Oh she knew! For weddings and all, they will specially call my grandmother and my mother. They can sing very well, with nice voices and a tune. If they are not there, there is nobody to organize the songs. Till the women finish singing, no one will get up from the table. All the men will sit down. That's the respect for the Jewish table, the *shulḥan arukh* [the set table]. Today that value is gone. Nowadays when you go to a party in Israel, the women are talking in such a loud voice, when the men sit down and sing at the table, they don't even hear. Even if they have a book, and even if they know how to sing the Malayalam songs for a Cochin wedding, they say "I forgot my glasses."

BIRTH CUSTOMS

Among the Cochin Jews, on the seventh month of a woman's first pregnancy, they have a party for the ladies. They buy a number of glass bangles of different colors to put on the wrists of the pregnant woman. Twenty-two are put on each hand, and then they break one so that there are twenty-two on one hand and twenty-one on the other hand. When her labor starts she pulls the bangles off and distributes them among the ladies who attend her.

The women also make a party the week before the baby is expected, to prepare the bed for her labor. The special thing they make for this party is a kind of cake which is made with coconut mixed with rice flour and a little salt. It is poured into coconut shells with a few pieces of bananas on the top and cooked by steam. It is very tasty.

When a child was born in the house, all the neighbors and friends were there to help, at night especially. Some stayed with the family overnight. When a woman was in labor, all the women in Town had no sleep that night. If she is in the hospital, all the women visited, one after the other. One of the medical officers of the hospital once said, "If a Jewish woman is in labor, all the Jewesses in town get the pain." When she comes home they go to help to look after the baby at night so that the mother can rest. The mother is given health treatment for at least a couple of weeks: good food, oil bath, massage, and bath with water in which different kinds of leaves are boiled.

CIRCUMCISION CELEBRATION FOR A BOY

If a baby boy is born, the celebration starts with a party on the Saturday evening after the next Shabbat. The night previous to the day of circumcision, they put a chair in the hall where the ceremony is to take place—a chair for Eliyahu Hanabi, asking his blessings for the baby who has to undergo this

Ruby's relatives join with more than sixty members of the Paradesi community for a festive meal, prayers, and songs the night before a *brit mila* in Israel, 1988; (*from the left*) Benny Gil, Ruby's late brother Bingley Daniel, her sister Raḥel Kala, and her cousin Eliezer Saggie. (*Photo, Barbara Johnson*)

great operation on the eighth day of its birth. Again there is a party, and people sit in prayer the whole night keeping watch over the baby before the *brit milah*, or circumcision.

Just before the *brit*, the men sing a Hebrew song "*El Elyon*," and after the *brit* the women sing a Malayalam song "*Oruvenai Vazhuvanna*," which is a translation of "*El Elyon*":

ORUVENAI VAZHUVANNA

May the Creator of the world, who governs the world single-handed, watch over this baby.

May the child be blessed like Adam, and may his blessings and ways be like Hannoch.

May you be redeemed from all sins and may the holiness of Noah be upon you.

Wherever you go may there be prosperity, and may you have long life like Abraham.

Much respect and kindness toward me, prayed Isaac to God.

God, who always does good, will protect you like Jacob.

Children, the fruits of the womb, will increase like Ephraim and
Manasseh the children of Joseph.

May God give you beauty and charm, and brightness of face like Moses
the teacher.

Years and good luck may you inherit, like Aaron inherited the Torah
and wisdom.

May you be blessed forever, as was Pinhas the lover of peace and truth.

Like the favorite of the mighty God, Joshua Bin Nun, the companion of
Moses.

May you be the greatest among the great hordes, like God's prophet
Samuel.

Follow strictly the path of King David the anointed.

At the time of sacrifice and afternoon prayer may you have name and
fame like King Solomon.

Enemies will not stand before you. The Prophet Eliya stands for
good luck.

May your prayers be heard when in need of mercy, like Elisha at the gate
of Jordan.

May your face shine like the list of Prophets, ten and another two.

May your happiness increase; may you have long life and beauty like Isaac.

Secret voices you will hear, as did Prophet Jeremiah and Ezekiel Ben
Bussi.

A breach will open up in the wall for you without knowing that
redemption would come, like Daniel.

God Shaddai will be your help amidst water, fire, and the burning flames,

He who gives water and food as to Hannaniah, Mishael, and Azariah.

You will be one who follows virtue always, and people will say you are
a child of holiness.

May you be redeemed like the righteous Mordecai.

Naming Ceremony for a Girl

The naming of a girl is not a grand affair. A party is made on any of the
auspicious days or on a Shabbat before Purim. The baby is taken to the synagogue, where the *hazzan* gives her a name and blessings after reading the
Torah portion of the week and giving the baby drops of milk and honey. After the synagogue is over, the ladies sing a short song:

KALLATHU POTHIL

In a hole in the cave sits a pigeon.
Graciously may she see the sights.
Pleasure and scent shall anoint you,
Honey and milk under your tongue.

For a mother, God created a daughter,
Born perhaps to dearly flow.

Four be the blessings of the seven mothers,
God will bless the baby.

The naming and a row of virtue:
May blessings and greatness be yours.
May the happiness of your marriage be seen.
May the fruits of your womb be full.

CEREMONIES BEFORE THE WEDDING

A wedding ceremony is a grand affair, because in Cochin they marry once and forever. There are very few divorces. In fact divorce is not talked about publicly. The word is spoken only in a whisper. At one time weddings were celebrated for a couple of weeks; then gradually the celebration was reduced to a week.

People used to get married on Sunday evenings or Tuesday evenings, but the celebration started on the Thursday afternoon before the marriage was to take place. On that Thursday a tea party is made for ladies only, and at that time seven young ladies help to make a bed in the connubial chamber. These ladies do not include widows or women who have been married more than once. The canopy for the bridal bed, which is called *manarah*, is decorated with silk curtains and small shiny balls of different textures. Even the entire room is decorated. Sometimes the Kadavumbagam ladies would come to borrow photographs from us to decorate their walls when they were making a *manarah*.

Then comes the Sabbath before the wedding, which is called in Malayalam *Nadakana Shabbat*. On Friday night the bridegroom makes a party for the whole community, or just his friends, according to his means. Next day he invites the bride and her relatives for a festival lunch. After the lunch one of the bride's relatives takes her home with the ladies, where they are treated with cakes and a cool drink called *shirbet*. At the end of the Sabbath, on Saturday evening, the bridegroom is brought home from the synagogue with a musical band.

Later in that same Saturday evening, the bride is dressed up beautifully in a *lungi* [lower garment] of colored velvet or satin, and a blouse of colored satin or silk, all decorated with tinsel work. People are invited, and they accompany the bride in a procession through the street from her house to the house where the marriage celebrations are to take place. On the way they explode fireworks and they sing all kinds of love songs. The bridegroom and the men walk backwards facing the bride, clapping hands and singing in Hebrew. When they reach the house, they have a festive dinner.

The bride stays there in that house till the wedding day. The night previous to the wedding is the happiest occasion, with singing and dancing. The seven young married ladies (only once married) are to make wine for the wedding. They usually used dry grapes boiled with water, maybe because they could not get kosher wine at that time. The Jews of Cochin usually made this raisin wine called *mai* for their ceremonies, such as circumcisions, Shabbat, and specially for the Passover seder. There were also some Jews who made real wine at home for such occasions.

On that same night, at three o'clock in the wee hours of the morning, all the ladies gather again in the bride's house to warm water for the bride to wash her face. This is the morning when they sing songs in praise of the royalty, describing their dress and how they went in procession on palanquins and on elephants, singing in praise of Joseph Rabban, who was granted the copper plates. One song tells how he went in a grand procession to receive the honor. Another song of this type is the following. At the end of each line comes the refrain "*Nalla!*" ("Good!").

PONNANANTHINDU

("Dressed with Golden Orbs")

Dressed with golden orbs and riding in a palanquin, he came to see the wedding ceremony. *Nalla!*

With gold jewelry on his breast, seated under a canopy of flowered saris. *Nalla!*

The king was surrounded by a procession of dancers, who were like peacocks, dressed in silk. *Nalla!*
In front of him were spread new carpets.
There were four rows of soldiers carrying peacock fans towering above him. *Nalla!*

Then follow four files of soldiers and the Nayar bodyguard.
And the dancing girls with music and dancing, the thundering of the army band, and the drums and flutes. *Nalla!*

All the people who gathered presented him with a ring.
There were many others also who came in palanquins. *Nalla!*

The king and men came in shouting and cheering until the house shook
When the bridegroom came to stay with the bride. *Nalla!*

The other girls, talking and giggling, ran away sadly and hid themselves.
Then another woman came and invited him in. *Nalla!*

And made him sit on a platform fully decorated.
Is there anyone who could dispute that this is beautiful? *Nalla!*

With the special standing oil-lamp, the tray for the betel nut, and the
   cuspidor. *Nalla!*

The women also sing songs in praise of the bride, including the following,
which describes how beautifully she is dressed and praises her for the expert
needlework with which she made her dress.

PONNITTA MENI

("Gold-adorned Body")

1

Adorned with gold, you songbird,
Shining with diamonds,
Camphor and rose water mixed,
All kinds of good-smelling things.
In green silk she is robed,
The woman blessed by God is she.
In good luck may she live,
More than a hundred years may she live.

2

Adorned with gold, you songbird,
Shining like gold is that woman,
With a proud walk and waving of the hand.
Dexterity was given her by God,
For leaf and needle golden,
Expert in beautiful needlework.
Wearing *tali* on a thread,
More than a hundred years may she live.

This party for the ladies lasted until early morning, when it was customary
to go in procession from one end of the town to the other and with all kinds
of bands and drums. In Cochin the traditional native band is made up of a
group of a hundred and sixty drums that go with it. These are made like

wooden barrels covered on both sides with cowhide and decorated too. They are beaten by two thick pieces of wood. But people usually hire only a few of them instead of a hundred and sixty drummers. These drums are beaten during the whole day of the wedding. And this is not the only kind of musical instrument.

After a wedding all the people of the Town have a sore throat from speaking loudly to one another in order to be heard above the din. Nobody cared and nobody complained about having lost a night's sleep or having disturbed a sick person. Everybody was happy. "Disturbance" is a word the Indians learned only in Israel. Even the Muslims, who also had their marriage procession at the middle of the night, sometimes passed through the Jews' Street with songs and bands. Everybody opened the doors to watch it. If there are any Jewish friends of the bridegroom, they would stop the procession in front of that house also and the bridegroom's friends honor him by garlanding him around the neck with jasmine flowers and sprinkling all the people in the procession with rose water.

THE WEDDING DAY

The day of the wedding is a very busy day for the whole community. At about nine o'clock all the ladies go to the bride's house. A goldsmith is called to the house and one of the bridegroom's relatives brings a one-rupee silver coin to the goldsmith. This he makes into a plain ring, which the bridegroom will put on the right-hand little finger of the bride during the wedding ceremony.

One of the relatives of the bride brings a quarter sovereign gold coin to the goldsmith, which he shapes into a *tali* pendant, which will be tied around the bride's neck by her mother or elder sister. The *tali* is also a symbol of marriage for Christians and Hindus, for whom the bridegroom ties it round the bride's neck. Perhaps the Jews adopted this custom to quietly show their neighbors that they are really married. The Christian *tali* has a cross on it, and the Jewish *tali* is bigger than the Hindu one, shaped something like a ladle.

My only memory of my Aunty Sipporah's wedding, which occurred when I was a small child, involves the making of the *tali*. My father brought a piece of a gold coin and dressed me up nicely. I remember standing near the goldsmith and putting the gold piece on a sieve. On the sieve was a coconut and some rice and other things. I am not sure whether I actually remember seeing these things, or afterwards I came to know they should be there.

Then the ladies go with the bride to the *mikveh*, or ritual bath, which is done in the well behind one of the houses. There will be only women around.

"*Ponnitta meni*" ("Adorned with gold, you songbird/Shining like gold is that woman.") The last Paradesi bride to be married in Jew Town, Glenys Simon, is dressed in the traditional wedding costume and taken in the women's procession to the synagogue. To her right is her mother, Esther Pearly Simon. Sarah Cohen holds the royal umbrella, and Lily Koder walks on her left, under paper streamers, which are hung between houses on the narrow lane, Cochin, 1978. (*Collection of Leslie and Glenys Salem*)

After this, the bride is dressed up and goes in a procession, with all kinds of drums and bands, to the synagogue. There she kisses the scroll of the Law, and on her way back she enters every house where there is an old person or a sick person who could not attend the wedding. She kisses their hands and they bless her.

After light refreshments, the people go to the bridegroom's house, where all the men are waiting, and there they have lunch. Only fish curries with rice are served at this time. All these different kinds of curries and rice are cooked in butter. They do not eat meat at that time, because in the morning they had all kinds of sweets made with butter and again at four o'clock there will be a party where all the sweetmeats and cakes are made with butter.

The afternoon party is a grand one, the grandest you have ever seen. All the cakes in the world will be there. When the party is over, the women sing this special song for the bridegroom:

In the synagogue, Glenys Simon kisses the Sefer Torah before her marriage to Leslie Salem, Cochin, 1978. (*Collection of Leslie and Glenys Salem*)

THAMBIRAN MUYIMBU

(Wedding song, sung before the bridegroom goes to the ḥupah)

First, let God's help come forward. There came a proclamation to
  Abraham our father:
I shall make you a great nation. I shall bless and raise up your name.

I shall bless those who bless you; I shall curse those who curse you.
God, who gives dew from heaven and food and drink from the fat of the
  earth.

God Shaddai shall bless you and cause you to increase among nations.
Through God's blessings of Abraham you shall possess the land of your
  forefathers.

God's blessings will be on you. The eternal God will bless you.
The blessings of your forefathers shall be upon you; like Joseph you shall
be the leader.

Increase justice and kindness and cling to God. Your legs will not falter.
The One who protects you does not drowse.

Curses will not affect you; illness will not attack your house.
God sends an angel to you, and He will protect you on your path.

Israel! At the time of your good luck, God's redemption will come to
you.
All the blessings pronounced in the Torah are included in the composition of the twenty-four books.

All those blessings will be on you, before the Father of heaven and earth.
All those blessings and long life will be showered upon those who
follow the spirit of the Torah.

The command came to Moses that Aaron should bless Israel.
Let all the blessings be yours and may you be protected forever.

His spirit will be upon you; He will keep you in peace.
Let your promise shine upon them and bless your children Israel.

Surely, by the order of God, Jacob heard the proclamation.
He heard the song sung by the girl Sarah bat Asher, containing the
message that Joseph is alive.

Listening, he happily sat up and called the girl to him.
By God he blessed the girl that she would never die.

As the women are singing this song, the bridegroom gets up and kisses the
hands of all the elderly people. Then he and the other men go to the synagogue for the evening prayers.

When the men leave for the synagogue, the ladies go to the bride's house.
There she is dressed in a white dress all embroidered in gold. Often this dress
was lent to her by some other woman in the community. All the brides, rich
or poor, were dressed up in the same style, with all the ladies bringing their
own jewelry to decorate the bride. All the brides, rich or poor, were wedded
with a silver ring, which both rich and poor could afford. A bride should not
feel sad on that day if she were to get only a silver ring and her rich friend
were to get a golden one.

All the other women were also dressed in grand style. From the way the
women dress, one can tell the relationship to the party concerned. The mothers and sisters use diamond jewelry and a more distant relation usually wears
pearls, and others wear golden jewelry. At the time of a wedding, when it was

very important for the ladies to put on jewels, those who had them used to lend to those who did not own the diamonds and so on, to wear for their children's wedding.

When the bride is dressed up and ready, either the mother of the bride or the elder sister ties the *tali* around the bride's neck. Seven pieces of thread are twisted together and put through the ring attached to the *tali* for this purpose. There is also a special song for this occasion. The women might have another five or ten minutes to wait while the men are finishing the evening prayers. Then when they hear that the men are ready, they accompany the bride in a procession, with singing and clapping, to the synagogue.

As the bride—and also the bridegroom—leave the houses for the synagogue, there is the custom of waving betel leaves and a few small coins over their heads. Children of the non-Jews who came to watch were happy to get a few of these coins, as a kind of charity to make them also happy.

The song which is sung to accompany the bride to the synagogue, by the Paradesi Jews only, is "*Ezhunettu neeradi*" ("Got up after having bath"). There is such a rush at this time, with the different kinds of bands roaring outside, all the ladies inside talking at the same time, children running around, the last-minute adjustment of the bride's dress—that this song is scarcely heard or noticed by many. It is sung by the few ladies standing close to the bride. I, for one, and many like me have never heard more than the first two lines of the song, the meaning of which is difficult to understand:

EZHUNETTU NEERADI

("Got up after having bath")

Got up after having bath to go to the synagogue,
Riding a horse held in front,
[Someone] went and gave the information.
The hero gave the riding horse.
Rubbing the hand, got on the horse.
[Someone] bent low and held the reins.
As the creation was done together,
Many years may [she] live.

In the synagogue a chair is placed next to the *heykhal,*where the Sefer Torah is kept. On top of the chair they put a circular frame with a white silk veil tied around it, hanging down to cover the bride.

The bride is brought from the house by her father—or by her brother or uncle if she has no father—and he makes her sit under this *ḥupah*. Nobody can see her face. Then the bridegroom is brought in by the two best men, called *shoshbinim*, whom he chooses by putting a garland around each one's

"The *ketubah* is read in a special tune by a young boy." Brian Hallegua reads the marriage contract at the wedding of Leslie and Glenys Salem, Cochin, 1978. (*Collection of Leslie and Glenys Salem*)

neck. At that time they sing a paragraph from the Book of Esther describing how Mordecai was dressed up and taken on a horse like the king. Then the *shoshbinim* help him to put on the prayer shawl, and the ceremony starts.

In Cochin there is no special rabbi to conduct the marriage ceremony, but the eldest man in the bridegroom's family helps in the ceremony, and he reads the seven blessings.

The *ketubah* is the marriage contract, with an additional stanza at the beginning. It is written on a parchment—by one of the men who knows how to write it—only on the day of the wedding itself. In the past it used to be written on a decorated paper. This contract is read in a special tune by a young boy of six or seven years old from the bridegroom's family, and then the bridegroom signs it, with two *shoshbinim* as witnesses, and it is then given to the bride.

It is to be noted that the wedding ring is placed inside the cup of wine which the bridegroom blesses, and after he drinks the wine, the ring is taken out and presented to the bride. The Cochin Jews have a specially composed verse for the marriage ceremony, which then the bridegroom reads, also in a special tune. Thus the man marries the woman, and no priest has to pronounce them man and wife.

When the wedding ceremony is finished, the mother of the bride raises up the veil and shows the bride's face, which everybody is eagerly waiting to see. At that time they sing a Hebrew song starting "Beautiful like the moon," and usually the bride's face has a special, satisfied look.

Then the bride and groom, walking side by side, are taken by the whole congregation and guests in a grand procession with all kinds of bands and fireworks. People from other communities would come to see the procession, sitting at the verandas of nearby houses. I used to go too if I am not in the procession, if the wedding is from another community. Then comes the big dinner and dancing. After the dinner there is more singing, and the bride and groom are blessed by the fathers of both, alternately putting the right hand on their heads.

AFTER THE WEDDING DAY

Usually on the day after the wedding there is a party for non-Jews who are also invited to celebrate the marriage. These include friends of the bride and bridegroom and of their families, sometimes the tenants who lived on the land owned by the families, and sometimes important guests such as officials. The guests bring presents, some say according to the grandeur of the wedding.

The bride and bridegroom are well dressed—the bride decorated with more jewels—and they are seated on a stage. In front of them is laid a table with sweetmeats, and the Jewish ladies sit on both sides singing a Malayalam song called "*Polika Polikedo*" ("Multiply, multiply"). The song refers to Chirianandan* as the raja of the place and begs the rain not to fall at the time of the wedding. One group sings the portion about the bridegroom, and the group on the other side answers with the portion about the bride.

POLIKA POLIKEDO

("Multiply multiply": a wedding song sung when the guests give presents)

Multiply, multiply in the wedding hall.
You multiply, you multiply, Chirianandan, multiply.
Multiply according to standard, and multiply in mind.

---

*BJ: The title "Chirianandan" refers to Joseph Rabban, the Jewish leader who received the copper plates from the emperor in Cranganore. For discussion of this title, see Barbara C. Johnson, "Shingli or Jewish Cranganore in the Traditions of the Cochin Jews of India, with an Appendix on the Cochin Jewish Chronicles," M.A. thesis, Smith College, 1975, pp. 69–70, 125–126, 130–131.

Multiply consciously the bridegroom's children.
Multiply consciously the bride's children.

When our bridegroom is going for his bath,
Blessed rain, you don't fall then.
The best men going with him won't get wet.

When our bride goes for her ritual bath,
Blessed rain, you don't fall then.
The best women going with her won't get wet.
The hands with the bangles and the bangles won't get wet.
The finger with the ring won't get wet.
The hair with the garland and the breast won't get wet.

Who is there to catch the deer?
"I will catch it, I will catch it," called out the groom.
What is the mark of the deer you caught?
There are many spots as the sign.

Who is there to cut the deer?
"I will cut it, I will cut it," says the bride.
What is the mark of the deer you sliced?
There are many spots as the sign.

As the ladies sing, they add the names of the donors and a few words in praise of them. The father of the bride or the groom, whoever invited them, brings a lot of presents kept on the side. According to the value of the present which each guest gave to the pair, the father presents that guest with a gift, perhaps a half sari with tinsels on the borders, or a golden ring, or other things according to their position.

On that day food is cooked specially for non-Jewish guests. Hindus have a Hindu cook, because they won't eat meat or fish or egg. Christians have Christian cooks and victuals of their own kind. They are also rich, high-class people and are so treated.

The Sabbath after the marriage (called in Hebrew *Ḥatan Shabbat* and in Malayalam *Perapadi Shabbat*) is celebrated according to the means of the families concerned. Some families have a grand party on that Friday night. After the Hebrew *birkhat hamazon* is sung by the men; the ladies sing this song in Malayalam. The words are translated from the Hebrew blessing.

ARULE PRAMANICHU

(Song sung during the Shabbat after the wedding)

The orders have been obeyed. Graciously you have blessed us.
In your hands there is only justice.

Don't wait when you hear the proclamation.
There is only you to clear the doubts.
Think on this before committing a sin.

To those who are kind-hearted, He will be the light.
Obeying the mitzvot that were commanded renders much benefit.
Even death will stand aside, and other griefs too.
If what is given is not enough, order happily more.
Obstruct the war. Seeing the approach of Pharaoh, He cleaved
The water of the sea, provided quick passage on dry land.
Put the golden bracelet according to rule,
Got to the land of Sinai safely.
Sure You are the One. Stoutly worship Him.

It is ten times advisable with love to worship.
To those who serve, no calamity will befall them.
Those who worship are rewarded beautifully.
Do favorably to us, oh God! Send goodness, universal God.
Send deliverance, God, and goodness send us in the future too.
The one we are waiting for, send as soon as possible.
The one who will find the people who have been dead for a long, long
    time.

You are the past and the future and the middle too.
Such is this nation, expecting Eli.
As in the past, You have ordered everything: myself and my nation.
You alone will save.

On that Saturday morning the bridegroom is called to the Torah with special songs. Then he reads a piece of the *parashah* "Abraham *Zaken*," where
when Abraham was old he called his servant Eliezer to find a woman for his
son from his family and not to take a woman from the Canaanites. Afterwards
they usually have yet another party. Many years ago the bride was expected
to learn a Malayalam song with a hundred and forty stanzas, all translations
from the Torah *parashiot*, which she would sing on the afternoon of *Hatan
Shabbat*. Every stanza she sang was repeated by the ladies. When we grew up
this custom was no more.

COCHIN WEDDINGS IN ISRAEL

Many of our boys and girls are getting married here, and we keep some of
our old wedding customs from Cochin. We still have a grand party on the
night before the wedding, with plenty of Cochin food and singing. In some
families the bride is dressed up in the traditional Cochin dress on that night,
with embroidered *lungi* and blouse and gold jewelry.

"Our tunes are very sacred to us, and we will never give them up—I hope!" (*Top*) Ruby sings traditional Cochin songs with her sister and visiting relatives, after serving them a meal in her apartment, 1993; (*bottom; from the left*) Abe David, Lillian David, Honey David, Raḥel Kala. (*Photos, Dan Kala*)

The wedding itself is usually held in a wedding hall, with both the bride and the bridegroom wearing Western-style dress, and an official rabbi has to be present at the ceremony as the notary. But the bridegroom still conducts the ceremony, as is the Cochin custom, while the rabbi is looking on with folded arms with a smile on his face. Either he thinks these are a peculiar kind of people or he approves of our way.

When the bridegroom is from Cochin, it is understood that he conducts the ceremony. When he is an outsider, he will be taught how to read it with the correct tune, and usually he is willing. A young boy will still read the *ketubah* in a Cochin tune. Our tunes are very sacred to us, and we will never give them up, I hope!

Chronology of Important Events and Periods

IN THE HISTORY AND LEGENDS

OF THE COCHIN JEWS

Tenth century B.C.E.   Ships of King Solomon may have traveled to Malabar coast

First century C.E.   Period of active trade between the Roman Empire and Kerala; possible beginnings of a colony of Jewish traders on the Malabar coast

1000 C.E.   Copper plates given to Joseph Rabban, leader of the Jewish community in Cranganore, signed by the Chera emperor

1341, 1524, 1565   Dates given in different accounts of exodus of the Jews from Cranganore to Cochin

1498–1663   Portuguese rule of the Malabar coast

1568   Building of the Paradesi Synagogue in Jew Town, Cochin

1663–1795   Dutch rule of the Malabar coast

1766–1792   Mysore Wars (invasions of Kerala by Muslim armies under Hyder Ali and Tippu Sultan)

1795–1947   British rule of the Malabar coast (indirect rule over kingdoms of Cochin and Travancore)

1848–early 1880s   One faction from the Paradesi community moves to Fort Cochin, under the leadership of Abraham ("Avo")

1881   Rabbi Asher Abraham Halevy visits Cochin as emissary of the Chief Rabbi in Jerusalem

1947   Independence of India

1948   Founding of the State of Israel

1950–1954   *Aliyah* of most of the Cochin Jews to Israel

1970s–present   Gradual *aliyah* of most of the Paradesi community

Supplement to Family Tree*

1. Dr. Venetia Esther (Minoo) Salem, *m.* Dr. Rao; children, Usha, Prakash; 2 grandchildren—India.
2. Dr. Malka Salem (*d.*), *m.* Antony; children, Rose, Mathew; six grandchildren—Ernakulam.
3. Dr. Leslie Salem, Ph.D., *m.* Dr. Glenys Simon (*b.* Cochin); children, Galya, Gilad—Haifa.
4. Dr. Cynthia Salem, *m.* Dr. Murali Dharan (*b.* Kerala); children, Nadiv, Dvir, Raviv—Afula.
5. Linda Salem, *m.* Steve Hertzman (*b.* Canada); children, Nathan, Joshua—Toronto.
6. Morris David, *m.* Reenie Ashkenazy (*b.* Cochin)—Haifa.
7. Sippora (Venus) David, *m.* Herbert Lane (*b.* USA); children, Aaron, Duncan—Tiberias.
8. Abraham (Abe) David, *m.* Lillian Ashkenazy (*b.* Cochin)—Tiberias.
9. David Davidson, *m.* Matilda Hallegua (*b.* Cochin); children, Leroy, Neil—Petah Tikvah.
10. Pinhas David, *m.* Zipporah (*b.* Israel); children, Mirav, Mettalia, Beniyahu Mosheh, Yoseph Hai, Yishai—Immanuel.
11. Shalom Zebuloon, *m.* Hannah, Bombay; sons, Joseph (*m.* Matilda; eight children), Shmuel (*m.* Maggi; six children), Jacob (*m.* Flora; five children)—Kurdani, Israel; daughter, Miriam Zebuloon (*d.*), first wife of Eliezer Saggie.
12. Shula, *m.* Kevin Foley (*b.* USA); daughter, Tal—Minnesota.
13. Ari Kala, *m.* De-ina (*b.* Israel); daughter, Metar—Tel Aviv.
14. Daniel Kala, *m.* Alona (*b.* Israel); son, Yarden—Kefar Saba.
15. Ruby also had three brothers who died young: Daniel (1918–21), Benaya Zion (1924–26), Binyamin (1928–29).
16. Eli Daniel, *m.* Elisheva (*b.* Israel); children, Yedidia, Hanania, Yonathan (*d.*), Ronit—Dimona.
17. Yair Daniel, *m.* Kathy (*b.* Israel); daughter, Chen—Beersheva.
18. Benaya (Benny), *m.* Ruth; children, Sara, Karen; granddaughter, Seena—England.
19. Eliezer Saggie, *m.* Miriam Zebuloon (*d.*); five children; second wife, Matty (*b.* Cochin)—Nazareth.

*See "Family Tree," page 14.

20. Sylvie, *m.* Ronen Koren (*b.* Israel); children, Elad David, Dvir—Jerusalem.
21. Annie, *m.* Ron Ben Haim (*b.* Israel); daughter, Linoy—Haifa.
22. Zeru Joseph, *m.* Mali (*b.* Israel); children, Karen, Shirley—Mizpe Ramon.
23. Margaret, *m.* Ivan Burgess; children, Paul, Aliza—England.
24. Aileen, *m.* Michael Santer; children, Mark, Steve, Graham; three grandchildren—England.
25. Molly, *m.* Ben Moss (*b.* Calcutta); children, David, Julia—England.
26. Raimond, *m.*? (*b.* China); children, (Jon, Lionel)—Canada.

Glossary

afikoman   Final "dessert" matzah eaten at the Passover seder

aliyah   Literally, "going up"; immigration to Israel; being called (up) to the reading of the Torah

Ashmodai   Legendary king of the demons

azarah   Entrance room of a synagogue (in Cochin)

Bar Minyan   Cochin term for Bar Mitzvah, the celebration of a boy's acceptance into the minyan at age thirteen

berakhah   Blessing

bimah   Pulpit or platform from which the Torah is read; Cochin synagogues are unusual in having two

brit mila   Circumcision ritual for a Jewish boy, held on the eighth day after birth

dewan   Prime minister of a native state (semi-independent kingdom, such as Cochin) in pre-independence India

Gemara   Part of the Talmud, the collection of rabbinic commentaries on the Torah

Habonim   Ihud Habonim, a Zionist youth organization

Haggadah   Book containing the liturgy for the Passover seder

hakafah   Procession around; procession carrying the Torah scrolls on Simhat Torah

hakham   Wise man, a title given to one who is learned in the Jewish Law; in Cochin, title of respect for a learned shaliah. from the land of Israel

halakhah Body of rabbinic law

ḥametz Leaven; any substance that must be removed from the household in preparing for Passover

Ḥanukkah Eight-day Jewish Festival of Lights, celebrating the victory of the Maccabees in the second century b.c.e.

ḥaver (pl. ḥaverim) Member (of a kibbutz)

ḥazzan Cantor or prayer leader, who chants the liturgy in the synagogue

ḥeder Jewish elementary school

heykhal Ark in which the Sefer Torah is kept

ḥupah Wedding canopy

Ima Raḥel Mother Rachel

jaggery Unrefined brown sugar

jati Caste

-ji Honorific suffix (as in Gandhiji)

Kabbalah Form of Jewish mysticism, which originated in medieval Spain

kabbalist Practitioner of kabbalah

Kaddish Prayer in the Jewish liturgy, recited by mourners

kapa Long robe worn by Cochin Jewish men for festivals

kapiri A small, mischievous supernatural being, in Kerala folklore

kashrut Jewish laws regarding the preparation of food

katyusha rocket Short-range missile, used by Arab forces in bombing the northern Galilee region where Kibbutz Neot Mordecai is located

Kerala "Land of the coconuts," the southwestern coast of India, now one of the Indian states

kibbutz A collective agricultural community in Israel

kolas Cochin Jewish songbook of liturgical hymns and prayers in Hebrew

lulab (lulav) Bundle of branches that is waved during Sukkot ritual

lungi One-piece lower garment worn by women and men in Kerala

Malayalam The language of Kerala

manarah In Cochin, a ritual canopy: the *ḥupah* in a marriage ceremony; the canopy built over a wedding bed; the canopy built over the temporary ark during Simḥat Torah

Mashiaḥ Messiah

matzah (pl. matzot) Unleavened bread eaten during Passover

megillah Scroll

meshuḥrar (pl. meshuḥrarim) One who is set free; manumitted slave

mezuzzah Piece of parchment with biblical passage, placed in decorative container, which is nailed to doorpost

midrash In Cochin, a *beit midrash* (house of study); a Jewish school

mikveh Ritual bath

minḥah Afternoon prayer

minyan Quorum for worship; traditionally, ten or more adult Jewish males

moshav Semi-collective rural community in Israel; village

Moshe Rabenu Moses our Teacher

musaf Additional prayers recited on Sabbath and holidays after the morning Torah service

-mutha (m.), **-muthi** (f.)   Honorific suffix referring to an elderly person in Kerala

Nayar   Hindu caste of high status in Kerala

neshamah   Soul or spirit

ola   Manuscript written on palm leaf

Orthodox   Strict in observance of traditional laws

palli   Synagogue; in Malayalam, a building for congregational worship (Jewish, Muslim, or Christian)

Paradesi   Synagogue and community of the "foreign" Jews in Cochin, whose ancestors began arriving in the sixteenth century

parashah   Weekly Torah portion

pastel   Filled pastry prepared by Cochin Jews for Shabbat and other festive occasions

Pesaḥ   Springtime festival of Passover

rab, rabban   A man who is learned in Jewish Law

Ramadan   Forty-day period in which Muslims fast each day

rimon   Decorative ornament for a Sefer Torah

Rosh Hashanah   Jewish New Year

rupee   Basic unit of Indian currency

sahib   Foreign (white) man; Englishman

sambhar   Sauce made from lentils, eaten with rice in Kerala

seder   Ritual meal for Passover

Sefer Torah (pl. **Sifre Torah**)   Parchment scroll on which the Torah is written; in Cochin, kept in a decorated silver case

selihot   Penitential hymns sung in the early morning for forty days preceding Yom Kippur

Sephardi   Pertaining to the Jewish communities of Spain or their descendants

Shabbat   Sabbath

shaharit   Morning prayer

shaliah (pl. shelihim)   Emissary from a Jewish community or organization

shalom   Peace, well-being; a greeting

shamash   Caretaker of a synagogue

Shavuot   Holiday celebrating the giving of the Torah on Mt. Sinai

shehitah   Authority to be a *shohet*

Shelomo Hamelekh   King Solomon

Shema Yisrael   "Hear, oh Israel"; a central prayer in the Jewish liturgy

Shemini Atzeret   Festival at the end of Sukkot, the day before Simhat Torah

shemorah   Special unleavened bread (matzah) made for the Passover seder in Cochin, from wheat harvested by Jews (from matzah *shemurah*, "guarded matzah")

Shimon Bar Yohai   A second-century rabbi, legendary author of the Zohar, whose death anniversary is celebrated on Lag B'Omer (in Cochin, called the Feast of Shimon Bar Yohai)

shofar   Ram's horn, blown on certain ritual occasions

shohet   Slaughterer certified to butcher animals according to Jewish Law

Simhat Torah   Holiday celebrating the conclusion and new beginning of the yearly cycle of Torah readings in the synagogue; second day of Shemini Atzeret; in Cochin, the most festive holiday of the year

Sokhnut The Jewish Agency; executive body of the World Zionist Organization, responsible for organizing immigration to Israel and absorption of new immigrants in Israel

tali Symbol of marriage in Kerala; pendant tied around the bride's neck during a part of the wedding ritual

tarwad Nayar matrilineal extended family

tebah (tevah) *bimah*, or pulpit

tebilah (tevilah) Ceremony of immersion in a ritual bath

tefillin Leather boxes containing words of Scripture; tied on the arm and forehead by Jewish men reciting morning prayers

Torah First five books of the Hebrew Bible; in a broader sense, Jewish law and learning

tzitzit In Cochin, a prayer shawl; literally, the ritual fringes in the corner of the prayer shawl

vallam Covered boat propelled by a long pole, which carries goods and passengers on the Kerala backwaters

vatik (pl. vatikim) Old-timer; one of the earliest members of a kibbutz

vesha Screen traditionally hung in front of the doorway in Kerala; doused with water to cool the interior of the house

Yom Kippur Day of Atonement

A Note on Caste in Kerala

In India, a caste (*jati*) is an endogamous social group, its membership inherited at birth. It often has a traditional occupation, particular religious beliefs and practices, behavioral norms regarding ritual purity and pollution, and a ranked status in a hierarchical caste system. The Cochin Jews could be seen as constituting one such caste. Other Kerala castes mentioned by Ruby Daniel in this book, with their traditional occupations or other designations, are as follows:

Hindu:

Brahmins (priests, at top of social hierarchy)
Nayars (warriors, another high-caste group)
Conganies (Konkanis, a high-caste group from the state of Maharashtra, north of Kerala)
Kanaka ("toddy tappers," traditionally a low-caste group)
Parayas, Pulayas, Cherumies (low-caste agricultural laborers, traditionally bound to the land as serfs or slaves)

Muslim:

Nainas (consider themselves descended from Brahmins who were forced to convert to Islam)
Other Muslims (the large majority, descended from converts from other castes and the offspring of Arab traders)

Christian:

Ancient community of Syrian Christians:
Roman Catholics, whose ancestors converted under Portuguese rule
Protestant Christians, whose ancestors converted during the period of British rule

Annotated Bibliography: The Jews of India

Abraham, Margaret. "Ethnic Identity and Marginality: A Study of the Jews of India." Ph.D. dissertation, Syracuse University, 1989.

A sociological study of reasons for Jewish emigration from India to Israel since the early 1950s, based on interviews in both countries.

Bar-Giora, Naphtali. "A Note on the History of the Synagogues in Cochin." *Sefunot* 2(1958):214–245. Hebrew.

A valuable collection of Hebrew primary sources on the Cochin Jews.

———. "Sources-Material for the History of the Relations between the White Jews and the Black Jews of Cochin." *Sefunot* 1(1957):243–278. Hebrew.

Additional primary sources in Hebrew.

Elias, Flower & Judith Elias Cooper. *The Jews of Calcutta: The Autobiography of a Community. 1798–1972.* Calcutta: Jewish Association of Calcutta, 1974.

First-person reminiscences of Jewish life in Calcutta, collected from members of the community who emigrated to England, and edited by two community members there.

Isenberg, Shirley Berry. *India's Bene Israel: A Comprehensive Inquiry and Sourcebook.* Berkeley, CA: Judah Magnes Press, 1988.

Comprehensive is the word! An extremely thorough collection of materials on the Bene Israel, based on many years of reading, archival research, and field-work in India and Israel.

Johnson, Barbara C. "Cochin Jews and K'aifeng Jews: Some Thoughts on Caste, Surname, 'Community' and Conversion." In *Jewish Diasporas in China: Comparative and Historical Perspectives,* ed. Jonathan Goldstein. Forthcoming.

An ethnohistorical comparison of two ancient Asian Jewish communities.

———. "The Emperor's Welcome: Reconsideration of an Origin Theme in Cochin Jewish Folklore." In Timberg, 1986, q.v., 161–176.

————. " 'For Any Good Occasion We Call Them': Community Parties and Cultural Continuity among the Cochin Paradesi Jews of Israel." In Katz, 1995, q.v.

An anthropological analysis of contemporary ritual celebrations in Ruby Daniel's community in Israel.

————. " 'Our Community' in Two Worlds: The Cochin Paradesi Jews in India and Israel." Ph.D. dissertation, University of Massachusetts, 1985.

An anthropological study of the transition of Ruby Daniel's Cochin Jewish "community" from India to Israel in the 1970s and 1980s, based on historical research and fieldwork in both countries.

————. "Shingli or Jewish Cranganore in the Traditions of the Cochin Jews of India, with an Appendix on the Cochin Jewish Chronicles." M.A. thesis, Smith College, 1975.

A detailed study of historical documents (including unpublished Hebrew texts from Cochin), legends, and songs relating to the early Jewish community in Cranganore, north of Cochin.

Katz, Nathan, ed. *Studies of Indian-Jewish Identity.* Ann Arbor, MI: Association for Asian Studies, AAS Monograph Series; and New Delhi: Munshiram Manoharlal, 1995.

A collection of new scholarly articles on the Jews of India.

Katz, Nathan and Ellen S. Goldberg. *The Last Jews of Cochin: Jewish Identity in Hindu India.* Columbia, SC: University of South Carolina Press, 1993.

A recent study of the small Paradesi community remaining in Cochin, from the perspective of comparative religions.

Kehimkar, Haeem Samuel. *The History of the Bene-Israel of India.* Tel Aviv: Dayag Press, 1937.

A classic study written in 1897 by a prominent member of the Bene Israel community.

Lord, Rev. J. Henry. *The Jews in India and the Far East.* Kolhapur, India: Mission Press, 1907.

A valuable early source on the Indian Jewish communities, from a Christian missionary perspective. Presents the viewpoint of the Malabari Jews of Cochin, as opposed to that of the Paradesis.

Mandelbaum, David. "The Jewish Way of Life in Cochin." *Jewish Social Studies* 1(1939):423–60.

Earliest academic study of the Cochin Jews by a Western anthropologist, based on his visit to Cochin and thorough review of available sources.

———. "Social Stratification among the Jews of Cochin in India and *Israel.*" *The Jewish Journal of Sociology* 17(1975):165–210.

Update of Mandelbaum's 1939 study.

Marks, Copeland. *Sephardic Cooking: 600 Recipes Created in Exotic Sephardic Kitchens from Morocco to India.* New York: Donald I. Fine, 1992.

Wonderful recipes collected from all three of the Indian Jewish communities. Readers could bypass the discussions of the exotic history and cultures.

Musleah, Ezekiel N. *On the Banks of the Ganga: The Sojourn of the Jews in Calcutta.* Quincy, MA: Christopher Publishing House, 1973.

A comprehensive overview of the history of the Calcutta Jews, compiled from archival sources and personal knowledge by a rabbi who comes from a leading family of that community.

Musleah, Rahel. *Songs of the Jews of Calcutta.* Cedarhurst, New York: Tara Publications, 1991.

A collection of songs from the Calcutta Jews, with Hebrew words, English transliterations, and musical notation; accompanying cassette tape is available. Includes many photographs from the Musleah family in Calcutta.

Reinman, Solomon. *Masa'ot Shelomo,* ed. W. Schur. Vienna: Georg Breg Press, 1884. Hebrew.

A nineteenth century Ashkenazi traveler's account of Jewish communities in Asia. Reinman settled for some time in Cochin, where he married a woman from the Hallegua family.

Roland, Joan G. *Jews in British India: Identity in a Colonial Era.* Hanover, NH: University Press of New England, 1989.

A scholarly historical account and analysis, focused on the history of nineteeth and twentieth century Jews in Bombay and Calcutta.

Saphir, Jacob. 1874. *Eben Saphir.* Lyck, Poland [?]: Silberman, 1874; Reprint Jerusalem: 1966/67. Hebrew.

Another nineteeth century account by a traveler who visited Jews in Cochin, Bombay, and Calcutta. Saphir was an Ashkenazi Jew from Jerusalem.

Segal, J. B. *A History of the Jews of Cochin*. London: Vallentine Mitchell, 1993.

A comprehensive history of the Cochin Jews based on written sources.

Shaham, David, ed. *The Jews from the Konkan: The Bene Israel Communities in India*. Tel Aviv: Beit Hatfutsoth, 1981.

Catalog of an exhibit, with photos by Carmela Berkson and an essay by Shalva Weil.

Strizower, Schifra. *The Bene Israel of Bombay: A Study of a Jewish Community*. New York: Schocken, 1971.

A sociological study, with emphasis on community institutions, based on fieldwork in the 1960s.

Timberg, Thomas, ed. *Jews in India*. New York: Advent Books, 1986.

A useful anthology of old and new articles.

Walerstein, Marcia S. "Public Rituals among the Jews from Cochin, India, in Israel: Expressions of Ethnic Identity." Ph.D. dissertation, Los Angeles: University of California Los Angeles, 1987.

A lively folkloristic study of community life and ritual performances of Malabari Jews from Cochin living in several Israeli moshavim.

Weil, Shalva. "Bene Israel Indian Jews in Lod, Israel: A Study of the Persistence of Ethnicity and Ethnic Identity." Ph.D. dissertation, University of Sussex, England, 1977.

An anthropological study, based on fieldwork in Israel.

———, ed. *MeCochin leEretz Israel*. Jerusalem: Kumu BeRinah, 1984. Hebrew.

A volume issued for the fortieth anniversary of Cochin aliyah, a 1984 celebration in Moshav Nevatim. Includes photographs, articles, reprints, and translations of older articles. Ruby Daniel responds to the reprints from Bar-Giora, Reinman, and Saphir in this volume.

Index

Note: Page numbers in italics indicate photographs or illustrations; page numbers followed by *n* indicate footnote.

Printed in the United States
18089LVS00007B/64-126

9 780827 607491